P9-AER-592

The Rise of Rhetoric and Its Intersections with Contemporary Critical Thought

Polemics Series

Series Editors

Michael Calvin McGee and Barbara Biesecker
University of Iowa

John M. Sloop
Vanderbilt University

*The Rise of Rhetoric and Its Intersections with
Contemporary Critical Thought*
Omar Swartz

Judgment Calls: Rhetoric, Politics, and Indeterminacy
edited by John M. Sloop and James McDaniel

Without Apology: Andrea Dworkin's Art and Politics
Cindy Jenefsky

808
Sw26

The Rise of Rhetoric and Its Intersections with Contemporary Critical Thought

Omar Swartz

WITHDRAWN

Westview Press
A Member of Perseus Books, L.L.C.

LIBRARY ST. MARY'S COLLEGE

Polemics Series

All rights reserved. Printed in the United States of America. No part of this publication may be reproduced or transmitted in any form or by any means, electronic or mechanical, including photocopy, recording, or any information storage and retrieval system, without permission in writing from the publisher.

Copyright © 1998 by Westview Press, A Member of Perseus Books, L.L.C.

Published in 1998 in the United States of America by Westview Press, 5500 Central Avenue, Boulder, Colorado 80301-2877, and in the United Kingdom by Westview Press, 12 Hid's Copse Road, Cumnor Hill, Oxford OX2 9JJ

Library of Congress Cataloging-in-Publication Data
Swartz, Omar.
  The rise of rhetoric and its intersections with contemporary
critical thought / Omar Swartz.
    p. cm.—(Polemics series)
  Includes bibliographical references and index.
  ISBN 0-8133-9089-3 (hardcover)
  1. Rhetoric. 2. Criticism. I. Title. II. Series.
P301.S935 1998
808—dc21   98-13855
                                                                                 CIP

The paper used in this publication meets the requirements of the American National Standard for Permanence of Paper for Printed Library Materials Z39.48-1984.

10   9   8   7   6   5   4   3   2   1

This book is dedicated to my wife, Rui Zhao.
Without her love I would have long ago succumbed to my alienation.
This book, and my scholarship generally, is an attempt to conquer
alienation. All such battles require hope. In other words, they require
love. For what is love, if not a hope and a commitment to a life of
happiness that continues well into the future.

Contents

Preface

This book has its roots in three circumstances, two of which derive from my experience teaching a class entitled "Persuasion in the Western World." First, in reading student papers and in cultivating class discussion, I am frequently disappointed by the students' lack of connection with the subject matter. Time and again I am told that the material is "boring" and that it is "history"—a subject matter of no consequence to people's lives today. Only a few students recognize the heuristic nature of rhetoric and see how it can contribute to an understanding of the contemporary world. Furthermore, as survey classes in Western persuasion are frequently offered as lower level, university-wide general education requirements, students often under-appreciate the benefits of the class in relationship to their other humanities course work. As Karl Wallace explains: "The student who learns to think rhetorically can hardly miss the relevance of his [sic] formal studies. He sees that rhetoric constitutes a general introduction to the subjects, ideas, values, and rational operations that specialized studies extend and refine."[1]

Second, as a result of my teaching experience, my *own* appreciation for rhetoric began to change. It is one thing to be a student of rhetoric, which involves mainly reading and writing, but it is another thing altogether to be a *teacher* of rhetoric; the demands of clarity, simplicity, and communication force the scholar to reengage the material on an entirely different level. More than relating to rhetoric as an intellectual exercise, as so much scholarship urges, I began to recognize, in an applied and pedagogical way, that "classical rhetoric helps us to specify what it means for invention to be an intellectual method, a method of thinking."[2] In other words, by teaching the course, I began to see for myself, in a new light, the dimensions of rhetorical theory that I was encouraging my students to see. I realized that I am just as much a student in the class as they are.

Third, I have repeatedly noticed that students as well as the general population of this country are increasingly alienated from the political life of the nation. Professionally, I have always felt a responsibility to speak to this alienation, since a great deal of it is linguistically and rhetorically situated.[3] In so doing, I have come to see rhetorical thinking as a critical activity. Thus, great effort is extended in this book to situate our discussion of rhetoric squarely in a modern political framework. This is, after all, a book on rhetoric, and even though I will be mainly discussing *classical* rhetoric, there is no meaningful way to do so without in some sense discussing *contemporary* rhetorical perspectives. Rhetoric—old and new—can lead to a vital discussion of ourselves and our world because rhetoric is always about people and the possibility for change. Thus, rhetoric is inescapably political.

As the above three sentiments matured, and as the relationship between pedagogy, politics, and my intellectual pursuits became more focused, I was confronted with a "rhetorical situation." The form of this situation was a growing professional urgency to unite theory and pedagogy (and to highlight praxis—or a political awareness—in my professional pursuits). This book is a product of this exigence. Under the influence of the above factors—the enforced apathy of my students and my own growing sense of rhetoric's practical, pedagogical, and political heuristics, I began a broad survey of primary and secondary source material in the literature of classical rhetoric in order to highlight the contemporary usefulness of the rhetorical tradition. I have come to believe, through the course of my studies and my teaching, that rhetoric is more than a cerebral activity; it is an important *dynamis* in the creation and perpetuation of human political culture.

In the survey of the literature that I undertook to write this book, I found myself almost immediately overwhelmed by the sheer volume of the material. To make my study more manageable, I limited my focus to the general contours of the rhetorical tradition and reviewed the work of the most prominent historians. My goal was to synthesize what these scholars have written about classical rhetoric and to present that material in such a way as to have its greatest appeal. In so doing, I have woven together what I hope others find to be an interesting narrative. However, the story told here about where we came from as a culture and what that means for us today in our modern communication environment says as much about who I am as a person and as a teacher as it does about history and rhetoric itself. My biases and assumptions should be clear as readers proceed through this book.

The intended audience for this book is diverse. First and foremost, it is a *scholarly* treatise designed to illustrate the feasibility of merging a left critical politics with scholarship: in a fundamental sense, it is my attempt to broaden the boundaries of disciplinary thought. As this is a "crossover" book, it should appeal to scholars in communication studies as well as in departments of English.

Second, and perhaps more importantly, this book is an attempt to *share* a rhetorical and critical scholarship with a wider audience of non-disciplinary readers. Students in particular, as well as activists and intellectuals outside of the academy, should find this book stimulating and useful in challenging their positions as spectators in a late twentieth/early twenty-first century U.S. political environment.

Omar Swartz

Notes

1. "The Fundamentals of Rhetoric," in *The Prospect of Rhetoric*, eds. Lloyd F. Bitzer and Edwin Black (Englewood Cliffs, NJ: Prentice-Hall, 1971), 12.

2. Eugene Garver, "Demystifying Classical Rhetoric," *Rhetoric Society Quarterly* 10 (1980), 75.

3. See Omar Swartz, *Conducting Socially Responsible Research: Critical Theory, Neo-Pragmatism, and Rhetorical Inquiry* (Thousand Oaks, CA: Sage, 1997).

Acknowledgments

I would like to thank several people who have contributed in direct and indirect ways toward the completion of this project. Sue Swartz, my mother, has supported me and has cared for me as I have built my career. I thank my grandmother Bubby Rose, who has given me so much love over the years. I also thank my father, Robert Swartz, for bequeathing to me a critical perspective. I thank Edward Schiappa, Charles Stewart, and Don Burks for their mentoring when I was a graduate student at Purdue University. Not a day goes by in my scholarly life that I do not return, in my thoughts, to my conversations with them. The strength of this book lies, in part, in the excellent education they gave me.

I want to thank Craig Allen Smith for his warm collegiality while I was writing this book at the University of North Carolina, Greensboro. Craig is a kind human being and mentor who helped me acclimate to the demands of being a new professor. Also, I owe a belated thanks to Julia Wood for her help in getting my previous book published.

Chris Bachelder has earned my gratitude and respect for reading and commenting on earlier drafts of this book. Chris prodded me in significant ways to improve my thinking about many of the topics contained herein. My two graduate students, Charles Catalano and Judith Szerdahelyi, provided welcome support during a difficult period of my professional life. To them I am grateful.

Portions of this book have been published elsewhere in a slightly different form. Part of Chapter 2 appeared as "Understanding Rhetorical *Kairos* by Means of an Analogy," *Speech Communication Teacher* 11: (1997), 12–13 and is used by permission of the Speech Communication Association. Part of Chapter 3 appeared as "Toward an Understanding of Marxist Discourse: Major Ernesto 'Che' Guevara's February 26, 1965 Address to the Conference on African-Asian Solidarity," *Speaker and Gavel* 30: (1993), 1–18. Also in Chapter 3, my discussion of praxis draws heavily upon my entry "Praxis" in *The Encyclopedia of Rhetoric and Composition: Communication from Ancient Times to the Information Age*, edited by Theresa Enos (New York, Garland Publications, 1996), 553. I am grateful for the permission to reproduce the material here.

O.S.

A humanistic discipline is in good shape only when it produces both inspiring works and works that contextualize, and thereby deromanticize and debunk, those inspiring works.

Richard Rorty
"The Necessity of Inspired Reading"
The Chronicle of Higher Education
February 8, 1996
A48

*   *   *

[A] nation which believes the mythology of its past at such expense to historical truth will not be inclined to free itself from self-righteous illusions about its more recent actions—especially since today's events act upon us with an urgency that makes dispassionate assessment all the more difficult.

Michael Parenti
The Anti-Communist Impulse
New York: Random House, 1969, 124.

Introduction

The classical period of rhetoric began around 500 BCE with the rise of democratic consciousness in the Mediterranean city states of Greece. This period ended with the solidification of Christian power in the Roman Empire during the fourth century of the Common Era. Within this context, the Ancient Greeks provided important intellectual work on the conceptualization of rhetorical theory. With the Greeks, rhetoric, as an area of knowledge, is given structure and cultural significance. This does not mean, however, that rhetoric can *only* be conceptualized in the ways found in the Ancient Greek texts.

Rhetoric as Culturally Experienced

By what standard should we conceptualize our understandings of rhetoric and rhetorical theory? Do we use the standard that a society uses for itself, as in the case of the Ancient Greeks, or do we look for more nuanced expressions of a rhetorical consciousness that may exist without being so overtly conceptualized? Consider, for example, James Murphy's position, representing one that scholars have traditionally held: "As far as one can judge from surviving evidence, the Greeks were the only people of the ancient world who endeavored to analyze the ways in which human beings communicate with each other. There is no evidence of an interest in rhetoric in the ancient civilizations of Babylon or Egypt, for instance. Neither Africa nor Asia has to this day produced a rhetoric."[1]

Murphy is able to make such a claim because he takes the existence of rhetoric literally. The Greeks had rhetoric because they *named* it, *defined* it, and *reified* it. In other words, rhetoric is "real" for Murphy and for the Greeks because of the systematic attention and tremendous resources that the Ancient Greeks devoted to understanding it. In this light, Murphy's claim is not unreasonable. There is clearly a rhetorical tradition in Ancient Greece and, by the standards of that tradition, there does not appear to be a similar tradition existing elsewhere.

Such a position, however, is Eurocentric; it views the European experience as the defining experience for our understandings of the world. In contrast to this view, a more holistic view of the ancient world's civilizations suggests that all had some sort of conceptualization of the communication phenomenon. By broadening our view as to what is and what is not rhetoric, we may be able to learn something about persuasion and communication from non-Western societies. For example, centuries before the rise of Greek civilization, Ptah-hotep, an Egyptian author, wrote a text called "The Ethics of Argument." Michael V. Fox explains, "[T]he Egyptians attained a fair degree of rhetorical consciousnesses some 1500 years before the golden age of Greek rhetoric."[2] In China during the third century BCE, a man named Han Fei Tzu authored a text titled *Difficulties in the Ways of Persuasion*. In India, about the same time or earlier, various writers discussed a rhetorical awareness in poetics and in preaching. All of these writers can be seen as illustrative of a concern with communication and persuasion that parallels the concern found in Ancient Greece. The difference is, however, that they did so differently. The art of persuasion was just as important in Imperial China as it was in Athens during the era of Pericles. However, what counts as evidence, argumentation, and proof is vastly different. In fact, it would be presumptuous of us in the West to assume that persuasion in the East involves the constructs we recognize as "evidence," "argumentation," and "proof."

Nevertheless, some scholars still argue that students of language must distinguish between the systematic study of something that has been *named*, and the more or less general inquiry into the nature of human symbolization.[3] All humans are symbol users, no matter where they are born. All humans use language to construct their societies. In these different societies, there are unarticulated "theories" that guide the construction of communication and discourse, and these may or may not take the form of written rules to guide presentational skills. However, this may not be the same thing as stating that they have a *theory* of rhetoric. They may or they may not; it depends on how the term is conceptualized. Proceeding from the logic that an area of knowledge only exists once it is defined as such, George Kennedy, considered by many to be the most important historian of rhetoric in the twentieth century, concurs with Murphy that rhetorical theory is largely a Western phenomenon: "Neither in India nor in China . . . did rhetoric become a separate discipline with a fully developed theory, its own logical structure, and a corpus of pragmatic handbooks. Such a degree of conceptualization is apparently found only in the Greco-Roman world, where it begins to appear coincident with the rise of Greek philosophy and other forms of conceptualization in the fifth and fourth centuries BC[E]."[4]

Some communication scholars have tried, with increasing success, to explore non-Western forms of rhetoric and rhetorical theory.[5] Such an effort is healthy and it ultimately expands our knowledge of how human symbolization works to create structures of meaning, and hence culture itself. These efforts mark a shift away from traditional efforts that represent non-Western rhetoric as if it were an incipient Western rhetoric. In other words, some scholars in the past have tried to universalize rhetoric by defining an Eastern rhetorical tradition in light of their Western assumptions.[6] The philosopher Richard Rorty warns against this type of scholarship by reminding readers that people must always bracket, to the best that they can, the assumptions they make about the past, when trying to describe the past. He explains that we need "to recognize that there have been different forms of intellectual life than ours."[7]

It is with Rorty's caution in mind that this book discusses Greek and Roman rhetoric in terms of a specific literature and tradition. The systematic development of a body of knowledge that we call "rhetoric" (as another systematic body of knowledge may be called "biology") can be associated with Greco-Roman culture and, by extension, with the wider Western culture as well. This does not exclude, however, *another* system of structure and influence that can be used to explain the effects of language on thought and that mediates the tensions between the individual and the collectivity. Thus, what we call Greek "rhetoric" must be seen as a *specific literary development*, one that has early origins in the Greek practice of speaking and culture, and becomes conceptualized in various terms with varying degrees of professionalization to meet growing cultural and intellectual needs.

Need for the Liberal Arts Curriculum

As we will explore in this text, what has become known to us as "rhetoric" was, in Ancient Greece, central to (and grounded in) the ideal of a civilized society, as well as to the concept of a higher education. Even today, to be fully educated, students must be able to think beyond the immediate technical training that they receive in college. The contingencies of life in the twenty-first century will demand a more encompassing thinking than the type of thinking currently encouraged in the humanities disciplines. In other words, the economic pressures that are leading the university to stress specialization as an institutional norm will be challenged, in the long run, by the growing recognition that, first and foremost, society needs people who can think, as well as people who are adept at running the machinery of the modern state.

As the integration of civilization and education was fundamental to Greek thought, so too is it necessary for ours. The Ancient Greeks had the luxury of living in a period of time during which human existence did not depend on the wise decisions of a generation to protect the environment and to provide for a stable world that is based on an equality for *all* nations. Athens, for example, could afford to perpetuate its selfish policies of imperialism, to practice its slavery and its misogyny, and to engage in its xenophobic aggressions. Athens had only its empire to lose, while we and our grandchildren have responsibility for the entire world, and can destroy it all in our deal with the devil for our technological vanity. This paragraph is not written with intended hyperbole. Rather, it is intended to emphasize the need for a cultural synthesis between the technological needs of an advanced industrial society such as ours, and the humanistic ideals of harmony, balance, and well-being. These ideals cannot come from a curriculum loaded with scientific or technical training. It is not that this training is unimportant; rather, it is incomplete. It does not train the entire person.

Paradigms and Logos

The practice of rhetoric as a self-conscious activity began during the so-called "Greek Enlightenment." This Enlightenment was characterized by a paradigmatic transition, as old ways and common cultural beliefs were being set aside or severely questioned. Paradigms are large scale belief structures that underlie societal assumptions. When these are questioned, or when they are in transition, people lose faith in their previous ways of thinking, feeling, and acting. These periods are marked by dynamic change, and are frequently associated with significant technological or intellectual changes.[8] In Ancient Greece, that technological change was literacy, and the intellectual change was the development of logos.[9] Particularly in Athens, the most important intellectual and political center of the Ancient Greek world, the human being began to challenge and replace the gods as the standard of experience. Belief in the gods and in theology—one paradigm—slowly gave way to a different sort of explanation for how the world and society were structured. The new paradigm that replaced it involved the belief in the human mind as an instrument for the construction of the social world and for the meaning and understanding of its material dimensions.

Central to the process of a new rationale for articulating what it meant to be human was an intellectual commitment to understanding the word "logos." As understood by the early Greeks, logos is reason and rationality as derived from the use of speech. The Greeks perceived the human being as the rational animal; within this capacity for rationality, human culture was able to emerge. Belief in this first principle of rationality as the dynamis of human society is clearly articulated in Isocrates' *Antidosis*: "[B]ecause there has been implanted in us the power to persuade each other and to make clear to each other whatever we desire, not only have we escaped the life of wild beasts, but we have come together and founded cities and made laws and invented arts. . . ."[10]

To a great degree, classical Greece was based on the spoken word in its new sense of logos. The classical Greeks believed that excellence in speech came from a mind well trained in thinking. Thought, the power to reason, was the focal point of the human experience. The study of rhetoric was the study of the human mind itself. As classicist Friedrich Solmsen explains, speech and language "[W]ere and are the indispensable vehicle for all of reasoning."[11]

What Is Rhetoric?

What is rhetoric? Why is it important? How can it become conceptualized? What is the significance of this conceptualization? These questions and related inquiries into the process of humanist reasoning demand our highest attention as thinkers in the liberal arts. As we will explore in this book, the conflicts, concerns, and situations that surround the early formation of a rhetorical awareness inform many of our present day academic concerns in diverse fields such as Communication, Philosophy, English, History, and Political Science. More specifically, the study of classical rhetoric helps us to learn what it means to know and how to establish systems of knowledge. In this sense, rhetoric is a "meta" discipline. It is a way of talking about how *all* disciplines come to understand themselves. This said, however, we are no closer to answering the question posed at the beginning of this section. What is it that we are studying in this book?

There is no easy answer to this question. As James Berlin documents in his study of North American English departments, there is not one rhetoric, but many. He urges us to talk about "rhetorics" and not just one monolithic entity that we reify in the image of one particular ideology.[12] In other words, every theory of rhetoric presupposes a politics of communication. For example, as we will see, Protagoras and Gorgias, two of the more influential Sophists, can be seen as having a more or less democratic political position as manifested in their belief that logos is a way of argument and debate in order to bring people together to construct their understandings of self and society. Plato's view of rhetoric and communication, on the other hand, supports an oligarchic politics or a monarchy, since communication is predicated upon the communicator's "True" understanding of the world and of an individual's position within that Truth. In between these two polarities, we find other views of communication and a different set of implicit politics. Aristotle's view of rhetoric implies an aristocratic politics, as he limits rhetoric to civic discourse and to formalized generic settings—the courthouse, the governing body, and the ceremonial encomium (all involving *free men* persuading free men). Aristotle does not recognize the rhetoric of dissident, the persuasion of social movements, the rhetoric of women, or the rhetoric of slaves.

In contrast to these three views, a fourth view of rhetoric can be offered. Kenneth Burke, the most important twentieth century theorist of rhetoric, gives us a rhetoric that implies a socialist politics.[13] Rhetoric, for Burke, is a form of cultural politics that strives to increase cooperation among individuals and to elucidate the strategic locations where ambiguity is created by powerful elites to protect and serve their material interests.[14]

None of these above four perspectives are any truer than any other—all reflect a way of slicing up the world. Neither one offers a complete perspective of what rhetoric *is*. The first thing that any student of rhetoric needs to learn is that *rhetoric is a way of cutting*. Each of the four examples illustrates how theorists use language to argue that their particular understanding is "true." None of the above theorists is wrong, but none is completely correct, either. Thus, the question becomes: which view of rhetoric do we choose to guide the construction of our lives?

As a form of knowledge, rhetoric is a way of emphasizing one set of relationships at the expense of others. It is useful then to use rhetoric itself to talk about rhetoric. This is what makes rhetoric the meta-subject mentioned above. In studying rhetoric, we learn many things that we may not anticipate; this is one of the things that makes the study of rhetoric so fascinating.

Because of rhetoric's meta-characteristics, it is no surprise that it is often seen as a "chameleonic" notion. "Few words have covered more different and diverse concepts—and provoked more different emotional reactions."[15] Because the meaning of the word "rhetoric" is difficult to pin down, it is often accused of not meaning anything at all. Thus, when people talk incoherently, deceivingly, propagandistically, dogmatically, and otherwise at the expense of substance, they are often seen as using rhetoric. Consider the following scenario. A politician for one country engaged in war with another says, "In our negotiations with the enemy, we welcome every honest act of peace. We care nothing for mere rhetoric."[16] What is happening in this instance? For one, the speaker establishes a binary between "action" and "rhetoric." Rhetoric is language that exists at the *expense* of action.

In exploring the mass media environment, we quickly see that this is the popular conception of the term. We are told that politicians need to use less rhetoric and more action. People tend to act as if what they say is "true," and what their enemies say is "rhetoric." Or, more specifically, if I agree with you, then you are logical and reasonable, but if I do not agree with you, then you are guilty of using rhetoric. Needless to say, this is *not* the view of rhetoric taken in this book. Rhetorical action *is* action, and a very important action.

Political Uses of Bifurcation

One of the purposes of this book is to correct for the misuse of the term "rhetoric." Yet we must acknowledge, before we go much further, that such misuse is not accidental. To create a bifurcation between two concepts, such as the bifurcation between "rhetoric" and "action" (or between "rhetoric" and "reality" as is more often the case) is to impose on the world an anti-rhetorical politics. This position assumes that there is "the world," on the one hand, and language on the other, and that the two seldom interact. When they do interact, we should be on our guard, as nothing but trouble can follow. When the world is seen as existing independent of language, then our methods of knowing themselves must be purged of any linguistic connection. This means that we have to control what we say—as not to interfere with our perceptions. If we cannot control what we say, there is always someone else waiting to do so for us—the censor whose job it is to protect the explanation or justification given for the existing order.

The censor takes on many forms: the teacher, the priest, the rabbi, the editor, the television producer, the business manager, the industrialist, and even the government. When censorship takes these forms, it is relatively easy to recognize (at least when *we* are being denied the ability to articulate a particular position). An obvious example of this type of censorship is when school boards decide to ban a book from the school library. Mark Twain's *Huckleberry Finn* and Kurt Vonnegut's *Slaughterhouse Five* are two frequently censored books for the implicit threats they contain against established authority. Students and people in the community are aware that such books have been banned, as the people who do the banning usually do so with much public fervor, as if silencing a book is a great moral achievement.

Sometimes, however, we do the work of the censor ourselves. Anytime that we believe that we know something and do not let ourselves be open to the position that what we know may change, given a conversation that we have with others, or given a new book that we read, then we are censoring our own minds. In totalitarian governments like Nazi Germany, censorship was overt and largely done for the Germans by their government. In governments where social control is more subtle, the need for self-censorship is more pressing. This is why rhetoric is seen as such a threat to our society and why the term has been demonized in the mass media. *Rhetoric is, first and foremost, an invitation to change.*[17] It is a not-so-subtle reminder that the world is constructed through language and that it can be reconstructed if people are committed to talking about things differently. This is why rhetoric is often burdened by such negative connotations. If people pay too much attention to rhetoric, they may see themselves victimized by it, and they might find that they can fight back through a language and vocabulary of their own. This is precisely what people are not encouraged to do. They are encouraged to see things as "real" and "given," existing in precisely the state in which they are given to them. As an act of resistance to this substantial form of social dominance, this text attempts to demystify rhetoric and to reveal the centrality and importance of rhetoric in our own society.

Rhetoric as Prescriptive Art

At its most basic level, rhetoric can be understood as a set of rules that can aid a communicator to be a more effective. In the words of Murphy: "Rhetoric is a prescriptive or preceptive art. By laying down specific prescriptions, based on analysis of observed speaking practices, rhetoric enables the experience of skilled speakers to be transmitted to later generations in the form of direct suggestions for conduct."[18]

The prescriptive nature of rhetoric is strongly evidenced in Aristotle's definition of rhetoric as "an ability, in each [particular] case, to see the available means of persuasion."[19] Another way of thinking about this is to see rhetoric as a "faculty," a way of thinking, a trained capacity by which a person can experience—and react—to the world in a particular way. Thus, Aristotle's assumption is that rhetoric is prescriptive, it is a training. The "available means" can be studied and taught, as his treatise instructs. As we have just seen, Aristotle assumes that rhetorical training can help a person to see the objective conditions that comprise the "rhetorical situation" or the context the persuader must address.[20] In addressing the situation, the persuader can do it "rightly" or "wrongly." That is, "better" or "worse" forms of rhetoric are measured by how closely they approximate the needs as determined by an objective situation. Such a view is useful, but it is not without its shortcomings. By viewing rhetoric only in this prescriptive way—tightly rule bound and passively dependent upon the situation—the more creative or epistemic functions of rhetoric are obscured.

"Epistemic" refers to the quality of language and persuasion to suggest, and thus to contribute, to a *new* understanding of the situation. People who believe that rhetoric is epistemic believe that our way of knowing is fundamentally bound up in our ability to exchange and debate ideas, thus making them meaningful.[21] Rhetoric, then, in its more broad sense, is not determined by the objective conditions of a situation, but can fundamentally act upon that situation in a meaningful way. Notice a fundamental difference between the two perspectives. In Aristotle's case, rhetoric can be judged by its *effect*. Does it or does it not lead to persuasion? In the second instance, rhetoric can be judged less on the effect of persuasion, and more on its strategic ability to influence our sense of self and society.

Television commercials can be understood by the two senses of rhetoric discussed above. On the one hand, they explore all the available means (often unethically) to get people to buy their products. Certainly, advertisers invest a great deal of money and expect to get that money back in the form of increased sales. But television commercials do something much more dangerous; they represent the epistemic function of rhetoric by creating a climate in which people come to accept television advertising as normal. From this perspective, it does not matter if a particular commercial is successful or not. Rather, advertisements must be considered persuasive because they help to structure our experience of U.S. society in such a way that the condition of commercialization and commodification seem to be natural.

Contemporary Definition

As suggested above, any contemporary definition of rhetoric must take into consideration the epistemic characteristics of language. Thus, a very simplistic, but useful contemporary definition of rhetoric is that it is the *strategic* use of language (strategic in the larger sense of a rationale, rather than in terms of a specific action).[22] By strategically structuring a speaker's thoughts, rhetoric aids the orator in becoming a more effective communicator. The measurement of persuasion, then, is not its end, but the product itself. Effective communication may not lead to persuasion. A persuasive appeal can fail, but can nevertheless be considered "good." Aristotle's perspective leads to a combative mentality where two orators face each other, battling for the soul of the community, one side prevailing over the over. The measurement of rhetoric, in the new sense of the term, is not success, but competency. A rhetorical theory, then, leads to our growth as communicators. As we shall see below, however, "competency" involves more than just skill: it involves an actual integration of a person's message and the audience to which it is intended. What is important is the integration, not the intent. In other words, we have "theory" on the one hand, and "practice" on the other, and what brings them together in a meaningful way is praxis—integration, influence, and the application of thought to meet the needs of the moment.

Effective Versus Ineffective Rhetorical Theory

As an example of an effective rhetorical theory and how it works in aiding the speaker toward the goal of competent communication, consider the following: All public speaking, as suggested in Roman rhetorical theory, can be broken down into five component parts: Invention, which is the conceptualization of the project at hand; Organization, which involves the placing of ideas into a sensible position; Style, which incorporates language to describe ideas; Memory, which is the retention of the above process; and Delivery, which is the actual communication of a speaker's ideas. These five points are called the "canons" of rhetoric and represent an important, although rudimentary, rhetorical theory. The assumption behind the theory is that a speaker can approach a particular discourse through these parts and give attention to each part individually. In so doing, the sum total of the effort would be a more competently prepared discourse. Of course, speakers often engage in a similar compositional practice without being aware of what they are doing. The practice of communication existed long before theory was designed to understand it. Nevertheless, the advantages of theory, any theory in any discipline, is that the more that the human mind reflects on its material practices, the more awareness and reflexivity can be brought to bare on a particular practice. Thus, the more consciously a person studies rhetorical principles, the more he/she can be sure that he/she is using language as effectively as possible. Since, by many standards, the ability to use language effectively is the most important thing we can do as individuals, citizens, employees, or leaders, the rationale for its study is even more clear.

Now that we have seen what an effective rhetorical theory is, and how it functions, we will contrast it with an example of an ineffective rhetorical theory. What is identified as "ineffective" rhetorical theory is actually more an assumption than a theory. A rhetorical theory, after all, is only as good as it is useful. So there is really no such thing as a "bad" theory of rhetoric (just degrees of usefulness).[23] There are, however, assumptions that people make about communication which actually detract from people's ability to achieve communication competency, as well as from their sense of agency in the construction of their communities and of their social lives.

The greatest detractor from a communicator's ability to communicate strategically is the belief that communication is not important, or that it interferes with "meaning." This will be discussed in greater detail when we explore the tensions throughout the history of Western culture between ontological and epistemological approaches to language, communication, and "truth." For now, however, a few words will suffice to help us understand these terms. If a person believes that units of meaning exist outside of human beings, then that person has articulated an ontological view of the world. Truth is what we find outside of our experiences. With such a view of truth in mind, language and communication can function only to transmit that knowledge—always a risky task. It is important for the communicator to transmit the information correctly, accurately, and precisely. Anything that interferes with the correctness, accuracy, and precision of that communication (things like subjectivity, style, emotions, and delivery) must be guarded against. Under such a perspective, it is not very fun to be a communicator. Communication itself is not seen as contributing anything to the world (which effectively cuts off criticism). The only way to talk genuinely is to "know" and the only way to "know" is to be an "authority." Communication, under this view, becomes simply a vehicle to transmit information or to mirror knowledge.[24] The more mathematical a language becomes, the better it is suited for this task.

Examples of this perspective, and the counter-perspective of epistemology, are scattered throughout this book. With Plato we will see that rhetoric (or communication) has an extremely subservient role to play in a world in which ontology or Truth is given an extra-linguistic prominence. In contrast to Plato, we will find that an epistemic view—one that recognizes truth as localized in subjective language communities—presents us with an opportunity to benefit from the rich experience language has to offer in the construction of our lives. We will see that our political reality—from our government down to our everyday interactions with people—is dependent upon a shared sense of community that is constructed through persuasion and is grounded in historical conditions. Before we move on to these more detailed discussions, however, we need to look at one example of a poor rhetorical perspective, and to understand how it is evoked by a world view that does not see communication as being very important to the structuring of our lives and to our societies.

Limitations of the First Amendment for Understanding Rhetorical Action

Consider the widely held belief that if one has something to say, then one ought to say it. Such a belief is an assertion of an individual's freedom. In the United States, citizens are frequently reminded that the right to speak one's mind is the most basic freedom ensured to Americans by the United States' Constitution. However, what is being asserted here is the right to speak, not the power to speak (or even directives on how to speak well). For example, while much of our speech is protected to various degrees, very little of it is encouraged. While it is politically important to have free speech as the basis for human liberty, it is more important, practically, to have something meaningful to say, and to have a forum available through which to have one's ideas widely disseminated. Freedom of speech, by itself, is a weak and insignificant freedom when it is not coupled with the material conditions to make that freedom a reality.

In the current United States, both of the above conditions are constrained, seriously undermining an environment in which rhetorical interaction can occur on a substantive level. First, to have something meaningful to say presupposes an educational system and a mass media that allows for a range of divergent viewpoints to be expressed, and is dependent upon a historical consciousness so that those viewpoints can take on substance and meaning. The fact that few Americans know the history of

their nation in any detail, or have a working sense of the political potentialities that lie outside of the two mainstream political parties, highlights
an important curtailment on our ability to think in meaningful ways.[25]
The implications for this on rhetoric and communication are immense.
Second, even supposing that we could find ourselves in a position where
we can be exposed to the necessary education to begin thinking historically and more broadly from a political point of view, we would find that
the forums available to us to communicate our ideas in a meaningful way
are limited at best. The mass media is representative of the limitations
that we have on our thought, and is unlikely to give us opportunity to
communicate or to give exposure to our ideas.[26] Even in the unlikely
event that our ideas were communicated, they would be couched in such
a way as to render them unattractive (for instance, they would be described as "radical"). Thus, we can see that the freedom to communicate
is dependent upon the ability to think differently than other people *and*
to access the media to share those ideas in a way in which they can have
influence.[27] After all, the public sphere is supposed to be public. The condition of democracy and a monopoly on public communication by the
wealthy media owners are incompatible constructs—each mutually implies the exclusion of the other.

In a sense, both the First Amendment and the widely held belief that
all a person needs to be an effective speaker is to have something to say,
are examples of a poor rhetorical perspective. Both offer an incomplete
vision of what communication in a democracy can and should mean.
The effect is the same, no matter which of the two views of rhetoric offered earlier we take. That is, if rhetoric is the art of matching formulaic
precepts with material situations to locate the objective spots where persuasion is likely to occur, or if rhetoric is the strategic use of language to
construct community and to become competent communicators,
rhetoric's epistemic effects are severely compromised. By implication,
rhetoric is incomplete without a wider social commitment to communication as a source of individual and community empowerment. A perusal of the "Letters to the Editor" section of any newspaper quickly reveals how ineffective it is just to "speak one's mind." Such faith in the
First Amendment creates the illusion that what one has to say matters. In
the world of corporate control, however, communication and influence
are not anywhere the same thing (although writing a letter to make our
point might make us feel better). Feeling "good" is certainly one function
of communication, but a lesser function of rhetorical communication.
Rhetoric, at least "good" rhetoric, aims above immediate gratification.
Rhetoric is not about *feeling* "good," it is about *doing* "good." Good
deeds, inspired by rhetorical persuasion, are one of the highest aims of
the educated mind.

So what is wrong about these letters to the editor that we find in hundreds of newspapers throughout the country? First, many of these letters are not well written and are rhetorically unsound at the most basic level. Second, even if they are well written, they tend to be representative of a world view that lacks a larger historical perspective and a wider education on the various dimensions of important issues. Granted, such a statement involves a sweeping over-generalization, and thus must be held very suspect. Nevertheless, it is the case that viewpoints that diverge from acceptable patterns tend not to be represented in the mass media, and this is evidenced from the broadcast news down to the editorial section of the local newspaper. In other words, viewpoints that seriously challenge the established beliefs that underlie our social institutions and justify the status quo simply do not appear in the mainstream press and mass media. The more original the thought (in terms of a political imagination), the more informed and challenging the thought (in terms of a substantive analysis of the present historical situation), the less likely it will be given the opportunity to be communicated.

When I speak of the mass media being about social control, this is precisely what I mean. The media does not control us by forcing us to think in a particular way, it controls us by limiting the terrain on which our thought is possible. Besides the above restraints, there is no objective reason why we cannot talk meaningfully about the injustice and criminality of much U.S. foreign policy, or about the benefits of socialized medicine, or the worthiness of unions and their contributions to a widely inclusive democracy. There is no reason why we cannot talk about democratizing the workplace, or about a whole host of other important issues, such as homelessness and its causes and solutions. These topics cannot even be raised for the purpose of debate. It is difficult for us even to *think* in terms of these issues. The mass media has eviscerated them as potentialities.[28]

A good rhetorical perspective, on the other hand, is one that helps the speaker to approach a speaking engagement with the ability to be proficient in the enunciation of one's position within the context of a meaningful exchange of ideas. In an important sense, rhetoric is inseparable from the democratic community that gives it significance. Even at the interpersonal level, persuasion is only significant when two people share enough of a communal awareness that they recognize each other as being an instrumental part of their collective social reality. Communication, after all, is always *for something*. In an ideal world there would not be much communication, at least not much persuasion. We would all understand each other so thoroughly and identify with each other so completely, that community would be assumed, and we would act in accordance with each other's needs. The extent to which we do not act in accordance with community reaffirming principles is the extent to which we have to compensate through persuasion to reestablish the social bonds that we have destroyed through a language that excludes, rather than affirms solidarity.

The First Amendment is an assertion of communicator rights, not a prescription of how to be an effective or ethical communicator. The fact that we are told that it is okay to speak our minds confuses an important distinction that most Americans fail to make. There is a difference between a freedom in the abstract and a freedom that is defined in action. We are all free to quit our jobs at any time, for example, a very important abstract freedom that keeps us from being slaves. Yet, in terms of the realm of actions, quitting our jobs would put us in a precarious financial situation. In order for our freedom to quit our jobs to become meaningful, some important prior conditions need to be met. We need to be independently wealthy, have someone take care of us, or be reasonably sure that we can find employment somewhere else. If any of these conditions is not met, then our "freedom to work" as it is called, can be reframed as "freedom to starve," "freedom to be homeless," and "freedom to be denied health care." In the same sense, the belief that freedom to speak is important is only half of the rhetorical equation. Communication is fundamentally about building community, and that cannot be done unless a person has access to an audience.

Conclusion

To speak one's mind is not necessarily to practice rhetoric in the sense defined here. A communicator engages in rhetoric only to the extent that discourse is addressed strategically. To be strategic, one must speak well, but one also must have the opportunity to confront the issues in a meaningful and public way. This is becoming exceedingly difficult as the public is defined in ways that limit popular participation.

Now that we know some of the ways in which rhetoric can be meaningfully conceptualized and some of the issues that surround what a good rhetorical perspective is supposed to accomplish, let us turn to ancient Athens and explore its approach to rhetoric. The purpose for doing so is less for historical reasons (although we will cover important historical ground). Rather, this study of Ancient Athens can be better seen as a study of ourselves. Thus, in the pages that follow, I will work from out of the classical literatures, but will do so in a way that reacts in light of our present contingencies. There is a fundamental bias to this book, and it can be stated as follows: a study of Greek rhetoric can tell us much about who we are. This may sound strange, when contemplating the more than two thousand years that separate the Ancient world from us.

If it is true that rhetoric is a way of establishing community, and if it is true that rhetorical theory helps to create competent communicators within the framework of a democratic community, then the first thing we have to do is to question all the assumptions we hold as Truth. We have to look very carefully at what we mean by "rhetoric," what we mean by "democracy," and what we mean by "community." If communication is the study of who we are and what we can do, then we need to study the present. But to do so we need a vantage point. We need to look at ourselves from somewhere. While Ancient Greece and modern North America are very different, there are some large philosophical issues and trends, as well as rhetorical patterns and tensions, that are common to both societies. Furthermore, since we are trying to chart the intersections between communication and community, there is really no better place to start than Ancient Athens, where many of these ideas are given their first detailed attention. Certainly, Ancient Athens is not the only place where this is true, but it is a place that we find more or less familiar. We may be other things, and we may come from other places. But as a modern nation caught up in the cultural tensions of the present, we can learn a great deal about ourselves by exploring the tensions that existed in the days of the Ancient Greeks.

Notes

1. "The Origins and Early Development of Rhetoric," in *A Synoptic History of Classical Rhetoric*, ed. James J. Murphy (Davis, CA: Hermagoras Press, 1983), 3.

2. "Ancient Egyptian Rhetoric," *Rhetorica* 1 (1983), 21.

3. See Edward Schiappa, "*Rhetorike*: What's In a Name? Toward a Revised History of Early Greek Rhetorical Theory," *Quarterly Journal of Speech* 78 (1992), 1–15.

4. *Classical Rhetoric and its Christian and Secular Tradition from Ancient to Modern Times* (Chapel Hill: The University of North Carolina Press, 1980), 7.

5. Karen Foss, Sonja Foss, and Robert Trapp's chapter, "Challenges to the Rhetorical Tradition," provides a good starting place for students interested in exploring non-Western forms of rhetorical theory. See their *Contemporary Perspectives on Rhetoric* 2nd ed. (Prospect Heights, IL: Waveland Press), 273-314. For two specific studies see J. Vernon Jensen, "Rhetorical Emphases of Taoism," *Rhetorica* 5 (1987): 219–229; and Henry Louis Gates, Jr., *The Signifying Monkey: A Theory of Afro-American Literary Criticism* (New York: Oxford University Press, 1988).

6. Robert T. Oliver, who for years was the only scholar to produce articles on Asian rhetoric, tended to approach non-western rhetoric from an Aristotelian perspective. See his "The Confucian Rhetorical Tradition in Korea During the Yi Dynasty (1392–1910)," *Quarterly Journal of Speech* 45 (1959), 364–373; "The Rhetorical Implications of Taoism," *Quarterly Journal of Speech* 47 (1961), 27–35; and *Communication and Culture in Ancient India and China* (Syracuse: Syracuse University Press, 1971).

7. "The Historiography of Philosophy: Four Genres," in *Philosophy in History: Essays on the Historiography of Philosophy*, eds. Richard Rorty, J.B. Schneewind, and Quentin Skinner (Cambridge: Cambridge University Press, 1984), 51.

8. See Thomas S. Kuhn, *The Structure of Scientific Revolutions* 2nd. ed. (Chicago: University of Chicago Press, 1970).

9. Eric Havelock, *The Literate Revolution in Greece and its Cultural Consequences* (Princeton: Princeton University Press, 1982).

10. *Against the Sophists and Antidosis*, trans. G.B. Norlin. Loeb Classical Library, vol 2. (Cambridge: Harvard University Press, 1956), 327.

11. *Intellectual Experiments of the Greek Enlightenment.* (Princeton: Princeton University Press, 1975), 5.

12. *Rhetoric and Reality: Writing Instruction in American Colleges, 1900–1985* (Carbondale: Southern Illinois University Press, 1987), 3.

13. *Permanence and Change: An Anatomy of Purpose* (Berkeley: University of California Press, 1984).

14. See Frank Lentricchia, *Criticism and Social Change* (Chicago: The University of Chicago Press, 1983).

15. A.D. Leeman, "The Variety of Classical Rhetoric," in *Rhetoric Revalued*, ed. Brian Vickers (Binghamton: Center for Medieval and Early Renaissance Studies, 1982), 41.

16. The words are President Eisenhower's. See *Peace with Justice* (New York: Columbia University Press, 1961), 34–44.

17. John Poulakos, "Rhetoric, the Sophists, and the Possible," *Communication Monographs* 51: (1984), 215–225.

18. Unpublished files on the instruction of graduate and undergraduate courses in classical rhetoric. These notes were given to me when Professor Murphy retired from the University of California, Davis, in 1991.

19. *On Rhetoric: A Theory of Civic Discourse*, trans. George A. Kennedy (New York: Oxford University Press, 1991), 36.

20. See Lloyd F. Bitzer, "The Rhetorical Situation," *Philosophy and Rhetoric* 1 (1968), 1–14.

21. Much of the vast literature on this subject stems from an article by Robert L. Scott, "On Viewing Rhetoric as Epistemic," *Central States Speech Journal* 18 (1967), 9–17.

22. See Donald Bryant, "Rhetoric: Its Functions and Its Scope," *Quarterly Journal of Speech* 39 (1953), 401–424.

23. See Barry Brummett, "Rhetorical Theory as Heuristic and Moral: A Pedagogical Justification," *Communication Education* 33 (1984), 97–107.

24. See Richard Rorty, *Philosophy and the Mirror of Nature* (Princeton: Princeton University Press, 1979).

25. To test the reasonability of this assertion, readers should compare their understanding of U.S. history with Howard Zinn's *A People's History of the United States* (New York: Harper and Row, 1980). The extent to which Zinn's history diverges from what most Americans understand about U.S. history, is the extent to which a historical awareness is lacking in this country, severely compromising Americans' ability to react intelligently to political issues.

26. Edward S. Herman and Noam Chomsky, *Manufacturing Consent: The Political Economy of the Mass Media* (New York: Pantheon Books, 1988).

27. For further analysis of this sort, as well as documentation of specific studies that more clearly establish these claims, see Michael Parenti, *Inventing Reality: The Politics of the News Media* (New York: St. Martin's Press, 1993).

28. Noam Chomsky, *Necessary Illusions: Thought Control in Democratic Societies* (Boston: South End Press, 1989).

1

The Circumstance Behind the Development of Rhetorical Theory

In Classical Athens, as well as today, rhetoric can be understood as a system of communication that has the power to alter and shape an audience's way of thinking or acting. It is a dynamic force that influences our lives in various ways. From the very beginning of Western culture, the Greeks felt that persuasion could color our experiences and even beguile us, as if by magic, to sway us toward particular ends. The Ancient Greeks began a systematic study of this phenomenon in order to understand its influence, and to tame and control it. In so doing, they stripped it of its magic, and turned it into an art. More specifically, they developed a vocabulary by which they could meaningfully interpret their social world. This vocabulary, like any vocabulary, reified the concept and gave it a substance that could be studied and understood.

Persuasion became, over time, "rhetoric"—the art of speaking. Yet this "art" did not spring up from nowhere. Its articulation as a body of knowledge, its boundaries, and its implications, are the results of historical conditions that give a cultural resonance to the need for such a language and literature. In other words, the vocabulary and knowledge that the Greeks recognized as being important were the result of historical accidents and conditions, indicative of their particular historical moments. While it is tempting to look to the past and to maintain that because something exists (i.e. "rhetoric"), it *must* exist, we must resist such temptations. It is impossible to know that which we do not have a language for, and the language that we do have is dependent upon the way knowledge has been conceptualized in the past. Rhetoric is a historical contingency, as is all of our knowledge in the West. All knowledge is dependent upon the need for its use. If this is true, how do we know anything? More importantly, how do we know that we know?

The Need for Historicization in the Study of Ideas

There are two ways to answer the question of what it means to know. The first is to acknowledge that the quest for certainty is the vain attempt to control the material world within the constraints of the limited human mind. Nothing is for certain: even scientific knowledge, based on the inductive model, is never more than a commitment to accepting as true a proposition that has repeatedly been shown to be constant over a number of instances. Yet the phenomenon itself cannot be true: strictly speaking, what is "true" or "false" is not the phenomenon, but the sentences we use to describe those phenomenon.[1] Furthermore, the truth value of any scientific claim is dependent upon the probability that because some phenomenon occurred x amount of times, it will continue to occur. Even an understanding of death, as a phenomenon, eludes us. We can say with a good deal of certainty that a specific person will die. But we do not know what that *means*. What does it mean to die? What does it mean to live? The condition of death is colored by our definitions of what death is; thus our behaviors or reactions toward the death of others are never behaviors directed toward the phenomenon of death, but toward the meanings we construe surrounding death.[2] The condition of life is similarly constrained. If these questions seem philosophical and meaningless, consider the controversy over abortion and euthanasia, and it quickly becomes apparent that the quest for "certainty" never leads to solid ground. What we are left with is reasoning, argument, persuasion, and rhetoric.

The second way to answer the question of what it means to know is very much tied to the first. It is also rhetorical and involves the historicization of ideas. Once again, the thinker or knower is not driven by a desire to reach absolute certainty on an issue; rather, what becomes important is seeing things as they evolved over time and the context in which they were evoked. The more access we have to this data, the better we are able to synthesize some sort of understanding about the thing we wish to know. If we are careful enough in our methods, we can get a good understanding about what it is that we know. However, we can only get a very small glimpse of certainty, and the things that we tend to feel that we know for certain usually become associated with the truth or falsity of sentences. In other words, there is little to know besides our descriptions of the world. This does not mean that we simply make up the world; on the contrary, what it means is that we have a responsibility to engage with the world as it exists in order to make it meaningful and useful to us. For example, while various legal, legislative, religious, and medical authorities might debate on what it means to know when someone is alive or dead, we, as a society, have to decide how it is we are going to treat people. There are no easy answers to these or to most questions that have cultural or scientific significance. But it is not the answers that matter, it is the way we form the questions and the way we go about searching for usefulness that becomes important to us.

In order to know what these questions are, we have to historicize our search for them. The more that we historicize our language and our ideas, the better able we are to understand the context or situation that called such language into existence. Thus, in order to understand better the implications of the Greeks' system of rhetoric and its relationship and usefulness to our own, we must, prior to discussing the specifics of rhetorical theory as it began to exist in the fourth century BCE, touch on some of the major influences in Greek life that existed previous to that time so that we can see how the *need* for a rhetorical theory arose.

To go back to our prior example, death exists. However, our theory of death, or our explanation of death, does not exist independent of our need for such a theory. To the extent that religion is an explanation for death, and perhaps our oldest explanation, then death becomes meaningful for us. To the extent that science gives us an understanding of death, then death is made meaningful to us. In either case, such meaning is not natural. We may react to death on a personal level, and we may even mourn our loved ones who die. But this does not mean that we have a knowledge of death, or that we would even care if people not in our immediate circle die. We must not confuse our personal experiences of a phenomenon with an assumed knowledge of it. The same applies to an understanding of rhetoric or of communication. People communicate. That is clear. Without communication, books would not exist and human culture would not have progressed to the state it has now reached. Nevertheless, the way we talk about communication, the way we conceptualize it, theorize about it, reflects the needs we have: our need to be political, our need to be religious, our need to be social, etc.

Just as doctors, lawyers, politicians, and theologians exist because of societal needs to understand the dimensions of life and death, and everything in between, rhetorical or communication theorists discuss language in such a way that that it becomes meaningful. As mentioned in the Introduction, these discussions always imply a politics. Our theories of life, such as those that inform the question "When is a fetus a baby?" and of death, "When can we terminate a life support system on a comatose patient?" reflect our political biases. We cannot help but to blur the political, personal, and the perceptual, as knowledge is based on need, and the question of need is always political and dependent upon our perceptions. Need starts from a subjective sense of what one is in relationship to others. Thus, all understanding reflects a desire to see something as important to one's self. People undertake to construct knowledge (or systems of knowledge) when they feel that some part of their experience is lacking. As the philosopher Michel Foucault has argued, knowledge is like a knife: its purpose is to cut the world in certain ways. Knowledge, in short, is the result of a political economy that invests in a particular knowledge institution. This point should be kept in mind as we explore the rise of rhetoric as an area of inquiry in ancient Greece, for such a knowledge cannot be appreciated without a prior understanding of the culture that created the space for rhetoric to emerge.[3]

To the above ends, this chapter discusses the circumstance behind rhetoric as an area of conceptualization, highlighting the implications of the oral tradition in the development of rhetoric, and exploring the major institutions of Greek culture. This overview should illustrate the centrality of rhetoric in Greek life. Moreover, our analysis will uncover certain contradictions that existed in Greek society, and will discuss those conditions, in relationship to the concept of rhetoric as epistemic. This chapter concludes by applying the lessons garnered from the Greek experience to the contemporary political environment of the United States (in an effort to make sense of the U.S. political experience).

The Circumstance Behind the Rise of Rhetoric

Since rhetoric is a social phenomenon, to begin our exploration of it we must look at Greek social life. At its most fundamental level, Greek social life was political and community based. Politically, these communities were organized in the forms of independent city/states known as the polis. Our own words "politics" and "police" come from this root. Politics is the art of governing the polis, and the police are agents that control the populace on behalf of the politicians. Some of our current cities in the United States have the word polis in their root (for example, Annapolis, Maryland; Indianapolis, Indiana; and Minneapolis, Minnesota). The fact that our current words "politics" and "police" contain the root "polis" gives us some clue to the similarities that exist between the Greek and the modern worlds. Our modern understanding of what it means to govern and be governed are socially constructed and linguistically tied to past theory. In a sense, the Greeks "invented" politics (at least in a Western sense) by conceiving of the polis in the way they did. Having done so, they needed to have a way to talk about what the polis was, how it functioned, and what were its characteristics. Having objectified an abstract mass of people as a political entity, the Greeks found that it was now possible to discuss relationships among them. Of the hundreds of Greek communities that flourished during the Classical Age, Athens was by far the most important. During the classical period of rhetoric, which corresponds to the so-called "Golden Age" of Greece, Athens became the standard against which Greek culture was measured. It was Athenian definitions that came to prefigure the relationships among the Greek city states. Furthermore, it was Athenian intellectual developments that prefigured the intellectual terrain of the region. This does not make Athens "right" or "better" or even important in a metaphysical sense. It simply means that Athens was the most hegemonic of all the Greek city states. It set the standards because it informed the standards. Similarly, the United States seems to have affected and influenced much of the world's culture in the twentieth century. This does not mean that the United States is the most important country in the world, as North Americans like to imagine. Rather, it means that the United States, like Athens, has successfully forced its standards and definitions upon the rest of the world. Much of the world is increasingly modeling itself on the "American" standard. This is not a sign of our brilliance; rather, it is a sign of the rest of the world's inability to resist the U.S. on military and cultural terrains.

The only other *polis* that approximated Athens in military or political strength during this time was Sparta. Sparta, however, developed upon different lines than did Athens. As a slave society, like Athens, and like the U.S. before 1865, it feared the large portion of its population that was consigned to servitude. In order to defend itself against this population, and in order to compete militarily with Athens, Sparta developed into a society of police and soldiers. To anticipate a point made later in this chapter, societies that repress others, in their own country or outside, develop into militaristic powers that eventually constrain the liberties and freedoms of their own people. For example, the victims of the Nazis certainly suffered much more than did the German people themselves, yet it cannot be denied that the repressive apparatus of the German state curtailed the liberty of the average German citizen. The American South under slavery was occupied by roaming armies of state and private militia groups whose ostensible goal was to monitor the slaves. In the process, however, white people who were critical of slavery or of other aspects of Southern life (such as the economic conditions of white tenant farmers) found themselves in less than comfortable situations. In the United States during the cold war and now, the formidable intelligence and police power of this country, purportedly created to fight what was demonized as "communism," has often been turned to monitor and control dissent. The recent crime bill signed by President Clinton will also serve a similar function.

For example, during the 1960s, the Civil Rights movement came under attack from the Federal Government. The CIA, the FBI, and other government agencies targeted civil rights leaders for harassment and worse. Martin Luther King Jr. and Malcolm X were assassinated, as were scores of Black Panther Party members. Stokely Carmichael and Eldridge

Cleaver were forced to flee the country. Similar acts of repression were directed toward the anti-Vietnam War protesters. In the 1980s, to take a more recent example, government agencies harassed people associated with the various grassroots movements to resist U.S. intervention in Central America, particularly in El Salvador and Nicaragua, where the U.S. government was financing bloody civil wars. In the case of Nicaragua, the United States was attempting to topple the peasant backed government, and in El Salvador, the U.S. was defending the fascist oligarchy against the insurgent population.[4]

Sparta suffered for its slavery, but it did learn a valuable lesson in terms of its future conflicts with Athens: social austerity has its military benefits. In its rivalry with Athens, Sparta was eventually forced by Athens into a series of open military conflicts. This eventually led to the defeat of Athens, wider instability in the region, and the eclipse of Greece's political might. More on this area will be discussed when we highlight the limitations of the Athenian "democracy." The price that Sparta paid for its military preparations was cultural. Athens had it both ways: the Athenian people had their cake and were able to eat it too, for a while. The success of Athenian imperialism, as we will discuss later, enabled it to support powerful armed forces while, at the same time, to maintain a prosperity and cultural life at home. Once again, the analogy to the United States cannot be overstated: imperial powers often justify their policies to their own citizens with the artistic, scientific, and intellectual developments that are supported by the spoils of foreign conquest. The choice that aggressive governments have to make is between guns and butter. The more successful ones are able to give both to their citizens. The less successful ones often opt for guns.

This said, where does this leave us in terms of rhetoric? Rhetoric, we will see, was one of the intellectual developments that the wealth of Athens was able to buy. It served certain needs among the citizens of Athens; more importantly, it was useful for the government in influencing the decisions that contributed to specific political realities.

Sparta, on the other hand, had no use for rhetoric, or for art or for philosophy, generally, because its cultural and monetary resources were invested in other areas; it had other needs. This is not to say that rhetoric was invented by the Athenians to serve their hegemonic political needs. Rather, it is to suggest that Athens needed rhetoric and thus developed it. Its internal political structure as well as its foreign policy were informed by that decision. Its advancements in the arts and sciences were fueled by the resources commanded by its politics. Thus, rhetoric is a symptom of Athens' wealth as well as a factor in its internal politics that led to its military superiority. Similarly, culture and progress in the United States during the twentieth-century must be seen as reflecting, as well as contributing to, the wider political environment of North American global hegemony. The question that can be asked at this point is: How much affluence is needed to justify any self-serving foreign policy? In the face of such affluence, at what point does the citizen say "enough!"? This is a sensitive question, but its difficulty does not obviate the struggle for an answer.

Geographical Conditions.   In part because of a hot climate with poor, dry farm land, the Athenians were forced to import by ship many of the raw resources needed to run their city. Aided by its geography, which included a large natural port, Athens became a central city in the Mediterranean. As Moses Hadas explains, "It has been suggested, plausibly enough, that the physical configuration of Greek lands shaped Greek character and political institutions."[5] For example, the same mountains that favor the development of independent city states—because of arduous land travel between neighboring communities—encouraged the development of Greece's sea-faring culture. In short, it was easier to travel by sea than by land. Also, because of the harsh land conditions, the Athenians developed into an interdependent people. For example, it took the labor of about three people to grow enough food for those three to support themselves and sustain a fourth.[6] Such slim margin of survival is important to consider when pondering the Athenian character. The climatic conditions encouraged the interdependence of people for education and survival. As W.C. Hardy explains, "[T]he homeland of the Greeks was a bare, rugged, and poor country."[7] Such a situation bred sociability among the Athenians, who depended upon each other for support. The fact that the Athenians could not produce much of what they needed to survive meant that they had to import much of what they consumed. This condition led to an important cultural factor: trade.

The Importance of Trade.   Similar to any port city, Athens became flooded with material objects. However, with merchandise comes people, and, as Hardy points out, "ships are freighted with ideas as well as with goods."[8] This historical condition can be seen repeated throughout the world. All the major civilizations have started on or nearby large bodies of water. Egyptian civilization grew up bedside the Nile. Chinese civilization grow up beside the Yellow River. Indian society grew up on the Ganges. Mesopotamian society grew up on the Euphrates. In addition, the intellectual centers of many countries are associated with their points of trade. In the United States, for example, Boston, New York, San Francisco, and Chicago have tended, historically, to be intellectual centers of this nation, due to the fact that they were centers of trade. With trade and commerce comes culture.

The Rhapsodes.   For the ancient Athenians, the most important purveyor of culture before the development of rhetoric was the rhapsodes. The rhapsodes were oral poets who preserved the work of Homer and passed on the religious and cultural traditions found in the pre-literate Greek society. The rhapsodes traveled throughout Greece, performing for pay and competition. They were, in the words of Donald E. Hargis, the "public reciters of epic poetry."[9] The function of epic poetry in Greek society at this time should not be underestimated. Prior to the fifth century, Greek society was oral. There was no alphabet, no written language of any kind. Without a written language, knowledge had to be codified in some way. The method of codification was narrative and the form was epic poetry. The rhapsodes, in other words, were the repertories of Greek knowledge as Greece existed in a pre-literate state. Both Richard Enos and Hargis provide excellent surveys of the rhapsodes in terms of their evolution and cultural implications. For example, Enos explains how "[t]he rhapsodes were the principle force in composing, transmitting, and codifying the oral literature of ancient Greece prior to the time of Corax, Tisias, Isocrates, Plato, and Aristotle."[10] Enos and Hargis agree that the rhapsodes provided an important educational opportunity in Greek life. "[T]he rhapsode became an 'educational instrument' as well as an entertainer, with the *Iliad* and the *Odyssey* as his 'textbooks' of reference."[11] In elaborating on this sentiment, Enos explains, "[R]espect for the rhapsodes was widespread, particularly among sophists such as Protagoras, who admired rhapsodes for the attempt to use Homer as a means of providing a practical education."[12]

The rhapsodes "prospered as highly regarded and esteemed representatives of Greek culture for at least nine centuries."[13] Thus, any account of rhetoric's development during this time must take into consideration who and what the rhapsodes were. While they were not theorists of language, and while they had nothing to say about rhetoric or rhetorical theory, they did serve an important pre-theoretical function by 1) providing examples of oratory as found in Homer, and 2) highlighting for the Greeks the power of speech in captivating an audience and in instructing people in morality. By providing access to the works of Homer, the rhapsodes provided people with means of accessing culture. Within the works of Homer, people learned the proper ways of being Greek. The rhapsodes were important gatekeepers; they transmitted and controlled cultural knowledge from generation to generation.

In the intellectual climate of Athens, the rhapsodes exalted the deeds and words of the Greek gods such as Zeus, the ruling god, Apollo, the sun god, Athena, the goddess of wisdom, and Aphrodite, the goddess of love. In so doing, the "Rhapsodes played an important part in the development of oral and written expression. . . . "[14] Before the fifth century BCE Greek society was largely oral. The Greek poet Homer and the historian Herodotus record many examples of oratory as it was practiced before the advancement of rhetorical theory. George Kennedy notes, "[T]he

Greek hero was from the start a speaker of words as well as a doer of deeds. . . . "[15] The literature of both ancient writers illustrates that eloquence was both valued and feared within the Greek tradition long before theories were developed to explain the phenomenon of persuasion. John W.H. Waldon adds, "The Greeks were by nature a people of speakers, and from early times the art of oratory was highly prized among them."[16] The qualities most valued in a person were strong speech and powerful deeds as illustrated by the heroes found in Homer's *Iliad* and *Odyssey.*[17] This oral tradition represents Greece's early enthusiasm for the power of the spoken word: "When the study of rhetoric began in the fifth century BC [sic], much of what was said was merely a theorizing of conventional practice. Techniques of rhetorical theory are already evident in the speeches of the Homeric poems."[18]

Book IX of the *Iliad* presents discourse that offers the clearest evidence for an incipient rhetorical consciousness in Homer. The notion of skilled public speaking existing in Homeric times is developed by K.E. Wilkerson. Similar to Kennedy, Wilkerson argues that there exists "[a] close similarity between forms of discourse found in the eighth century and those found in the fifth. . . . "[19] Wilkerson's premise is that Greek oratory was functionally unchanged by fifth century theorizing. He explains, "Although preliterate speaking . . . was uninformed by theory, it did not differ very much from the speaking that was so informed in the fifth century."[20]

Other forms of entertainment in ancient Athens included dramas, politically based dinner clubs, and daily social contact in the Agora (market place). George Miller Calhoun expresses the political implications of these organizations: "The formidable political strength comprised in the membership of these clubs is attested by the two occasions which they were able completely to dominate the state. We know further that individual clubs were at all times factors of the utmost importance in the political and litigious activities of the Athenians."[21]

James Greenwood explains that the clubs served as a way of funding trials and "also were valuable for the pressure . . . that they could collectively apply to the prosecutor."[22]

Art and Ideology.   Permeating Greek cultural life was art, the presentation of which contributed to the spiritual and political life of the community. An example of this is found in Greek tragedy. In studying Greek drama, Aristotle argues that it utilizes a device called catharsis. The purpose of catharsis is to purge the emotion of an audience of its socially unhealthy elements and to reconnect the audience to the human condition, as defined by the status quo of the community. According to Kenneth Burke, the civic nature of Classical Greek tragedy is accentuated by its cathartic appeal: "[It attains] maximum cathartic effect to the extent that, whatever the disputes that plagued the city, the audience (which was composed of *all conflicting classes* among the citizenry) could be infused with a unified attitude. This would be the case if all members of the audience, despite the conflicting interests in their daily relationships with one another, could be brought to weep in unison at the pathos of an intensely dramatic fiction."[23]

Thus, one function of drama within a social community is to arouse safely certain negative feelings within the context of the theatre, feelings that, to the extent that they exist *outside* of the theater, may be considered harmful for the community (Aristotle gives the examples of pity and fear).[24] Certainly, art has other functions within a community, but one function is always control: by focusing our attention on some aspect of life—through aesthetic statements or representations—art necessarily distracts us from thinking about something else. Drama, in particular, by highlighting salient social issues, accentuates the importance of some issues over others and offers a resolution that supports some political position.

In other words, artistic expression serves as a form of "rhetoric," a strategic extension of the human desire to find or create order and meaning in human existence. Art, in this sense, is a transcendence or a definition. It either reifies the current position or persuades people to adopt another. More practically, art equips people for living by helping them to define and otherwise interpret their lives. Burke develops this theme in his essay, "Literature As Equipment For Living."[25] He writes that "art forms like 'tragedy' or 'comedy' or 'satire' [can] be treated as *equipments for living*, that size up situations in various ways and in keeping with correspondingly various attitudes."[26]

Burke's ideas about art and politics gain a great deal of their salience from the Greeks. The Ancient Greeks recognized that art is not inconsequential. The potential danger, as well as the potential beneficence of art, can be characterized in two ways—the Platonic "ideological" way and the Aristotelian "aesthetic" way. Burke calls the above characteristics the "censorship principle" and the "lightning rod principle."[27] He explains that, according to Plato's perspective, art is *overtly* ideological and serves "as a means of lining us up on behalf of the state, a theory now generally associated with totalitarian governments."[28] On the other hand, Burke explains that, in line with Aristotle's theory of catharsis, art is potentially therapeutic, as well as *inadvertently* ideological—it purifies society (or circumvents popular unrest) "by draining-off dangerous charges, as lightning rods are designed, not to 'suppress' danger, but to draw it into harmless channels."[29] As Burke recognizes, along with other social critics,[30] the propagandistic functions of art are not vulgarly repressive in our society as they are in more obviously totalitarian states. This lack of vulgarity, however, does not make the Aristotelian "lightning rod" principle any less severe in manipulating our beliefs, attitudes, values, and behaviors.[31]

Art, then, was taken seriously by the Ancient Greeks, in ways that are seldom appreciated today. As mentioned above, theatre, in particular, was a salient political and cultural feature of Greek life. As E.F. Watling observes, Greek tragedy "touched the deepest centers of man's [sic] individual and corporate consciousness."[32] The early Greeks realized, as we need to learn today, that art can be seen as an extension of social, economic, and religious identity, and it is frequently infused into the political agenda. Art is never innocuous; like rhetoric, it is always an opportunity to change, to revise, to accept or reject things as they are represented and reified by the status quo.

Solon. By the year 440 BCE Athens had become the political and cultural center of the Hellenic world. Athens had entered her so-called "Golden Age." However briefly this age may have lasted (about 30 years if we take as our standard the reign of Pericles, 461–429 BCE), Western culture has continued to look back to that period with reverence for the accomplishments the Athenians made. With regard to this period of time, Richard A. Katuala asserts, "No thirty year period of history can compare to it."[33] These accomplishments were in the arts, sciences, and politics, and they will be discussed in more detail as we move through this chapter. The important point now, however, is that these accomplishments did not come easily. In and prior to 594 BCE Athens was ruled by an oligarchy of aristocrats. Similar to oligarchies today in places like Central and South America, the oligarchy that controlled Athens was selfish and brutal. A few people controlled all the wealth and land, reducing the people to depravity. Living conditions were intolerable and landless debtors were forced into slavery or prison. This led to social strife between the common people and the ruling elite. Just as similar conditions in the twentieth century have led to revolution in places like Russia, China, Cuba, Vietnam, Korea, El Salvador, Nicaragua, Guatemala, Chile, and scores of other places throughout the Third World, the social inequities of oligarchic Athens were pushing society to the brink of an open conflict.

In a last ditch effort to stave off a wide-spread revolt, a man named Solon was chosen by the ruling class to serve as an arbiter between the common people and their aristocratic landlords. He was given the authority by the ruling class to negotiate a limited settlement with the people. His job was to alleviate some of the tensions, while keeping intact the bulk of class privilege. He was selected to serve as an arbiter because he was a poet and was thus respected by the people. In the pre-literate age, poets were respected to a degree that has not been seen since. Poets were the people responsible for the codification of culture. Poetics as a method was a way to help people learn things and to remember the past. Recall the role that the rhapsodes played in Greek society. Poetry was the currency upon which social knowledge was exchanged.

Solon surprised both the aristocracy and the citizens of Athens by dictating a set of revolutionary laws, thus creating conditions in which a future democracy could emerge. History remembers Solon as "The Law Giver." Solon may be regarded as the first known individual to articulate such a shift in political consciousness, one respecting the rights of the common people. Great ideas, however, seldom appear in a vacuum; Solon studied in Egypt and watched as challenges were made to the divine status of kings and to the rule of the gods there. In fact, Solon might not have been the only Greek to travel to places in Africa, in particular to Egypt and Ethiopia, and to have learned from non-European cultures. There is evidence to suggest that many of the Sophists and philosophers also traveled outside of Greece and may have picked up some of their important ideas from non-Greek sources. One scholar, in particular, has done important primary research in this area. The research of Martin Bernal challenges us to rethink the history of Western culture and our understandings of the evolution of civilization. Bernal's great contribution has been his two volume, *Black Athena: The Afroasiatic Roots of Classical Civilization.*[34]

Bernal's study documents the prehistory of the Mediterranean region and highlights the influence of North African culture on Greek society. Bernal's text challenges the Eurocentric or "Aryan" model of ancient history. The "Aryan" model was formulated by nineteenth century European classicists and philologists, mostly German, to justify the imperialistic policies of Europe. The European community, during this time, believed in the natural superiority of what they called the "white race." European nations had been practicing, for some time, an international slave trade as well as a Third World colonization. To justify, in part, this theory of race hierarchy, racist scholars perpetuated the notion that civilization "began" with the rise of Greek culture and they argued that African cultures have largely been devoid of world significance. To the extent that Bernal is correct in his appraisal, and his evidence is as sound as it is convincing, the West is challenged to reevaluate its understanding of history and to reject the political narratives that are often used to justify a continuing imperialist relationship with the Third World (cultural or otherwise). Gold is always theft, to a degree, and the "Golden Age" of any civilization must constantly be historicized so that its developments can be seen in relationship to the other cultures that enabled it to prosper.[35] The United States, for example, emerged as a leading industrial power within two hundred years of its birth because of its Third World imperialism, 400 years of African slavery, the subsequent disenfranchisement and accentuated economic alienation of Americans of African descent following emancipation, and its repressive labor policies that were particularly brutal prior to the 1930s.

Solon's laws were also a response to Dracon, who wrote the earlier laws favorable to the rights of the aristocracy. The term "Draconian laws" has come down to modern times as meaning laws which are harsh and cruel. Kathleen Freeman observes, "The Athenians had a saying that the laws of Dracon were written not in ink but in blood."[36] Naphtali Lewis explores the agrarian legislation that Solon authored and comments that this adjusted the concept of property ownership and debtor's laws. Lewis shows how, through these efforts, Solon helped enable a future democracy to emerge in Athens: "The landed aristocrat was interested in acquiring more land, the indignant debt-laden peasant in retaining at least his freedom. To their mutual, if unequal advantage, therefore, they had developed a legal fiction to accomplish those purposes. Solon removed the necessity, for the future, of recourse to the fictional sale. By forbidding the securing of loans upon the person, he ensured the people against enslavement: this was 'the beginning of Athenian democracy.'"[37]

Athens eventually developed into a "democracy" where all "citizens"—those who were male, non-slave, and born of Athenian parents—were able to participate in political discussion and decisions. Slavery was pervasive in the Greek world. Hardy notes that "[t]he number of slaves in fifth-century Attica is variously estimated at from 80,000 to 150,000; 90,000 is probably a fairly sound number."[38] In addition to slavery, the Athenians marginalized women and were generally abusive to the people that they conquered (as their siege and capture of the island of Melos indicates).[39]

Slavery, as well as misogyny, was well institutionalized in Athenian society, and was staunchly defended by the great philosophers, Plato and Aristotle. In subsequent chapters I will discuss the repressive politics of the great philosophers, and the politics of knowledge, generally. For now, however, it suffices to give a brief example. In chapters four and five of his *Politics*, Aristotle refers to slavery as "natural." He argues that people are born with an inherent inequality. Some people are meant to be ruled, some people are meant to be rulers. In respect to gender, all women are to be governed by men, just as some men are meant to govern others. He writes, "[A]s between the sexes, the male is by nature superior and the female inferior, the male ruler and the female subject."[40]

Exploring the Contradictions in
Athenian and American "Democracy"

As mentioned earlier, serious contradictions existed in Ancient Athens between its self-image and its behaviors. Once again, the purpose of pointing out these contradictions is not to laugh at the people of the past or to condemn them from our "superior" moral position. Rather, the point is to recognize that all societies have their contradictions and that our critical energies need to be spent on learning to recognize our own contradictions. We cannot go back and "improve" Ancient Greek society, nor can we ameliorate the suffering of its victims. What we *can* do is to recognize that the contradictions between our own self-images and our behaviors contributes to our own legacy of suffering. By acknowledging this point, we can direct our critical actions toward reducing the suffering that we have some control over. If we, as U.S. citizens today, look toward Ancient Athens and see the irony that Hadas sees, then we are hypocritical if we still remain stirred by the ideal, but do not put forth the action required to reconcile the contradictions in our own lives. He writes: "We are stirred by the democratic ideal of Athens as set forth in Pericles' Funeral Oration, but we are aware that the entire system rested upon the institution of slavery, that citizenship was rigidly exclusive, and that women were relegated to an inferior legal and social status."[41]

Whether it is Pericles' Funeral Oration, the Gettysburg Address, or even the American flag, the symbols of what we can achieve must not serve as their own ends. It is not the oratory of Pericles or Lincoln, and it is not the flag that deserves our respect and our reverence. It is not even the ideal that they represent that commands our attention. Rather, it is the *practices* that they are supposed to symbolize. Democratic states do not just mouth the words of "freedom" and "liberty," but conceptualize these words in a concrete freedom, one based in a mutual respect between human beings. In a democratic society, there is no room for racism, sexism, homophobia, a state religion, and a material inequality among social classes. Democratic nations are living a contradiction when they dominate the world militarily and deny the rights of people throughout the world to develop their own economies and to use their national resources in ways that they see fit.

Within the context of the limited democracy of Classical Athens, one that can make no excuses for its exclusionary politics, for its imperialistic policies, for its egoism and its destructive pride, rhetoric was seen as primarily having to do with public, persuasive speech making. Rhetoric, which involves the free exchange of ideas, thrives in the threshold of a "free" society. Kennedy writes, "it has long been noted that oratory flourished most in the democracies and least under tyranny."[42] He adds, "In a democratic state words change history."[43]

Brian Vickers concurs with the above analysis. As he explains, "It is a historical fact, more familiar in this century than in any other, that tyrants and totalitarian states destroy freedom of speech."[44] Kennedy substantiates the connection between the rise of rhetorical consciousness and the formulation of a more or less democratic rationality. He writes, "The immediate cause of the greatly increased consciousness of rhetorical techniques in fifth-century Athens was the application of the democratic process on a large scale to the judicial procedure."[45]

No society is ever completely free, but a society can be seen as more or less rhetorical when it views social and political knowledge as being dependent upon the wants and needs of its citizens. When people, rather than ideals, become the standard of what is important or useful for a society or community, then we can say that that society is committed to some sort of rhetorical process. While rhetoric does not cease to exist in totalitarian systems, it tends to regress into panegyric excess. Panegyric is a type of oratory which stresses elaborate praise at the expense of well reasoned argumentation. Traditionally, panegyrics have been seen as the servile prostration of a subject to his or her controlling power, as when the king's court sings praise to the king's honor. Yet panegyrics can also be seen as a type of discourse that celebrates national myths or unquestioned cultural norms in order to keep us from engaging in a critical or debunking analysis. In other words, it is a type of discourse that keeps us from thinking. It is jingoistic, distracting, and alienating. Examples of this type of discourse in our contemporary society are commercials and media displays of patriotism that tend to surround U.S. military invasions. In both cases, the American people are kept as consumers in a world that is handed down to them from the anointed. The privileged few control from an ideological position that is often far away from the wants and needs of everyday people, struggling for survival in a world that is becoming economically and ecologically unviable.

The Political Structure of Ancient Greece

In a participatory democracy like Athens, one limited to a very specific sub-section of its population, speeches were delivered primarily before a deliberative body for the purpose of creating or influencing public policy, or before a jury in the case of a trial. Speeches were also given in ceremonial contexts. In each of these cases, the political structure of Athens was reified through its rhetorical practices. In short, the context under which rhetoric was practiced corresponds to the political environment that calls that type of practice into being. Thus, there is a symbiotic relationship between the forms of communication and the political infrastructure of a society. In this reciprocal relationship, both forms reinforce each other. While the conditions of the court, the Assembly, and the public epideictic call into existence the forms of rhetoric (forensic, deliberative, and epideictic), those same forms reinforce and reify the existence of the political environment. Thus, we cannot talk about politics without also talking about rhetoric. Even in our contemporary society, the forms of public discourse—the Mass Media—reflect the form of government that we have—

a limited and politically alienating republic. Such analysis is not meant to reduce politics and rhetoric to the same phenomenon; rather, it is only meant to illustrate that any talk of democracy cannot be separated from a concern for how *public* our public is and for how democratic our methods of communication are.

In Ancient Athens, these connections were much more direct than they are now, at least among the narrowly defined citizenry. In Athens, the speaker or communicator was in many instances acting in a political way. This is not to write that people did not communicate in ways that had no bearing on the running of the state. Rather, it is to emphasize that the "public" was much more political than it is now. To speak in public in Athens usually meant to engage in dialogue on matters that did in fact have state or communal significance. Today, in contrast, very little of what we communicate can be considered "public." Certainly, we receive public dialogue in the form of the Mass Media, but few of us are involved in the actual creation of such dialogue. In our times, the public sphere is operationally defined as the practice of private consumption. Thus, in earlier pages, I referred to rhetoric being dependent upon the potential to connect to a wider audience. Rhetoric, according to the position offered in this text, is dialogue that has a chance to make a meaningful contribution to public life. The limited opportunities to do this in this country are one reason that most people would never identify as being rhetors. While politicians may be rhetors, and while cultural leaders and business personalities may be rhetors, it seems odd in this day and age to see our fellow citizens as being rhetors. In essence, when most of us speak, it is from a position of marginalization and powerlessness. We are free to say what we want in this country, but when we speak differently than we are expected to speak, we find ourselves without access to the communication channels that will give us cultural, hence rhetorical significance.

In Ancient Athens during the age of limited democracy, the communication channels were democratized within the body of citizens that comprised the political entity known as the state. In this context, to speak in the public arena was to be elevated to the stature of rhetor. Mogens Herman Hansen's description of the rhetor is particularly illustrative of this point: "*Rhetor* was a technical term which in the language of the law referred to any citizen who appeared before the people with a speech or a proposal: a citizen became a *rhetor* the moment he stepped onto the speakers' platform, and as a mark of his dignity a wreath was placed on his head like that worn by magistrates."[46]

The rhetor was not only honored and given the opportunity to talk, but was also held responsible and accountable for what he said.[47] This aspect of "accountability" is another dimension of democracy sorely missed in our contemporary political environment.

The people who led in the Athenian democracy were known as orator/statesmen. These were the rhetors, the leaders, the people who communicated with a cultural and political significance. Within the political environment, one that included the formal workings of the Assembly and the Courts, as well as the informal gatherings of epideictic display, every citizen had direct access to the means and methods of communication. Literally, every citizen had a voice; they were even encouraged to use it. Hansen explains, "[W]illingness to stand up and speak or make a proposal in the Assembly was encouraged by honorary decrees or by giving gold crowns worth 1000 drachmas to, for example, the best *rhetor* of the year. . . . "[48] Certainly, the wealthy could train their rhetorical skills and thus accrue more political power, and there were teachers who would turn the wealthy into polished speakers for a price. Yet even the poorest of the citizens, if he could muster his courage, could compete with the wealthiest over the right to communicate. No such liberty exists in our day. In short, we are a nation of spectators, not a nation of rhetors.[49]

The four components of the Athenian political system that will be discussed below are the *Ecclesia*, or Assembly, the court system, the Council of 500, and the Board of Ten Generals.

The Athenian Assembly

Central to Athenian politics was the Assembly. The Assembly was the policy-making branch of the Athenian political system and was made up of all interested citizens. Interest, however, was high among the Athenian people for they felt that it was the obligation of the citizenry to participate in the political processes of daily life. To be a citizen *meant* to be political. Politics was not taken for granted, but largely lived and interactive. The English word "idiot" derives from the Greek word, *idiotes*, which means to be non-political, literally a "private person." In other words, the Athenians considered it to be abnormal for a person to want to escape from his political responsibility in contributing to the state. Thirty to forty thousand citizens met frequently to deliberate and decide upon policy. This democratic body met about thirty-five times a year in and around a large building called the Areopagus. At each session, they would pass around ten decrees.[50] Consequently, the Areopagus was an important arena where rhetoric flourished.

As can be imagined, it is no easy task to gather so many people together to focus on some specific task. To ward off abuse, and to keep the business of governing serious, there was a system in the Assembly to keep unscrupulous people from wasting the Assembly's time. The system worked as follows: any citizen could submit a bill for popular deliberation and vote. However, if someone submitted a bill that was subsequently overturned before one year, that is, if the bill was so ridiculous or worthless that it could not stand the test of serious deliberation for twelve months, then the person was fined a heavy punishment for being negligent in his duties. This procedure helped ensure that an individual would give serious thought before proposing worthless or perhaps self-serving legislation. More importantly, it insured that *all* legislation had some degree of a wider social appeal. Unlike laws today that frequently benefit small sections of the population at the expense of the many, the Greek system held the law makers accountable for the effects of their legislation.

The Athenian Legal System

After the Assembly, the court system of Athens was the most pervasive political construct in Athenian life. The court system of Athens served the population in settling criminal and civil law suits. The citizens were responsible for making their own cases and defense. Large popular juries, consisting of 201–1001 people, were called *dikasteria*. As Kennedy explains, "A body of 6,000 was used as a pool from which individual panels of 201 or more jurors were chosen by lot for each case."[51] Decisions were made by a majority vote. All this occurred in the absence of what today we would recognize as legal "professionals" or "experts." There was no lawyer class, nor a professional judge. The courts were administered by people who served fixed terms and were drawn by lot. No state prosecutor existed to level criminal charges. Individual citizens rose to speak on behalf of the state.

In order to be successful in his case, a citizen would have to be able to appeal to a large crowd and be persuasive. The life, property, and freedom of an individual in the court system thus depended upon that person's ability to speak well. Edward Schiappa reminds readers that "Fifth- and fourth-century Athens was an exceptionally litigious society; careers and fortunes were won and lost in the law-courts."[52] At any given point in time, a citizen could find himself before a civil court and be held accountable for something that he may or may not have done. In light of the propensity for Athenians to engage in litigation, an ancient Greek wall inscription warns, "He who does not study rhetoric will be the victim of it."[53]

The Council of 500

After the Assembly, the Council of 500 comprised the next level of Athenian leadership. This council "exercised a sort of general supervision over the business of the State."[54] Thus, the Council of 500 "acted as a standing committee of the people and prepared business for the Assembly. . . . "[55] The Council was chosen by lot from 5,000 candidates who were popularly supported. The 500 represented 50 citizens from each of ten regions which were organized into ten political blocks called *demes*, which "were the building blocks of the Athenian system."[56] The council existed to insure expediency when decisions had to be made in a more timely fashion than allowed by the deliberative process of the Assembly.

Pericles and the Board of Ten Generals

The final component of the Athenian political system discussed here is the Board of Ten Generals, or *strategoi*. This group was elected directly by the Assembly. The function of the board was to command the Athenian armed forces. It also had a civil function, such as to preside over state affairs.

Pericles (died 429) is the most noted member of this group. Pericles was leader of the democratic party from 460 BCE until his death by plague during the Peloponnesian war.[57] Under his leadership Athens experienced its so-called "Golden Age." This was an era unprecedented in the development of art, literature, and architecture.

Pericles' domestic policy encouraged a massive public works project that gave employment to the jobless while simultaneously improving the city with architecture and other works of art and culture, many of which can still be seen in modern Athens. In addition, Pericles arranged for a salary to be paid to the Council of 500, the Board of Ten Generals, and jury members, broadening the participatory base of the government. The purpose for paying money to these people, most of whom where chosen by lot, was to insure that the needs of the Athenian people could be represented across class bounds. In contrast to Rome, for example, where the patricians (wealthy class) comprised the juries—thus ensuring that the law would represent a class bias against the plebeians (the poor class)— the Greek juries were comprised of many old and poor people. By enfranchising these people through the pay that made it possible for them to participate, a more popular justice was accessible.

The public works projects were also a similar type of welfare system that encouraged political unity for the state and tempered incipient class tensions by equalizing people, at least symbolically, across class lines. Even if such gestures do not actually equalize people, as there was still a clear division between rich and poor in Athens, the small expenditures paid to the poor made a big difference in their lives and contributed positively toward building support for the dominant ideology of the time. In light of class distinctions, the Athenian state under Pericles had enough sensibility to include the poor citizens in the workings of the government, and to provide them with the means of sustenance. *Any democracy worth its name must engage in a similar activity, otherwise democracy becomes available only to those who can afford its luxuries.* This is not to say that Athens was free of class antagonism and class struggle; rather, the wealth of Athens was such that it was able to buttress the contradictions of society that led to class hostilities. The decision by the leaders of the democracy to broaden their appeal was an example of political savvy that the modern U.S. political machine—by excluding labor—has yet to learn.

This is not to suggest that no parallel exists between Ancient Athens and the U.S. on the issue of buying people's loyalty to support what would otherwise be unpopular regimes (as plutocracies like the United States tend to be when their political contours become obvious). For example, while the U.S. systematically excludes labor from its mainstream political organizations, and while it tends to limit its appeal and opportunity for the non-wealthy to participate, it nevertheless shares its ideology of imperialism with Athens. And, like Athens, the U.S. uses some of the wealth gained from its foreign adventures to buy the support of the people (increasingly through television advertising and the public relations industry). Until recently, the vast wealth of the U.S. (the part of it at least that was not consumed on military expenditures) was used to buttress social contradictions in this country. This is no longer the case. Similar to Athens, all the wonderful things that this country produces—its technology, arts, higher education systems, and its industrial might—tend to be dependent upon our hegemonic role in controlling the world's economy, in particular the economies of our subject nations (most of the Third World).

As the U.S. experiences more economic difficulties, and as it responds to those difficulties by dismantling what little social welfare exists in this nation, and as public school systems and universities face disintegration from lack of money and become dependent upon private funding, the limitations of our "democracy" and economic system will become glaringly evident for the large masses of people who, until recently, were getting by materially. In a sense, these people have been "bought off" by the government. In exchange for things like access to education and cheap commodities (cheap from the perspective that they were produced by subsistence labor), people in this country have mortgaged their political, critical, and moral consciousness. As more and more people face these moral and economic contradictions, class antagonisms will come to a head. At such a time it will take a leader, such as Pericles, to revive a public sphere that involves a broad base of individual empowerment and material security. Yet such material security cannot come from the mouths of others. Poverty is never cured by theft. In such case, the poverty still exits; it simply has been transferred. To cure poverty world wide, the sources of poverty need to be addressed. A solution to poverty can only be found when the needs of *all* people are addressed, and not just the needs of those who have the power to take what they want and to subject others to their dominance.

The material development and technological progress of U.S. society is necessary, as it is in all societies. When we look back to Ancient Athens and see what it accomplished during its "Golden Age," we are proud. We see a city that was built on the idea of beauty. We see a vast system of public works and a political community that did not suffer from the egregious class tensions that plague modern U.S. society. Yet we cannot be lulled into an uncritical pride that does not reflect on the wider historical conditions. All the development in Ancient Greece, like much of the social and technological developments of the U.S. today, resulted from a criminal and monstrous foreign policy. Pericles' government, like the U.S. government for at least the past one hundred years, was an imperialist power. Pericles built for Greece an empire of more than two hundred city-states, with Athens at the center. This resulted in the proverbial "Glory of Athens."

Empires are evil. The Greek, Roman, Spanish, British, and the American empires were all built on the assumption that one race, one culture, one economic class had the right to subject as many other people as possible. Each of these empires had the ability to conquer other people and mistook its power for a mandate. In each case, the nation in question built for itself a privileged society for the few, while the great masses of people toiled and starved. This is why I refer to the "so-called" Golden Age of Greece. I do this to express incredulity and suspicion of the moral integrity of the Greeks during this time. Likewise, when we look at the United States and see all that it has justly to be proud of, we should express our incredulity, our suspicion. Behind the beauty of Greece lies a trail of blood and behind the strength and accomplishments of the U.S. lies a similar, if not longer trail.

This trail can be traced from Africa where millions of men, women, and children were snatched from their homes and placed in cargo ships to be brought to North America: "It is roughly estimated that Africa lost 50 million human beings to death and slavery in those centuries we call the beginnings of modern Western civilization, at the hands of slave traders and plantation owners in Western Europe and America, the countries deemed the most advanced in the world."[58]

This trail of blood also continues through the experience of the Native Americans, victims of a genocide more complete than the one created by Adolf Hitler in the twentieth-century. As Michel Beaud explains, "In a little more than a century the Indian [sic] population was reduced by 90 percent in Mexico (where the population fell from 25 million to 1.5 million), and 95% in Peru."[59] Granted, these figures are not of Native Americans in the territory we recognize today as the United States, but they do illustrate the gravity of the situation. Native peoples did not fare well when the Europeans came to the Western Hemisphere, and the United States government was as much responsible for the situation as Spain, Britain, and the other European powers.

For the U.S. government, the trail of blood only begins here. The U.S. did not start the slave trade, or the policy of extermination of the Native American, but it did vigorously pursue these goals. While it may be painful to look, to feel, to hear, to know that this history exists, there is nothing worse to do than to ignore it and to pretend that it does not matter. These sentiments do not commit us to an anti-American position; rather, to be an American means to be aware of who we are and where we come from. There is nothing more patriotic and loyal than to embrace one's history and to grow from the experience. If we love ourselves, and if we love our country, we must thus strive to "know thy self," to borrow a phrase from Socrates, and to know thy nation. Such knowledge is the beginning of wisdom and the foundation of all morality.

In reference to the Athenian Empire, W.G. Forrest makes the icy observation that "It was impossible to separate this imperialism from the democracy which had fostered it. . . . "[60] The same is true for us. Athens had its Pericles. We have our Kennedys and our Reagans. Athenian society had its contradictions and we have ours. The difference is that the Athenians represent a past civilization, having succumbed to their contradictions. One important consequence of the imperialist policy of Pericles was the Peloponnesian war which led to the downfall of Athens' empire.[61] As A.N.W. Saunders notes, "The Periclean age of the greatness of Greek, especially Athenian civilization ended with the outbreak of war between Athens and the Spartan alliance in 431 [BCE]."[62]

Even though Athens would cease to be politically important, it would remain an artistic and intellectual center for Western culture.[63] What similar thing can be said of the U.S.? When you take away our guns, and take away our army, and when you take away the money and power that comes from these weapons, what remains? We are a nation of poverty and crime amidst a ruling elite that controls more of the world's resources than all other oligarchies in history. What does that say about us as a people?

Comparison to U.S. Imperialism

The Athenians were in control of a vast empire that stretched across the Mediterranean, up through the Black Sea and into North Africa, Southern France, and Spain. The Athenians would send ships and troops to these places, conquer (and often enslave) the people living there, and set up their control of the economy and trade. People who resisted were fiercely terrorized or enslaved. In either event, the Athenians made sure that their control was unchallenged. The imperialism of Athens led directly to a condition of perpetual war and to Athens' eventual defeat. It weakened the Greek city states and enabled the subjection of the Greeks by the Macedonians and later by the Romans. It is easy to look back at the Athenians to judge their contradictions. Here was a society that was premised on democracy and freedom, yet it denied political freedom to its slaves, its women, and its "foreigners." It was also a society that imprisoned much of the Greek world and subjected them to its brutal and selfish will. It believed in rhetoric as an important tool for governance, yet tended to privilege military force outside of its borders to win by strength what it could not gain by negotiation. Such a society can justly be challenged for its inability to question its contradictions.

However, it is a more useful exercise to treat the past as a lesson as to how to approach our contemporary experiences. After all, our study of Greek rhetoric, or of any history, is not to make excuses for the past, and it is not to justify or glamorize the past, it is to understand ourselves. Western nations today are the heirs, in many respects, of Ancient Athens, and thus we can understand ourselves better if we can come to understand it. One point in particular that is ripe for introspection is the imperialist polices of the Industrial nations, particularly the policies of the United States. These have been discussed in the previous section, but it is so central to meaningful scholarship today that it cannot be over-emphasized. All scholarship, all writing, all learning, must be *for* something. That something is the future. We study for a reason, particularly to make something of ourselves and our lives. We study to know. But when we know something is wrong, when something is not just, we move to correct it—particularly if we see ourselves as being moral and just people.

The connections between morality, justice, and critical thinking, and their intersections with scholarship is particularly relevant in a book on rhetoric. If rhetoric is to have any significance as a concept, it must be, above all else, a study of these connections. More specifically, the question of imperialism, in whatever guise it takes, is the question of freedom—not just for the subjected countries, but for the citizens of our own. Any country that is an imperial power must also be one whose citizens are faced with the curtailment of serious political freedoms—for instance, the freedom to resist imperialism. If rhetoric is indeed dependent upon a political environment in which everyday people have an opportunity to debate the issues of the day and to exert their influence on social policy, then we must see Greek imperialism, as well as our own, not as anomalies in our larger rhetorical and political environments, but as fundamental threats to that environment.

This book is not the place to recount the full extent of Western and U.S. imperialism and its devastating effect on the peoples of the world, as well as its debilitating role in limiting and even eviscerating American democracy. These histories are well documented and appear in a number of easily accessible books.[64] To the extent that these histories go against the grain of much of what we are taught about our country, we should be thinking: what is the source of this conflict? The answer is not that these books are "un-American" or "radical." Nor is it that these books are biased to see only the "bad." Rather, the authors are pointing out what is an obvious fact: an imperialistic foreign policy in a country like the U.S. must be kept "secret" in order to keep people from acting democratically. In other words, if people do not like what they read when they read these books, then they certainly would not have liked it when the events were actually happening, and they may be angered enough to try to *prevent* future events from occurring. To the extent that some Americans try to do this, they are to be applauded.

Most Americans, however, are passive. Many are passive because they do not know any better. They are lied to by their government and the media and, exacerbating the problem, dissident voices are marginalized, ignored, or eliminated from the public sphere. In place of accurate information about their country and the world, the American people are fed stories of communist "expansions," brutal drug traffickers, and of the necessity for a permanent war economy. People are passive because the average citizen of the United States is systemically excluded from the democratic participation in this economy and is not allowed to interact meaningfully with issues that are personally important: things such as health care, meaningful employment, retirement insurance, healthy housing, clean food and air, and a livable wage. In such a restrictive environment, what can rhetoric mean? It becomes reduced to a form of social control. For students of rhetoric, in particular, the challenge is paramount. If rhetoric is to mean anything as a practice, a theory of discourse, or a philosophy by which to understand the world, it must be given the potential to transform the world. If there is to be a substantive difference between "rhetoric" and "propaganda," then it must start from the following distinction: propaganda is the invitation to envision the world according to the people who own and rule it. Rhetoric is the invitation to change the world.

The Epistemic Function of Rhetoric

In the courts, outside in the *Agora*, or in the Assembly, the single most important tool of the Athenian government and of people wielding power was the ability to speak. Speaking was the way to achieve a position of leadership, keep that power, and use it effectively. But it was more than simply power that was at stake, it was knowledge. Power and knowledge, as Foucault explains, have a symbiotic relationship. It is through power that we come to understand what it means to "know." More importantly, power, as it was wielded in Ancient Greece, and as it is wielded today, is not only economics, is not only the use of force, but is, more essentially, the internalization of a structure of relationships, a language that we use to distinguish that which is deemed "true" from that which is deemed "false." In other words, the language we use to talk about something effects the way we perceive it. At the level of rhetoric, this relationship between words and thought becomes amplified. A citizen's ability to speak in Ancient Greece, and our ability to speak today, is tied to the potential we have in changing the way people think about something.

Modern theorists of rhetoric have clearly isolated a relationship between rhetoric and the creation of a social reality. The theory, developed to explain the epistemic function of human communication, has been promoted in several sources, most notably in the work of Robert L. Scott, and later by Richard A. Cherwitz and James W. Hikins.[65] Cherwitz and Hikins explain that "The processes by which we discover the world we live in and the methods we employ to articulate that world are intertwined."[66] Persuasion results when two separate epistemological knowledge bases confront each other, with one of these structures influencing and fundamentally changing the other. Scott explains that "Man [sic] must consider truth not as something fixed and final but as something to be created moment by moment in the circumstances in which he finds himself and with which he must cope."[67]

This relationship between language and social reality has important implications now, as well as for the Ancient Greeks. However, it is prudent to proceed cautiously, as Susan Jarratt warns, when applying our twentieth century understanding of language to a culture which did not have this conceptualization.[68] Admittedly, it may be inaccurate to assume that epistemic discourse was consciously created in the Assembly or before a jury. Clearly, the classical Greek and Roman orators, for the most part, limited rhetoric to its Aristotelian function of persuasion. On the other hand, it is undeniable in the extant writings of the major Sophists that persuasion was a function of knowledge creation. If we want to take Gorgias seriously as an intellectual figure, and we clearly do as a flood of recent research in the humanities suggests, how else could Gorgias' "Encomium to Helen" be explained?[69] If persuasion was to work in that instance, the person persuaded would have to change his or her conception of Trojan history, which was socially constructed by Homer to begin with. Furthermore, rhetorical theorists believe today that communication contributes significantly to the creation of knowledge, a process embedded deeply within the symbolic nature of language. Such a process must necessarily have existed for Ancient Greeks, as well as for moderns, for the functions of language and human symbolicity have not changed in the last two millennia. Either way, some rhetorical scholars anachronistically attribute this knowledge to the Greeks. For example, William Benoit expresses this attribution when he explains, "Isocrates was proud of the epistemic qualities of rhetoric."[70]

In short, language is a way of *entitling* the material world.[71] Language, by organizing our experiences, helps us to order and make sense out of our environment. The citizens of Athens were able to understand their social and political options through a reality portrayed by their orators. Through rhetoric, Athens defined both itself and its relationship with the rest of Greece.

Conclusion

The social, political, and cultural circumstance behind rhetoric has now been explored. Special attention was paid to the epistemic function of language and its connection with rhetoric. Accentuated was the need for political freedom. Within conditions of such freedom, however, we must recognize that, if rhetoric is to be more than merely a form of social control, then the potential for criticism and change must also exist as a precondition for discourse. As stated in the Introduction, it is not enough simply to be given the opportunity to speak, or to live in a society in which a "democratic" infrastructure exists. Rather, as we saw with the limitations of Greek society, and as we ponder the limitations of our own, we must remember that rhetoric is less important when viewed as a thing. Rhetoric is a process; it is a way for constructing or deconstructing our environment in ways that matter, or should matter, to everyone no matter how alienated or marginalized they are from the workings of power in this country.

Notes

1. The general philosophical tone of my analysis is informed by Richard Rorty's neo-pragmatism. See his *Consequences of Pragmatism* (Minneapolis: University of Minnesota Press, 1982).

2. For a detailed discussion of this argument, see Edward Schiappa, "Arguing About Definitions," *Argumentation* 7 (1993), 403–417.

3. This discussion of knowledge is derived from the theory of Michel Foucault. For an introduction to his ideas, see *Power/Knowledge: Selected Interviews and Other Writings* (New York: Pantheon Books, 1980).

4. These are only a few examples. Many more, and their documenting evidence, are available in Michael Parenti, *Democracy For The Few* (New York: St. Martin's Press, 1995).

5. Moses Hadas, *The Greek Ideal and its Survival* (New York: Harper and Row, 1960), 16.

6. Carole Blair, 1990, unpublished lecture, Davis, California.

7. *The Greek and Roman World* (Cambridge: Schenkman Publishing, 1970).

8. Ibid, 8.

9. "The Rhapsode," *The Quarterly Journal of Speech* 56 (1970), 388–397.

10. "The Hellenic Rhapsode," *Western Journal of Speech Communication* 42 (1978), 134–143.

11. Hargis, "The Rhapsode," 396.

12. Enos, "The Hellenic Rhapsode," 141.

13. Ibid., 142.

14. Ibid., 138.

15. *The Art of Rhetoric in the Roman World* (Princeton: Princeton University Press, 1972), 57.

16. *The Universities of Ancient Greece* (New York: Charles Scribner's Sons, 1909), 5.

17. For a more thorough discussion of rhetorical consciousness as found in Greek history, drama, and poetics prior to the formal articulation of rhetorical "theory," see George A. Kennedy, *Art of Persuasion in Greece* (Princeton: Princeton University Press, 1963), especially pages 26–51. Richard Enos, "Early Concepts of Greek Rhetoric and Discourse: A Selected Bibliography," *Rhetoric Society Quarterly* 10 (1980: 49–50) can lead students into discussions of this sort. Also, see Enos, *Greek Rhetoric Before Aristotle* (Prospect heights, IL: Waveland Press, 1993).

18. Kennedy, *Art of Persuasion in Greece,* 35.

19. "From Hero to Citizen: Persuasion in Early Greece," *Philosophy and Rhetoric* 15 (1982), 105.

20. Ibid., 104.

21. *Athenian Clubs in Politics and Litigation* (Rome: "L'erma" di Bretschneider, 1964), 1.

22. "The Legal Setting of Attic Oratory," *Central States Speech Journal* 23 (1972), 185.

23. "Realisms, Occidental Style," in *Asian and Western Writers in Dialogue: New Cultural Identities,* ed., Guy Amirthanayagam (London: Macmillan Press), 30.

24. *The Rhetoric and Poetics of Aristotle,* trans. Ingram Bywater (New York: The Modern Library, 1954), 230.

25. *The Philosophy of Literary Form* (Berkeley: University of California Press, 1973), 293–304.

26. Ibid., 304.

27. *Counter-Statement* 2nd. ed. (Berkeley: University of California Press, 1968), xii.

28. Ibid., 160.

29. Ibid., xii.

30. Noam Chomsky, *Necessary Illusions: Thought Control in Democratic Societies* (Boston: South End Press, 1989) and Neil Postman, *Amusing Ourselves to Death: Public Discourse in the Age of Show Business* (New York: Penguin Books, 1985).

31. For more discussion of the relationship between art and politics in Burke's writing, see Omar Swartz, "Kenneth Burke's Theory of Form: Rhetoric, Art, and Cultural Analysis," *Southern Communication Journal* 61 (1996), 312–321.

32. Introduction. *The Thebian Plays.* By Sophocles. (Middlesex, England: Penguin Books, 1974), 8.

33. "Greek Democracy and the Study of Rhetoric," in *A Synoptic History of Classical Rhetoric,* 2nd ed., eds. James J. Murphy and Richard A. Katula (Davis, CA: Hermagoras Press, 1995), 10.

34. New Brunswick: Rutgers University Press, 1987.

35. This is an extension of Joseph Pierre Proudhon's argument that "Property is theft." See his *What is Property?* (Cambridge: Cambridge University Press, 1994).

36. *The Murder of Herodes and Other Tails from the Athenian Law Courts* (New York: The Norton Library, 1963), 15.

37. "Solon's Agrarian Legislation," *American Journal of Philology* 62 (1941), 154.

38. *Greek and Roman World,* 18.

39. On the condition of women in Athens during this time, see Sarah B. Pomeroy, *Goddesses, Whores, Wives, and Slaves: Women in Classical Antiquity* (New York: Schocken Books, 1975).

The island of Melos was populated by people who wanted to absolve themselves of Athenian influence during Athens' larger geo-political struggle with Sparta. In response, Athens attacked the island *polis* and killed the entire adult male population, then sold the women and children into slavery.

40. *The Politics,* trans. H. Rackham (New York: G.P. Putnam's Sons, 1932), 21.

41. *Greek Ideal and its Survival,* 11.

42. *Art of Persuasion,* 23.

43. Ibid, 34.

44. *In Defense of Rhetoric* (Oxford: Clarendon Press, 1988), 7.

45. *Art of Persuasion,* 27.

46. *The Athenian Democracy in the Age of Demosthenes* (Cambridge, MA: Blackwell, 1991), 144.

47. Ibid.

48. Ibid., 157.

49. This argument is extended in Postman's, *Amusing Ourselves to Death.*

50. *The Athenian Democracy,* 156.

51. *Art of Persuasion,* 27.

52. "Did Plato Coin Rhetorike?" *American Journal of Philology* 111 (1990), 465.

53. Graduate seminar in classical rhetoric, university of California, Davis, Fall quarter, 1990.

54. W.G. Hardy, *The Greek and Roman World* (Cambridge: Schenkman Publishing, 1970), 40.

55. A.W. Pickard Cambridge, *Demosthenes' Public Orations* (London: Everyman's Library, 1963), 18.

56. Hardy, *The Greek and Roman World,* 39.

57. See Thucydides, *The Peloponnesian War* (trans. Rex Warner. London: The Penguin Classics, 1954).

58. Howard Zinn, *A People's History of the United States* (New York: Harper-Perennial, 1980), 29.

59. *A History of Capitalism: 1500–1980* (New York: Monthly Review Press, 1983), 19.

60. "The Realities of Athenian Government," in *Democracy and the Athenians*, ed. Frank J. Frost (New York: John Wiley & Sons, 1969), 134.

61. Thucydides, *The Peloponnesian War*.

62. Introduction. *Greek Political Oratory*, ed. and trans. by A.N.W. Sanders (Penguin: Middlesex, 1970), 21.

63. John Waldron, *The Universities of Ancient Greece* (New York: Charles Scribner's Sons, 1909).

64. The best specific account of the U.S.'s long history of imperialism is Zinn, *A People's History*. For a more generalized world history, see Beaud, *A History of Capitalism* and Noam Chomsky, *Year 501: The Conquest Continues* (Boston: South End Press, 1993).

65. Robert L. Scott, "On Viewing Rhetoric as Epistemic," *Central States Speech Journal* 18 (1967), 9–17; Richard A. Cherwitz and James W. Hikins, *Communication and Knowledge: An Investigation in Rhetorical Epistemology* (Columbia: University of South Carolina Press, 1986).

66. *Communication and Knowledge*, 9.

67. "On Viewing Rhetoric," 17.

68. *Rereading the Sophists: Classical Rhetoric Refigured* (Carbondale: Southern Illinois University Press, 1991).

69. See Edward Schiappa, "Sophistic Rhetoric: Oasis or Mirage?," *Rhetoric Review* 10 (1991), 5–18 for his appraisal of recent research on the Sophists and the attempt of this research to treat the Sophists as important historical figures in the evolution of Western thought.

70. "Isocrates and Plato on Rhetoric and Rhetorical Education," *Rhetoric Society Quarterly* 21 (1991), 68.

71. Kenneth Burke, *Language As Symbolic Action* (Berkeley: University of California Press, 1966), 359–79.

2

The Beginning of Rhetoric in Ancient Greece

The previous chapter explored the general circumstance behind the development of Greek rhetorical theory. In particular, it explained that demographic, geographical, and cultural conditions created a need for rhetorical knowledge. Such discussion emphasizes the importance of "historicization" in the study of ideas.

Ideas, Representation, and Mythology

Ideas never exist outside of history, and it is only through the study of their history that we can actually claim to know anything. Everything that we know today only makes sense to us, is only recognizable to us, by virtue of the nexus between "form" and "history." Anything that exists has a form, even ideas. These forms are only recognizable because of the historical context that gives them substance.

Words have histories, etymologies that are embedded in the evolution of a culture. To know the word, a person has to know the cultural context in which the word is situated. Furthermore, ideas are nothing but words. The idea of "history," or the idea of "rhetoric" is nothing more than the language we use to describe it, to represent it. To place language, words, or ideas in the context of their history is to put them in focus. However, clarity in vision is not always what human beings strive for. Clarity in historical memory, for example, is often painful, as parts of the last chapter indicate. Because clarity in vision is often painful, people tend to avoid it, and that is a natural psychological reaction. If all of our personal contradictions, shortcomings, and faults were perfectly clear to us, if all our personal pain and tribulations were constantly accentuated in our day to day experiences, we would go mad. In addition, strategic ambiguities can be very useful, although they are often used to deceive us. For example, politicians often appeal to the mythical, all inclusive and powerful "middle class" to gain support for their positions. Nevertheless, strategic ambiguities are often a way for us psychologically to cushion the blow that we receive when our personal idealized worlds come into contact with the dominant narratives that surround us. If we look at something too closely, even those whom we love, we find that clarity of perception removes the mystique of ambiguity that colors our initial and often romantic impressions.

In addition, absolute clarity is not even possible, nor is it a practical ideal. Clarity of vision implies Truth and, more importantly, it implies representation. "Historical Truth," if we take it to mean events that actually happened, such as the atomic bombings of Hiroshima and Nagasaki, as two examples, is not a problematic concept. No one can deny that those events occurred. However, the representation of Truth is problematical. For example, how do we represent the Atomic attack on Japan? Even to admit that it occurred, in the language that we choose to communicate that fact, is to color our experiences of it. What does it mean to say that it "occurred?" To say it in those words is to deprive the act of its agent. Would a Jewish historian say that the Holocaust "occurred?" Perhaps, but he or she would probably stress that it was *created*. It was not just something that "happened" to the Jewish people, and to six million other people, but it was a planned event. It was the result of human intent, planning, and cooperation. The same applies to the Atomic destruction of two Japanese cities in 1945. Both the Holocaust and the Atomic bombings were crimes of the gravest magnitudes. Yet, the crimes of both events are not self-evident parts of the historical record. As material events, they are simply scars on the Earth. As history, they are significant events because of the meaning that surrounds them. That meaning, their crimes, are not ahistorical, but situational, rhetorical, and subjective.

In order to declare the Holocaust and the atomic attacks on Japan "crimes," we have to appeal to some standard that is context specific. For instance, we can say they were crimes because they were racially, selfishly, and cruelly undertaken, that they increased the sphere of suffering in the world, that they were done so that a few select people could perversely benefit from the terror they inflicted on the weak and the powerless. In other words, they are wrong because we can judge them as wrong by certain criteria. These criteria is not self-evident. This is why one event, the Holocaust, may appear grotesquely wrong, while the atomic bomb attack on Japan, the fire bombing of the German city of Dresden by Allied Forces in 1945, or the saturation bombing of Vietnam, Laos, and Cambodia in the 1960s can be made to appear justified. Such justifications, after all, are always the prerogative of the victors. Notice, for example, how historical meaning is accentuated by the Jewish people in their remembrance of the Holocaust; we do not find a comparable historical memory being popularly communicated in terms of the genocides of the African people and their African-American slave descendants, the Native Americans, and the Vietnamese, Laotian, and Cambodian peoples. Their suffering is no less great than the Jews, the enthusiasm of their tormentors was no less genuine, the degree of their destruction is no less comparable. Why, then, do certain events, like the Holocaust, as horrible as it was, assume a cultural significance, and other events, like those mentioned above, become shadows of memory? The answer has to do with the power and control of representation.

The best we can get when representing the past is caricatures. Look in any high school history book, and many college history books, and the crudeness of this caricature is painfully clear. Another word for this is narrative. Thus, what we find in this book, as in any text, is a narrative of a reconstructed past. This narrative should not be confused with the actual past, as this past is largely unknowable. *Complete historical clarity is impossible.* All we have left of our ancestors is our representations of them. With our language we can reanimate the fossils of those who went before us. But those fossils dance to our tune, even as much as we try to reconstruct the music of their day. We can never completely know the past, because we can never completely know what it was that people were doing. Even when we have their own words, we can never be sure that their words and our words mean the same thing. This is not to say that there is never the possibility for historical understanding. Rather, the question becomes, given what we know about events (two atomic bombs exploded over populated cities in Japan in 1945), what can we say about them? People respond in different ways. Some say the act was criminal. Some say the act was patriotic (which is often the same thing—"patriotism" tends to be the justification we give to state sanctioned crimes). Some say that it was necessary, that it actually saved lives (meaning *American* lives). Some say that this act was designed to put the Soviets in their place, and some maintain that this act was America's best effort to establish a climate of world peace. How this question is answered will inform the narrative by which the past can be known.

To return this discussion to our particular subject matter, the question becomes, what is it that we know about Ancient Greece, and how does that knowledge help us today? This is a very important question indeed, for as I have tried to show in the preceding chapter, the past is often precursory to the future, and serves at least as an analogy for how we live in the present. In a sense, there is no past in any other but in an abstract manner. What we have are shifting figures of language that only tenuously represent the past. We have mostly narratives, built upon narratives, built upon narratives. This condition brings us back to rhetoric. As we ended the last chapter, rhetoric has certain epistemic qualities. That is, it affects the way we perceive the world through the use of narrative.[1]

In the narrative we call the history of rhetoric, some interesting developments occur at this stage. This chapter explores the evolution of persuasion as a concept from its mythical associations with the goddess Peitho to its association with logos by the Sophists. On the way, the relationship between rhetoric and democracy will be accentuated. More importantly, we are going to start seeing how rhetorical thinking evolves. From the legend surrounding its "invention" by Corax and Tisias of Syracuse, to the phenomenon of the fifth century BCE Sophists, we will see how the need for a system of persuasive communication arises in a society that has given up its traditional moral system by rejecting theism as a governmental rationale. When a single transcendent standard for Truth is gone, people become faced with two options. People may look for "Truth" in the material world, which is what the Ionian philosophers tried to do (or what modern scientism has tried to do), or people may look for "truth" in a more socially relevant and historically contingent way, which is what some of the Sophists attempted (and what a rhetorical epistemology attempts). We will see, in this chapter, how the Sophists give us a set of parameters for rhetorical thinking and provide an epistemological rationale for "democracy." Human beings need the freedom to think creatively and rhetorically. Democracy, in its larger, libertarian sense, is the system that best provides for human creativity. This connection between persuasion and democracy has always been evident.

Peitho

In Athens there was a goddess for oratory and persuasion, and her name was Peitho (not to be confused with pathos). Peitho personified the nature of persuasion and was both feared and admired by the pre-classical Greeks. Peitho personifies the power of persuasion. The Greeks sensed that speech did something to the human being, but they were not quite sure what this force was. Persuasion was magic. Persuaders, in some sense, practiced a gift that was divine in origin. Over time, people started to feel as if they could control this force. The naming of gods as agents controlling the material world is actually the beginning of "science," for it is the beginning of causation. This is not to equate the creation of gods with the practice of science. Rather, it is the search for causation that is the trademark of scientific inquiry, and the act of naming is an act of assigning causation. At the very least, it is an act of defining, and all definitions are dependent upon an interdependent system of correspondence for them to make any sense. To name the various gods is also to establish a relationship among the gods, including hierarchy, lineage, and politics.

The fact that Peitho becomes embodied with the spirit of persuasion is indicative of the Greeks' attempt to control her, to understand her. Their effort was to place persuasion into the structured order of things.

By the fifth century, as oratory became more important in Greek political life and studied as an art, the fearful qualities of this goddess began to change. Representations are never permanent. Just as the meaning of the Holocaust and of the atomic bomb attack on Japan is not self-evident outside of the context in which those acts occurred, the meaning of Peitho, as a representation of persuasion, is also dependent upon its historical context. As that context changed, as speech become more and more subject to rational control and understanding, and as persuasion became a medium for political expression, Peitho eventually transformed into the spiritual representation of democracy itself. As I.F. Stone explains, "In fifth-century Athens, Peitho had developed into a civic goddess of democracy, a symbol of the transition to rule by popular consent and consensus, achieved by debate and persuasion."[2] In R.G.A. Buxton's elaboration, we see accentuated the influence of politics on the conceptualization of knowledge. He explains, "Peitho's connotations vary considerably between contexts, and in at least one respect—the importance of rhetoric—its associations alter over time in parallel with a development in Greek political life."[3]

From the early Homeric times, the powers of speech were recognized as impressive, and the Greeks felt that there was the potential danger of an unwary audience being swayed wrongly by an immoral speaker. Consequently, the traits most valued in a speaker were eloquence and wisdom. The combination of both virtues was deemed necessary in order to keep justice and the social order from becoming perverted and self-serving. But more was needed than simply a balance between "eloquence" and "wisdom." What was needed was the actual parameters of the "art" as well as a narrative to position its practice in a socially convenient way. In other words, such a powerful phenomenon needed to be brought into the service of the state. At least, its political economy needed to be established. Aiding Greek society in this task was the use of a myth to describe the origins of the art.

The Corax/Tisias Myth

Although rhetoric, in a sense, is found as organized discourse in the works of Homer (in other words, as a practice), the actual "invention" of rhetorical theory (the recognized relationship between rhetoric and persuasion) can be traced to a myth about a man from Sicily named Corax. According to legend, Corax codified "rhetoric" in 476 BCE and thus gave it conceptual life. He did this in order to give people something to use to function effectively within the context of a more or less democratic state. In democratic states, people need courts to resolve disputes, and they need assemblies of sorts to decide upon policy. Depending upon which strand of the myth one chooses to believe, Corax "invented" rhetoric to serve in either of these two state functions. The notion that he "invented" rhetoric is a politically biased concept. It implies an authorship that extends into the cultural economy of the state. "Rhetoric serves the function of the democracy," implies this myth, just as the invention of the atom bomb by the United States implies that its use serves in the defense of democracy. In both cases, the association of power with "righteousness" assumes the rational control of power. Thus, there is nothing to be fearful about; the "democratic" state controls the means of power. To a people who fear demagoguery, as the Greeks did, such a myth brings with it a degree of comfort. Likewise, to a people who feared atomic weapons, the fact that the U.S. controlled the "Bomb" evoked a sense of relief (as compared to August 1949 when the Soviets, tired of living under constant nuclear threat from the U.S., finally exploded their own bomb). Suddenly, the bomb becomes fearful, because it is no longer controlled by a "beneficent" power (meaning us). At this stage, we have to create new narratives, which, to a large extent, was what the cold war was about.

Whether or not Corax, the man, existed or not, does not really matter, just like it does not matter whether or not the Rosenbergs gave the Soviets the secret to the atom bomb. We still have the Corax story, and it served an interesting and important cultural function. Nevertheless, scholars have recently debunked that myth, just as some scholars are working hard to debunk U.S. myths and ideologies.[4] As we will discuss in more detail in chapter four, the word "rhetoric" did not come into existence until years after "Corax's" death.[5] If he did live, he probably used the word "logos" to describe what he was doing. Even if he was using the word logos, it was not likely that he was using it in the way that Isocrates or the Sophists used the word. Nevertheless, the myth is still very relevant: It is similar to the saying that if God did not exist, humans would have to invent God. Even if Corax never existed, the presence of someone like him is crucial for the Greeks to begin understanding just what it was they were talking about when they discussed "rhetoric." Ideas cannot be separated from the people who articulate them. The extent to which biology gained much of its identity from Darwin, or Marxism from Marx, or psychology from Freud, is the extent to which people need to associate ideas with people; doing so helps make ideas real. Certainly, biology is not reducible to Darwin, Marxism to Marx, or psychology to Freud. Likewise, rhetoric is not reducible to Corax, nor is it devalued by his mythic origins. Biology is not limited by Darwin, Marxism by Marx, or psychology by Freud; each represents starting points by which knowledge in a certain area could unfold. In a sense, each offered encompassing narratives, under which a certain type of knowledge could be localized.

The art of speech existed as an intuitive process prior to its codification, an act which gave it its conceptual structure. D.A.G. Hinks clarifies this position: "Let the practice of oratory have begun when it may, the first attempts known to us in Classical Antiquity to formulate a series of principles for the art of speech were made in the fifth century before Christ [sic]. These earliest systems were naturally very imperfect: they could not immediately be either comprehensive or well organized. But they were something that had not existed at all before."[6]

Thus, it was a significant moment when Corax (or whomever) recognized persuasion as an art to be studied and improved upon. Even if the myth is wrong about when rhetoric was named, naming itself is an act of power and mythologies are an attempt to control this power. In the U.S., the government tries to do the same thing when it associates all the popularly gained social and political rights of the underclass with its own narrative about the wonders of the free market to guarantee personal liberty. In actuality, it is at the expense of the "free market" that we get social development, usually under much political and personal repression. Nevertheless, the narrative of the government coopts this past and eviscerates historical memory. Images of Martin Luther King, Jr. at the opening ceremony of the 1996 summer Olympics in Atlanta, Georgia, is a case in point. Such representation reinforces the dominant myths of U.S. society and government; the U.S. government did everything it could to derail the Civil Rights movement, and it may actually have been responsible for King's assassination.[7] Likewise, in the myth about the "invention" of rhetoric, Corax names rhetoric on behalf of democracy. Such an "action" exists, regardless of its historical "truth," as King was made to endorse the U.S. government before the world during the Olympics. Historical memory often works this way, especially when it is controlled by a government. George Orwell was not far off base in his account of how governments can control the present by controlling our perceptions of the past.[8]

In all likelihood, the origins of "rhetoric" cannot be reduced to a person such as Corax, but, rather, its development is more of a cultural phenomenon taking shape in Greece around the fifth century, generally, throughout a population that was becoming increasingly literate.[9] In order for a concept to be studied, within the condition of literacy, it needs to be given parameters, and Corax represents the trends toward intellectual specification that began to give rhetoric conceptual identity. But it is not just rhetoric we are talking about here, we are talking about the beginnings of disciplinary thought in *general*. It so happens that "rhetoric" and "philosophy" are the two oldest disciplines, coming as they did from a split in the word logos, but any body of knowledge is similarly constructed. Biology becomes separated from natural history with Darwin. His use of the phrase "descent with modification" to imply a non-teleological development demarcates a new paradigm that is distinct from theology or natural history.[10] Darwin argued for a fundamentally different way of studying life, which gave way to the need for a new discipline. Freud did the same thing. By naming the human psyche in the way he did, he actually "invented" it; the human psyche did not exist in the same way it did before Freud. Marx did the same thing for sociology and politics. He gave us a language that forces us to think differently about our relationships to each other and to the state. In much the same way, the Corax/Tisias myth is an important legend in the Western paradigm in terms of a burgeoning critical consciousness.[11]

Myths are important for any discipline as well as for any community. All communities need the myths that call them into being. A community is defined as a group of people being something distinct from other larger groups. The defining characteristics of a group reflect its narratives. People study communication, for instance, because they have certain beliefs about the importance of communication in understanding society. The community of communication scholars, like all scholarly communities, is defined in part by these beliefs. These beliefs are common to the group and are shared because of a common education (or indoctrination). Within the indoctrination process, usually found in graduate school, students learn the myths of their disciplines. To the extent that they embody these myths, they are recognized as having been transformed into a scholar. When they "walk the walk" and "talk the talk" of their disciplines, they are rewarded with a Ph.D. This award sanctions their ability to perpetuate the cycle, and to produce knowledge that is reflective of their beliefs, assumptions, and paradigms. This is how professionalism works throughout the academy. Acknowledging this is not a cynical move; it does not undermine the importance of scholarship, or of disciplines. Acknowledging this simply reminds us that we should not take any of our knowledge for granted. What we know is dependent upon the questions we ask, and our questions are dependent upon the type of ideas we have been taught.[12]

Furthermore, all ideas need to have their genesis. Unless Plato was correct, and that Ideas exist independent of their creation by human beings, they have to be created from somewhere, and from something (see chapter four). Moreover, ideas have to appear significant, and this significance has to be learned. People have to be taught that an idea is "good" or "bad" as well as the conditions upon which it can be made useful. The more important the idea to a culture or a community, the more necessary it is for some significant genesis story to explain its significance. In U.S. history for example, we like to tell stories of the courageous rebels who fought to liberate the colonies from the tyranny of Britain. We hear the patriotic stories of the brave settlers who conquered a vast wilderness, empty of civilization, and brought forth the glory of God to the New World. We are told of the "Western expansion" and how hard work, sacrifice, and technological advancements tamed a hostile and forbidding land. Ignored in this narrative is the "Eastern invasion," the story of European encroachment on Native American lands. Also ignored is the struggle of many early Americans to resist the rising tyranny of capital and its practice of forced pauperism, slavery, and genocide.

The important part of the dominant narrative is its narrative intent. It is how people, usually the ruling class, assign meaning and perspective to the past, giving it purpose. In other words, all concepts, like nations or ideas, need a *telos*. A *telos* is the ends to which something strives, its locomotion. Narratives, history, and ideas themselves need to be *for* something, working *toward* something.

U.S. myths have been those of "progress," "Western development," "manifest destiny," and "freedom." The U.S. government presents itself as the great bulwark against the so-called "international communist conspiracy." These myths are invested with substantial political currency. After the First World War, Germany had a similar set of myths which served a related function. The myth of rhetoric's origins is not all that different (perhaps less violent) than the above two examples. We look towards Corax as calling rhetoric "the art of persuasion" and accentuate the importance of the arrangement of ideas in speaking successfully. One reason why we do this is because of the context of this "invention." The context was the overthrow of the theocracies and oligarchies of many nation states in the Mediterranean area. Rhetoric was used by Corax, supposedly, to help people to recover their property in court and to set up democratic governments.

From the point of view of Athens (where the myth derives, found originally in the works of Aristotle), the myth is a way of establishing the credibility of its own government and accentuating the rhetorical ideology of the day. As Peitho develops from representing "persuasion" to representing "democracy," it makes sense that rhetoric's origin will parallel the narrative structure of our modern government's moral economy: as we get democracy, we get rhetoric, so the narrative goes. Positioned in a different way, *if we have rhetoric, we have democracy*. That may not be true, but to the extent that we think we are engaging in the free expression of our ideas, and to the extent that we think that our ideas matter and that we are important as citizens, then it *appears* that a democracy is in operation. Thus, the myth of Corax and Tisias is important to us today, as it was important to the ancient Greeks: it gives us a reason to believe that we are acting in some sort of grand narrative, one that has the sanction of history itself.

The Concept of Probability

Even if Corax never lived, the myth of his accomplishments includes the earliest discussions that we have of the concept of probability as an important factor in rhetorical persuasion. Corax is said to have fathered the concept of probability (*eikos*) as a central tenet in argumentation. Again, it does not matter to whom we attribute this concept; it is, conceptually, the first important principle we have characterizing a rhetorical psychology. Corax may have been the figure who was made to embody an important cultural development. In a world that was rejecting its theology, its absolute standards for judging right and wrong, justice and injustice, and the qualities that constitute a political state, something needed to be created to replace it. In place of a theology that is increasingly seen as being irrelevant, is the notion of a rhetorical epistemology. With this, we see the eclipse of one system of representation, and the incipient rise of another. But what is this epistemology? What is its character? How can we conceive of its purpose? These were not the types of questions being asked at the time, but these are valid questions that we can ask of history. While we can never know what was going on in the minds of the Ancient Greeks, we can understand the importance of epistemological change and the type of uncertainty it brings to a society. In the absence of certainty, people are left with probability. In a world without theology, human beings are left to their own resources. This much is as clear now as it was in history. The concept of a God confuses culture by masking human agency behind the cloak of a supernatural moral standard. In the words of Michael Bakunin:

> God being everything, the real world and man [sic] are nothing. God being truth, justice, goodness, beauty, power, and life, man is falsehood, iniquity, evil, ugliness, impotence, and death. God being master, man is the slave. Incapable of finding justice, truth, and eternal life by his own effort, he can attain them only though divine revelation. But whoever says revelation says revealers, messiahs, prophets, priests, and legislators inspired by God himself to direct it in the path of salvation, necessarily exercise absolute power. All men owe them passive and unlimited obedience; for against the divine reasons there is no human reason, and against the justice of God no terrestrial justice holds.[13]

Bakunin's sentiment, while written in response to nineteenth century Christianity and its political and cultural influences, exemplifies the alienation created by religion. The certainty of God, or in the case of the Greeks, of the gods, confuses human beings into giving up their agency, their power to construct a meaningful world based upon the wants and needs of the human community. Divine certainty is comfortable, but it comes with a price, as Bakunin highlights.

In this struggle over what it means to know, we are faced with two different ways to approach the world. The world can be approached ontologically, that is, from the point of view that it can be known independent of human beings. Historically, that has been the purpose of religion: to bring certainty and order to the chaos and meaninglessness of human existence. The other is a more epistemological view, a position that can be characterized as rhetorical. This view holds that in the absence of certainty, we come to know in a much more limited, and socially contingent manner. In giving up a dependence on an ontological structure, the Greek people were beginning to struggle with more subjective ways of knowing, and this development has its representation in the Corax myth.

Probability, in its most basic sense, "is likeliness to be true; the first notation of the word signifying such a proposition for which there be arguments or proofs to make it pass, or be received for true."[14] Bromley Smith offers an example of how probability functions in an argument: Corax, supposedly, had a student named Tisias who disputed with his mentor in court over the paying of educational fees:

> Corax is said to have demanded pay for his lessons in rhetoric, arguing as follows: You must pay me if you win the case, because that proves the worth of my lessons. You must pay me also, if you lose the case, for the court will issue a decree against you. Either by our stipulation, or by the judgment of the court you fail. What's the use of going on with the case? To this Tisias replied: I will pay you nothing, because if I lose the case, your instruction has been worthless; whereas if I win, the court will absolve me from the claim.[15]

According to the legend, the case was thrown out of court with the following remark: "A bad *crow* lays bad eggs."[16] The word "*korax*," in Greek, means "crow."

The argument from probability is more substantial than it appears in the Corax/Tisias court dispute. In particular, Aristotle relies heavily on this precept when he declares that rhetoric and dialectic work to uncover contingent knowledge. Aristotle's discussion of persuasion, in particular his characterization of the "enthymeme" and the rhetorical "example" derive from the premise that certainty in human affairs is probabilistic and not scientific. A further advantage to the argument from probability is that probabilities, unlike oaths and witnesses, do not lie and cannot be subjected to bribes. The argument from probability assumes that auditors generally act rationally (an Aristotelian assumption) and that individual human action or a particular political position can be predicated on the assumption that people try to see for themselves that which the persuader wants them to see. Kennedy explains the circumstance in which an orator might engage in probabilistic reasoning: "If he [sic] has direct evidence to support him, an orator of course makes use of it. If he has not, he must rely on probabilities. Usually the situation is somewhere in between: there is some evidence, but it will not take the orator all the way."[17]

A useful (and classical) example of the argument from probability might be a small, unarmed man who defends himself on an assault charge where the victim is a large, armed man. The defense of probability is not based on evidence, but on the unlikeness that a small man can actually succeed in hurting a large man. The definition of "likeliness" is based upon the perception of the audience:

> Corax's notion seems to have been that such probable arguments, logically inconclusive though they may be, are nevertheless often more effective than stricter arguments from particular evidence, because they are based on general observations which every one will admit to be true: while the stricter reasoning which we might expect to carry more weight carries less, because its force depends entirely on the truth of particular premises which the hearer may be not at all disposed to believe; and far more people are impressed by admitted truth in the premises than by logical cogency in the reasoning.[18]

In the above quote, the author is highlighting perhaps the most important conceptual development in the evolution of rhetorical thinking. The principle of probability accentuates the importance of audience involvement in the persuasion process. Logic and evidence must be *perceived* as "logical" and "good." There are no external standards by which an argument or a piece of reasoning can be judged valid. All logical systems, all moral systems, reduce to a condition of human social contingency. All moral, logical, or ethical appeals are system dependent. As long as people are involved in that system, they have a potential to recognize the importance of any particular claim. But from outside of that perspective, they face what can be conceptualized as the "comprehensibility chasm."

Comprehensibility Chasm

The comprehensibility chasm involves the limitations of communication that derive when people from outside of a particular rationality system are asked to participate in the construction of an argument. In other words, there is a gap in perception that arises between people who speak from differing logological positions. Words imply relationships and the vocabularies we use predispose us to act in certain ways. For Rorty, such vocabularies act as our moral guides.[19] For Burke, these vocabularies lead to the condition of sight itself. In his discussion of "terministic screens," he explains, "Even if any given terminology is a *reflection* of realty, by its very nature as a terminology it must be a *selection* of reality; and to this extent it must function also as a *deflection* of reality."[20] Or, in other words, "A way of seeing is also a way of not seeing—a focus upon object *A* involves a neglect of object *B*."[21] Literally, our language implies structures of meaning. Even the structural framework of our language disposes us to think, act, and feel in particular ways. On a related note, the linguist Noam Chomsky advanced the thesis that the physiological structure of the brain makes language possible, but also places limitations on the way that the language, and hence knowledge can be actualized. As a result, certain forms of knowledge can be made known to us, for example, physics, while others things exist that we cannot even imagine because it does not fit the deep structure of our brains.[22]

What does all this mean? It means that we are only able to think and know according to structures of meaning that are made available to us. While there is not much we can do, according to Chomsky's biological model of human comprehensibility, there is a great deal that we can do within the limitations he postulates. In short, there is *everything* that human beings have the potential to do, and that takes us squarely back to rhetoric. Within this condition of potential, there are symbolic orders of structure, and these are created by our language. Different languages lead us to different structures. By "language" I do not necessarily mean to make the distinction that one might find between, say, Chinese and English. Certainly, the difference between these two languages leads to different interpretive structures. By "language," what I am trying to emphasize is the actual vocabularies people use to construct the world and articulate their positions. Within a single language, English for example, we find that different language communities occupy different epistemological positions. This, in turn, is reflective of ideological distinctions. *Ideology, then, is linguistic: its shape is formed by the contours of language.*

Here is where we find the crux of this position. Between any two positions there is the potential for conflicting vocabularies, epistemologies, or paradigms. Such conflict is the purview of ideology. Simply, the use of one language often excludes another. To talk of the "Aryan Race," for example, excludes a vocabulary that describes Jews in a positive light. To talk of the "free market" excludes our ability to talk about the rights of labor and the need or concern for ecological issues.

Within the comprehensibility chasm lies the condition of incommensurability. Incommensurability occurs when people from different paradigms look at each other from across the chasm of incomprehensibility and try to talk to each other without establishing, through definition or stipulation, some degree of common ground. For instance, incommensurability is what occurs when a strict argument from "evidence" fails to be persuasive. What might appear to be a strict argument from evidence to the persuader, is not perceived as such by the audience. Since persuasion is about the relationship between a communicator and an audience, it is that distance between the two minds that must be traversed. This bridge is often metaphoric. In moving from the known to the unknown, audiences cannot be asked to traverse too large a conceptual gap. Rather, they have to be aided in their task by the persuader who offers them a resemblance. That is where metaphor becomes important.

The Use of Metaphor in Establishing Commensurability

The use of metaphor is part of the argument from probability: it starts where the audience is, the known referent, and proceeds to hold the audience's hand so that it can make the conceptual move toward understanding the unknown referent, thus completing the comparison. Metaphors are not always logical, but they do not have to be: often, it is not logic that appeals to people, but the internal feeling they have about the believability of a particular set of propositions. To say that "Richard is a Lion," to take a popular example, involves more than the attribution of lion qualities (the known) to Richard (the unknown). Strictly speaking, the argument is not logical, as the analogy compares two things of different classes which do not have a demonstrable degree of similarity. Lions do not have courage in the sense that humans have courage, since "courage," properly speaking, implies heroism, or at least the sense that one has the ability to stand down a fear of mortality in the face of danger. "Heroes," however, are symbolic, and so are "death" and "mortality" as concepts. People die, lions die, but lions do not have an ability to transcend fear through honor or a sense that their virtue lies in facing down the fear of death (which is symbolically a way of transcending it).

In what sense, then, is "Richard is a lion" a useful metaphor? It is useful because, in the absence of logic, it is appealing. It is understandable. It is believable. Its argumentative force appeals to the inner sense of pride that people have the ability to feel. That is appealing, more so than the logical progression between premise and conclusion. They believe in themselves. They believe in what they could achieve and they recognize that they could be Richard. If I were to say that "Richard is a ball point pen," such argument would be ludicrous. It is unbelievable and people cannot imagine themselves as part of the argument. They cannot empathize, they cannot sympathize, and they cannot identify. The argument is improbable: it would take an extremely talented orator to bring to light, in a serious way, the recognizability of the comparison.

In order to bridge the comprehensibility chasm, the persuader must start from where the audience is (the first part of the metaphor), what they can see, feel, and know based upon its readily observable conditions. The importance of this for all further rhetorical theory cannot be underestimated: persuasion starts from the perception of the audience and builds an argument, not from evidence found in the external world, but from a command of the inner subjectivity of the audience's private world. The strength of Aristotle's enthymeme (discussed in chapter five) is based on this principle (metaphors themselves are enthymematic). In a world where there are no absolute anchors to secure our arguments, we are left with people's perceptions from which to fashion our rhetorical appeals. This is the strongest argument we have against the detractors of rhetoric, people who reduce it to the use of flowery language or talk at the expense of meaning. Rhetoric is how we make meaning. Rhetoric mediates external logical systems and invites people to participate in the construction of arguments. Without this function in our thinking, we would not be able to communicate with anyone who was not completely consubstantial with us.

Rhetorical communication works off the principle of consubstantiality. For rhetoric to work, there has to be a degree of identification or sameness between two minds. Once the two minds connect at the consubstantial level, persuasion increases those bonds, and develops even greater levels of identification. But there is no hook, no connection, if there is no sense of a perceived similarity between the two minds of the communication interaction. That is why persuaders always have to start from where the audience is and from what it is that they are willing to believe.

Rhetoric Comes to Athens

According to the legend, Tisias brought Corax's teaching to Athens and, in the course of his tenure, mentored three particularly noteworthy students: Gorgias, Lysias, and Isocrates. Here is where the history of rhetoric is placed on more solid ground. Each of these three people we know to have existed. Each also played an important intellectual role in the development of Athenian culture and in the formation of what we recognize today as a rhetorical environment.

As illustrated in the previous section, the dominant myth of rhetoric was that it rose out of the early need of democratic consciousness to assert itself after the fall of regional tyrannies in Ancient Greece. In this context, a man named Corax was said to have designed an early handbook called *The Art of Rhetoric* to aid speakers in the courts who were trying to regain confiscated property after the defeat of Thasybulus, the tyrant of Syracuse. His student, Tisias, brought these teachings to Athens where they found fertile soil to grow and develop into the rich rhetorical tradition that exists today. Notice the neatness and succinctness of this narrative. On its face, it is almost as unproblematical as the myths surrounding the founding the United States of America. The myth conceals its ruptures and focuses its task on the creation of an ideological environment. With the myth of Corax, rhetoric is given a telos, a purpose, a tradition. More importantly, it has a context, one that cannot be separated from the rationale of the politics that provides the context. In this way, and in others, knowledge is always political. Knowledge always exists because of its narrative context, and narratives are stories that people in power tell about their history in order to make that history appear in the image of their own making.

As suggested, the rhetorical tradition begins with "Corax." But if this is all that we could write, rhetoric would be an impoverished discipline. Things begin to develop quickly at this point in terms of the intellectualization of logos. Armed with the basic principle of probability, fueled by a political environment that endorsed a democratic ideology, and situated in a wider cultural context in which literacy increasingly becomes the cultural norm (along with the correspondingly decreased reliance on theistic or poetic reasoning), this phenomenon that we call an incipient rhetorical consciousness becomes gradually elaborated upon by the Sophists.

Preview to the Sophists: The Ionian Philosophers

Before moving into our discussion of the Sophists, we need to establish a sense of their historical position in relationship to other dominant ideas that were in circulation at the time. In particular, the Sophists, and their teachings, were a response to the materialism of the Ionian philosophers and to the inability of the Ionian philosophers to provide a rationale for political and ethical life.

The Ionian philosophers were among the first people in Ancient Greece to break from the Greek preoccupation with deity worship. Their materialism is their response to theistic or mythic reasoning. In the absence of a God, or a system of gods, to structure the daily workings of life, the Ionian philosophers sought material explanations for the way the world was structured. This was their attempt to find order amidst the chaos of the natural environment. In a sense, they were the first scientists. With Thales, notes F.M. Cornford, "Western science appeared in the world—science as commonly defined: the pursuit of knowledge for its own sake. . . . "[23] The Ionian philosophers set out to explore the empirical world in order to understand it. The way they did this was to study its elements. They sought answers to the question, "What is the world made of?" The following are four prominent Ionian philosophers and their hypotheses.

The first, Thales, believed that the world was composed of water, as evident in the following two fragments from his work: "The first principle and basic nature of all things is water . . . The Earth rests upon water."[24] This position is not altogether unrealistic. Human beings are roughly 70% water. The surface of the planet is covered by roughly 75% water. The Greek experience, being dependent on the ocean, was marked by a heightened consciousness of water. Outside of air, water is the most basic and fundamental element for the maintenance of life.

The second, Anaximenes, postulated that the world was air. Anaximenes wrote, "As our souls, being air, hold us together, so breath and air embrace the entire universe."[25] Similar to Thales' postulation, Anaximenes' thesis is not altogether nonsensical. He recognized that elements go through certain stages and that air is basic to those stages. For example, air condenses into wind and forms into clouds by trapping water particles. It contributes to rain and mud, and makes fire possible. On earth, air connects the spaces between physical places, and fills in the spaces between the atoms. In a sense, it gives substance to form. Air gives us displacement, as when the air that fills a cup moves so that it may be filled with water or wine. The importance of Anaximenes' thought has less to do with his specific principle of air, but his acknowledgment that air has different forms, and that, as matter, it has the ability to change properties in relationship to the environment—an important early scientific principle.

The third, Heraclitis, proclaimed that the universe was itself change; the notion of flux was the substance of all creation. Fragments from Heraclitis stress this observation: "Everything flows and nothing abides; everything gives way and nothing stays fixed. . . . You cannot step twice into the same river, for other waters and yet others go ever flowing on. . . . It is in changing that things find repose."[26]

This is a very Eastern approach to conceptualizing the nature of the world. Heraclitis, as far as we know, derived this principle independently of Taoism, which was rising at the same time in China. Compare Heraclitis' passage with the following from the *Tao De Ching*:

> *What is half shall become whole.*
> *What is crooked shall become straight.*
> *What is empty shall become full.*
> *What is old shall become new.*
> *Whosoever has little shall receive.*
> *Whosoever has much, from him shall be taken away.*[27]

The inverse of the above is also true: what is whole will soon disintegrate, what is straight will become crooked, what is full becomes empty, what is new comes old. Whoever receives has something to lose.

Lao Tsu's principle of change and flux is based on the Yin/Yang symbol. The Yin (black) and Yang (white) also denote femininity and masculinity. The symbol is pictured as a circle, and the circle is divided into two curves, with a smaller circle drawn in the middle of the thick part of the two halves. The color of the small circle conforms to the color of the opposing half. But "opposing" is not the most accurate word. White does not oppose black, maleness does not oppose femaleness. Within black is white, within white is black. Within male is female, and within female is male. The idea is that the cycle never breaks; white eternally transforms into black, and black eternally transforms into white. Male and female are likewise intertwined. Binary oppositions are thus de-emphasized in Chinese philosophy, unlike in the West where binary oppositions are invested with a terrible political economy (i.e. white *over* black, male *over* female).

The ideas of flux behind Heraclitis' writings have not found an hospitable home in the Western mind. A perusal of his extant fragments accentuates his distinctly Eastern tone. For example, he writes:

This universe, which is the same for all, has not been made by any god or man, but it always has been, is, and will be—an ever-living fire, kindling itself by regular measures and going out in regular measures.[28]

To be temperate is the greatest virtue. Wisdom consists in speaking and acting the truth, giving heed to the nature of things.[29]

Cool things become warm, the warm grows cool; the moist dries, the parched becomes moist.[30]

Opposition brings concord. Out of discord comes the fairest harmony.[31]

Heraclitis offers a philosophical strand that differs sharply from both Plato and from rhetoric.

The fourth Ionian philosopher, Democritus, made a remarkable observation for his time when he proclaimed that the world was made of atoms. A fragment from a lost Aristotelian treatise states the following: "According to the theory of Democritus it is the nature of the eternal objects to be tiny substances infinite in number. . . . His theory is that they cling together and remain in certain combinations until they are shaken apart and separated by outside forces."[32]

Like the other Ionian philosophers, Democritus' position is not as odd as it might initially strike us. Twentieth-century physics has much to say about these "tiny substances" that Democritus spoke about.

What is important about the Ionian philosophers is not whether or not they were "right" about the elemental nature of the world. There is a degree to which they were all correct. What is important is that their views contrasted sharply with a culture steeped in deity worship, introducing a critical perspective that would lead, eventually, to the birth of science. The Ionian philosophers made the unique assumption that everything in the world that appeared contrary to the true essence of the world was merely illusion. Notice the ideology that is being assumed here. While the logical extreme of their arguments points to an atheistic position, they have merely substituted one "material" standard for another. Granted, it is reasonable to assume the position of nature over God for the practical purposes of responding to the contingencies of the environment. Nevertheless, the position of the Ionian philosophers was missing something fundamental about the role of ideas in the functioning of society, something that was at least implicitly recognized within the system of the divine ontology, something that did not transfer once the ontologies switched.

What was missing involves the question of culture. Specifically, it involves the issues surrounding morality, justice, emotions, politics, and subjectivity. In short, it involves the failure to recognize that science is, first and foremost, a *human* activity. It was invented *by* humans *for* humans. It is limited both by human subjectivity and by the types of questions it can ask. Because its ability to question is limited, the breadth of its claims and terrain is limited. The limitations of the materialism of the Ionian philosophers is that they did not quite meet the cultural need that religion played in Greek society. While it is potentially liberating to devise an understanding of the world outside of a theistic influence, the task falls upon the philosopher to offer an alternative morality or structure to replace the one that religion used to hold. To ignore this responsibility is to be ignorant of the sociological functions of religion.

Religion is more than a metaphysics of spirit, it involves the day-to-day functioning of society. Religion provides an ethics and a morality structure. It gives meaning and cohesion to society. It does not matter which particular religion we are discussing, as most religions contradict each other on fundamental points of ethics and morality. But every religion does the same thing: it offers an explanation for the world, and it gives people the tools to cope with their lives. The Ionian philosophers, by overturning the dominant ontology of the heavens, did not replace its ethical dimensions. It is one thing to assert that the universe is air, water, flux or atoms. The universe may not have a metaphysics (organized religion, at least, has failed to offer anything more than force, dogma, or "faith" to substantiate its claims). Human spirituality and religion may in fact be a big illusion, and often a destructive one at that. There may be no absolute meaning to human existence (certainly, such position is privileged by a rhetorical epistemology). Nevertheless, this does not mean we cannot have small "t" truths. The absence of big "T" Truth and metaphysical hope in divine justice does not mean that we cannot as human beings be responsible for the creation of truth and meaning in our lives. Yet the base materialism of the Ionian philosophers did not allow for such subjective rationales. Unlike the materialism of Marxism which explores the dialectical relationship between the material world and human culture,[33] the discussion of the world by the Ionian philosophers left no room for a discussion of human involvement in the cosmos. It is into such an absence of space that the Sophists situated their appeal.

The Sophists

The Sophists rose as a cultural force in Athenian society during the fifth century as an initial reaction against the social irrelevance of the Ionian philosophers. The Sophists were nurtured by the political climate, which was thriving on the need for an educated and articulate citizenry. The political order demanded that its citizens be able to participate in a popular politics, and it demanded education and a reasonable degree of articulateness. As rhetoric, still largely defined as logos, was the means of political participation, it makes sense that the class of educators that were active at that time would be focused, to some degree, on questions of oratory and communication. Just like the rhapsodes before them who served the educational needs of a theistic and poetically-based oral society, the Sophists were teaching communication skills that corresponded with the nexus of political power. Communication channels are always associated with wealth and politics. Areas of vast wealth and power today are the computer, satellite, and the television cable industries: the communication technologies. Our study of rhetoric, then, is easily conceptualized as a study of power as it was manifested in Ancient Athens.

The Sophists were not a conservative movement working to reestablish an old order. On the contrary, they utilized the gains made by the Ionian philosophers in terms of questioning the natural forces in nature. On the other hand, it would not be accurate to call them "radicals" either, at least in our current political sense (some of the Sophists supported the oligarchic movements of the period). They were attracted by power and they were in control of a significant cultural resource. This made them very important people. As such, they were attacked by the conservatives for threatening the established order, and for encouraging more people to be actively engaged in the political economy of the city. Nevertheless, what made them special as a loose collective of people is that, while they joined with the Ionian philosophers in breaking from the servitude of the heavens, they did not replace their traditional ontology with a new material one. Rather, they uniquely made the human mind the focal point of human experience. In a loose sense, the Sophists can be considered the first humanists. Harold Barrett elaborates on the teaching of the Sophists: "They taught that human horizons were not predetermined, that humankind could understand and deal with natural forces. The Greek people could use their minds to improve themselves. They could be taught to conduct themselves more effectively as orators and thereby ready themselves for places of usefulness and standing in the community."[34]

The Sophistic movement revolted against the ideas of the Ionian philosophers as largely irrelevant and foolhardy. Even if the Ionian philosophers were correct, the Sophists reasoned, how could their observations affect the lives of people who had to contend with day to day reality? In other words, the impractical nature of Ionian philosophy did little directly to enrich the lives of the people. As Frederick Beck explains, "The scientific speculations of the sixth century had succeeded in stimulating intellectual activity but made no contribution towards offering a guide to conduct."[35] The Sophists believed that the human mind was perfectible, that education could improve the innate conditions of an individual. Education, they taught, was empowerment.

The Sophists, sensing the need for some system of practical morality, introduced a humanistic approach to human speculation and thus began to articulate what since has become known as the *nomos* vs. *physis* argument, an intellectual query that still engages thoughtful people today. The Sophists took the *nomos* position. *Nomos* is the concept that laws are not unalterable and dictated by divine or natural forces beyond the control of humans. Wheelwright defines *nomos* as "custom, convention; a received body of opinions as imposing an unwritten law."[36] Under the position of *nomos*, people govern the cosmos and make agreements and contracts. These contracts could become "law," but such a law is contingent upon continued validity of that agreement or contract. This position holds that the responsibility for human fate lies within the mortal realm. The structure and order that is imposed on human communities come from within the communities themselves. Thus, they are not immutable. They are open to debate and revision. Their moral or legal force rests upon the consent of the governed (to borrow a modern political concept). As Susan Jarratt explains: "On the level of the social, *nomos* determines the behavior and activities of persons and things through convention."[37]

The *physis* perspective, on the other hand, holds the view that natural laws are unchangeable, and people are helpless to do anything except act in accordance with these forces. Wheelwright defines *physis* as "the nature of anything but usually with a quasibiological connotation of growth or potential growth."[38] The *physis* position is a form of absolutism, while the *nomos* position is that of cultural interactivism. The position of the Sophists introduced the social agreement view: tables are tables because human beings have decided to call them such and to treat them as such. An Ionian (*physis*) retort to this position could be in the form of a question: Does gravity exist because we agree to be held to the Earth? Obviously, it does not. But that is not to say that we understand what is happening to us because of our ideas of "gravity."

Currently, it is useful to talk about gravity, because it helps us to explain certain things about the world. However, as our needs change, our ideas of "gravity" might not be able to keep up with those needs. When that occurs, we will need to broaden our understanding of the term. It does not mean that our understanding of gravity is wrong: it is merely incomplete. Yet *it will always be incomplete*. There is no big picture to apprehend, no prize that we get when we successfully solve nature's "mysteries." Nature does not "hide" "mysteries" from us. Nature just is. What we choose to "know" defines for us what we do not know or cannot know, and these things we call "mysteries."

The Sophists made their living as traveling teachers. Because of the Athenians' respect for speech and ideological commitment to debate, many Sophists gravitated to Athens where they were considered *metics* (resident aliens) or *Metoikoi*. They were allowed to work and had to pay taxes but were not permitted to intervene directly with the workings of the government. As *metics*, the Sophists could not appear before the Assembly, and were treated with a degree of suspicion. While they could not participate directly in the workings of government, they often wrote speeches for people who did, and trained many others to be effective politicians. In this way, the Sophists had a profound influence on the democracy through their teaching. This influence can be appreciated in the following statement by G.B. Kerferd who writes that the Sophists in general "produced for the first time in human history a theoretical basis for participatory democracy."[39]

Again, not all the Sophists did this. Nevertheless, enough of them were committed to the idea that language affects our ability to think, and that argument is a good way of determining a localized truth. While such a view is not the same thing as a direct support for democracy, it does open the door for justifying democratic processes. If democracy has any rationale at all, it is that the more people who contribute to the logos, the richer our understanding will be of our political realities. This is one of the reasons why, functionally speaking, we cannot really characterize the United States as a "democracy," as there is not much of a commitment to competing logos. What we have are practical disagreements on a highly specific range of ideas. Voices that hope to extend this range of topics and introduce new perspectives or otherwise challenge the characterization of the debate itself are systemically excluded. Also, enfranchised Athenians were all included in the political environment of Athens regardless of their economic status, while citizens in the U.S., while technically enfranchised since the passage of universal suffrage in 1921 and of Civil Rights legislation in the late 1960s, are functionally disenfranchised on economic grounds.

Six Traits of the Sophists

The group of men who belonged to what is called a Sophist "class" were never more than precisely that, a group of people acting as independent agents. There was never a unified movement. However, within this diversity of individuals, the Sophists can generally be classified as having the following six qualities in common.

First, all the Sophists taught or professed to teach virtue and character. The English approximation for the Greek concept of *arete* is virtue or excellence in human affairs. This sense of excellence has extreme moral overtones and is applied equally to athletic achievement as well as to philosophical inquiry. However, as Wheelwright observes, "Involved in the meaning of *arete* there was always an element or at least the overtone of political reference."[40] Because Greek life evolved around the functions of the polis and because the polis was, in effect, a small entity, political life was an exceedingly preeminent institution to which young men could aspire. Thus, *arete* was inherently political. Consequently, the Sophists' belief that they could cultivate *arete* in their students makes more sense: "The principle skill which the sophists taught, and of which an ambitious Greek youth would be eager to acquire mastery, was the ability to win debates and to influence public opinion through the art of persuasive public speech."[41]

If *arete* has a degree of political connotation, and if politics was mastered through the use of logos, through reasoned speech and other tactics and perspectives that would later be labeled "rhetorical," then the Sophists, in teaching this skill, would in fact be teaching people how to be virtuous. Barrett observes, "[T]heirs was a practical curriculum, designed to teach the Greek ideal of *arete*: the knowledge and attitude for effective participation in domestic, social and political life."[42] In the words of Magill, the Sophists "claimed to teach *politite arete*, competence in citizenship."[43]

Second (and related to the first), all the Sophists emphasized what we would recognize today as being "rhetoric": "Since the ability to sway votes in courtroom or Assembly was a fundamental political skill, the Sophists taught rhetoric and were the first to organize it into an art."[44] This characterization is a bit of an overstatement in terms of the intellectual conditions of the time, but it does not significantly misrepresent the environmental situation. Strictly speaking, the "art" of rhetoric did not exist until a) Plato coined the term, and b) Aristotle developed its *techne*.[45]

Practically speaking, however, the Sophists were teaching people how to persuade and how to contribute to the contingent affairs of the state.

Third, each of the Sophists charged many *drachmas* (money) for their educational services. This circumstance immediately points us in the direction of an apparent inconsistency. On the one hand, an immediate result of their teaching was an increased cultural bias toward democratic rationales. On the other hand, as Barrett writes, "Their immediate clientele were not the masses certainly, but people with leisure and sufficient money to pay the fees."[46] This "contradiction" makes sense, arguably, when one considers our earlier discussion of the Sophists contributing fundamentally to the move away from the old theocracies and power structure to newer, more "democratically" inclined ideologies. This move incurred the wrath of the conservatives, people whose power depends upon the appeal to a divine sanction. This does not mean, however, that the Sophists were not elitists, or that their vision of democracy was incompatible with slavery, misogyny, or their association with the wealthy. While class tensions were modified somewhat by the Athenian democracy, they were not non-existent. The Sophists privileged the rich, and the Athenian government, in the sense that it can be known as such by its orators, tended to be wealthy. The Sophists, to the extent that they contributed to this environment, did so by training the children of the wealthy.

Fourth, the Sophists tended to teach *eristic*, which is the ability to argue both sides of a particular question. This practice makes sense, given their predisposition toward a rhetorical epistemology. Unfortunately, the term is usually now associated with a poor way of reasoning, as when Barrett defines *eristic* as "a form of disputation characterized by wrangling or specious reasoning."[47]

Fifth, the Sophists tended to engage in frequent displays of epideictic oratory. Epideictic oratory is ceremonial speaking, a speech of display used for advertising and for entertainment (see chapter five). In the words of J.B. Bury, "It is probable that most of them were publicists; that was a useful and natural form of self-advertisement."[48]

Sixth and finally, "All the Sophists were versatile and could teach almost any subject. . . . "[49] Part of the reason for this was that the disciplinization of knowledge and its corresponding degree of specification had yet to occur during this period of time. There was less to know and easier ways to characterize knowledge in the days of the Sophists than there are currently. Another reason why they could converse well on any number of subjects was that, in their study of logos, they figured out, perhaps only intuitively at this point, that all arguments could be broken down into various *topoi* (or topics), a type of list that can be memorized or learned. (Protagoras, at least, seems to give us indication of such theorizing, and Gorgias seems to use it in his "Encomium to Helen"). This list consists of certain strategic concepts that are readily generalizable across subjects (in other cases, they can be dependent upon a certain subject). The topics have a wide applicability and were used by the Sophists to "invent" a wide range of knowledge by focusing their critical inquiry.

Protagoras and Gorgias

The two best known Sophists were Protagoras of Abdera and Gorgias of Leontini. To a large extent, our characterization of the Sophists reflects the conditions and personalities of these two figures. In a sense, our knowledge of them often colors our experience of the other Sophists. In part, this is because of convention, in part because of laziness, and in part because of their tremendous influence on subsequent thinkers.

Protagoras, Perception, and Communication

Protagoras was born circa 485 BCE and is attributed authorship of the famous statement which fully expressed the sophistic position. He argued that the "[Hum]an is the measure of all things: of things that are, that they are; of things that are not, that they are not."[50] This statement indicates that reality, at least in its more subjective sense, is not a given in nature, not universal. Nothing is true or real other than what is commonly agreed upon. However, it is not just agreement that matters. What Protagoras seems to be saying is that inner subjectivity is perceptionally based. In its crude form, Protagoras' statement can be taken as "What I as an individual human say is true, is true." Such statement is tremendously egotistical and solipsistic. This position can rightly be rejected. A more useful reading of this passage is that, in the absence of God, what can be considered meaningful for human existence must come from the human mind itself.

When Protagoras says that the human is the measure of "all things," he does not mean "things in themselves." Rather, he means "things as they are understood by humans." In other words, Protagoras is not saying that the human becomes God, but that we do not need the concept of God anymore. All we truly have as individual humans is our minds by which we make sense of all things, starting with the body, and extending to the world. In a human-centered universe, reality does not rotate around the human, as planets around the sun or a theological world around God. Rather, it is a world in which humans are freed to make their own way. In making their own "way" they make their own world. Everything we know, we know via our human subjectivity. Even the instruments that we make to do our science express our anthropomorphism—they are extensions of our primary senses and rationalities. As Protagoras points out, we cannot escape our human subjectivity. Any theory of knowledge or of communication must take this condition into consideration.

Protagoras' statement goes much further than the positions of the Ionian philosophers; he is not simply postulating another material explanation for the world. Rather, he is going beyond the need to seek material answers. In other words, he is changing the question, or trying to at least. He is not trying to find a way to match human beings to the order of the cosmos, as religions attempt to do. He is not trying to understand the world in terms of its elements. Rather, he is introducing a different type of rationality. He is not ignoring elemental factors, and he is not necessarily ignoring the gods, if they in fact exist. Whatever the material world is, does not matter; it can be a billion different things. Whatever it is must necessarily be perceived by human beings in order to be meaningful to us. God may exist, but as we cannot perceive it, or sense it outside of this nebulous thing called "faith," we must consider this unknowable thing irrelevant (even if it very much effects our lives through a logic and an influence of which we are unaware).

Our human perceptions may or may not be "accurate." This does not matter, either, as questions of "accuracy" are not part of Protagoras' epistemology: they are part of a world view that is alien to him. He is not interested in getting the world "right." Protagoras' interest (or at least our understanding of his interest) lies in accentuating human subjectivity as the yardstick of meaning for the human. From the point of view of the gods, they may be the standard of existence. From the point of view of turtles, they are the standard of existence. The human, in differing from turtles and gods, only knows what he/she can know, and that knowledge is experiential to him/her.

Protagoras' position directly challenges the social order that embraced God-given law, rights of birth, and the rule of the aristocracy. It does so by recognizing and privileging the ability of the individual human mind to express its own subjective reality, and to communicate that experience with others. This seems to be the most human thing we can do and may be the grounds upon which love can be experienced. Such a communication does not lead to a contest of wills with two subjectivities battling it out to force one's definition upon the other. Rather, such communication expresses one human's experience which, when shared with others, helps the larger collectivity to understand better the human condition. It leads to a richer life and, ultimately, to the state of irony. For example, if people in the United States took the time and effort to understand different cultures and to learn the needs of people living in countries that are non-European, non-capitalist-based, they will see that much of the world experiences the reality that we take for granted quite differently. However, since the U.S. cruelly forces much of the rest of the world to conform to its business and industrial needs, it ignores the localized needs and the localized expressions of human solidarity and national identity felt by the different peoples it subjugates. Such action might become unthinkable if we had respect for these people, and respect begins from accepting the world view of another as equally valid to our own. Likewise, by waging a relentless war against any expression of socialism throughout the world, the U.S. downplays important cultural, social, and economic expressions that developing peoples may have.

By taking this out of a Marxist model for a moment and by placing it into a Protagorian model, my point is this: the human experience of reality is not singularly defined by the United States. All peoples of the world have a right to communicate their subjectivity and desires. It is in the collectivity of all these expressions that human "nature" can be understood. But to get a better sense of this "nature," we cannot just look at all the existing human cultures. We have to look at all the past ones and all the future ones as well. Thus, it is difficult to talk about human "nature" in any meaningful way if we try to extend too far past Protagoras. The human mind provides our freedom and our limitations.

Protagoras' remark and its subsequent implications did not go unchallenged. Plato, for example, proposed a well developed metaphysics that contradicts Protagoras' claims (see chapter four). Among the politicians and day-to-day citizenry of Athens, Protagoras' remark was considered controversial. When pressed about the implications of his remark on the authority of a divine spirit, Protagoras retorted: "As for the gods, I have no way of knowing either that they exist or that they do not exist; nor, if they do exist, of what form they are. For the obstacles to that sort of knowledge are many, including the obscurity of the matter and the brevity of human life."[51]

While this remark earned him state censorship, banishment, and public destruction of his works (according to some accounts), it is his next statement, the two-*logoi* fragment, that would characterize the position of the Sophists for the next two millennia and court the condemnation of philosophers like Plato, Descartes, and Kant. Protagoras said, "On every question there are two speeches that oppose each other."[52] Protagoras' idea was for a speaker to learn how to bolster the weaker argument in his position in order to understand the parameters of the issue.[53] If the human mind is the standard of experience for the human, then the specific yard stick of that experience is language. Yet language is imperfect, as are our perceptions. How then do we improve on our language?

Language itself cannot be true or false, but our propositions can. Propositions can be true or false because they invite argument. But how do we evaluate argument? By itself we cannot evaluate argument, we need some sort of standard. There are internal standards for argument validity, but those principles had yet to be developed during the lifetime of Protagoras. Another way to evaluate argument is by external standards: to clash arguments. The force of the clash causes us to form an opinion on how well they maintain their integrity under pressure. The greater the clash the more able we are to form a substantive opinion. To assert a "truth" is not very useful. However, to create an issue is extremely useful for a community, for it keeps people for taking what others exert as "truth" for granted. Protagoras is essentially saying that reality is known through issues, and that the more salient the issue, the more useful our understanding of it. This is also a useful way of resolving the tensions created by individual subjectivities struggling to be the "measure" of things, as discussed above. Individual subjectivism does not become truth, it simple becomes one dimension of the logos that must interact with others.

The Greek term used to express Protagoras' sentiment is *dissoi logoi*. With this term, Protagoras introduces the following rhetorical precept: effective choice-making is largely determined by a thorough understanding of any situation. This principle does not just have an argumentative function. It has a reality-defining function, as well. It is a way to make sense of the environment. It is also an ethic, a morality. Thus, Protagoras begins to give the Athenians what the Ionian philosophers could not: a way to structure their moral and political lives. This morality is community-based and dialogical in approach.[54] Unlike the Judeo-Christian ethic which is imposed from the "top" and is selectively applied, a Protagorean ethic, or what we can retrospectively call a "rhetorical ethic," comes from the "bottom" up (it actually rejects the high/low binary). Such an ethic can be just as abused as the Judeo-Christian ethic, but it is much more difficult to do that and maintain the illusion of consistency (a communication platform cannot easily be both community based and anti-community at the same time). Judeo-Christian ethics are selectively applied because they come from outside of us. Thus, we can interpret them any way we want. War, slavery, predatory capitalism, and just about every criminal act that has occurred in the world since the rise of Christianity has been defended by the Church, comfortably couched within its ethics.

Contemporary supporters of the Church can look back on these instances and rightly condemn what they see as hypocrisy, and they can condemn the Church for its moral imperfections. Judeo-Christian morality is imperfect because it does not take into consideration the differing logoi of people. The Church has defined people, at least historically, in specific ways, from the point of view of culturally dominant Church power relations. Whatever else the Church may be, it is a cultural force, one with great consequence for the practice of politics in the last five hundred years. With variation, depending on the Church, and depending on the cultural situation, "people" generally have been defined as wealthy, white, and male. Thus, in a sense, the "hypocrisy" of the Church must be historicized. While the Church, or the Christian nations that developed into the Capitalist powers, committed genocidal acts against the poor at home and toward most of what we now recognize as the "Third World," there is a sense in which it was *not* being hypocritical. It *was* living up to its own moral standards, perhaps piously; the hitch is that the Church chose not to extend those standards to include a wider range of people (Native Americans, Africans, Asians, Jews, and the European poor). The Nazis did the same thing with their ethical positions. Many of the Nazis that we recognize as "monsters" were upright citizens, pious fathers and husbands, and religiously devoted to the ideology of the State. Their particular system of ethics may have been different than that of the Christians, but they were consistent in living up to their ideals, as contained in their philosophy of "nation" or "blood." They merely defined a great deal of humanity out of their moral universe.

It is difficult for a dialogical or a rhetorical ethics to exclude people selectively on ideological grounds because it starts from the proposition that community is essential, and that the wider the community the more beneficial the results. It starts from the wants and needs of day-to-day people and extrapolates from those needs to postulate the actual structure of the legal or political system. Such a system is superior, I argue, because it is more difficult to define people out of community. For example, if the United States were to treat Third World peoples as human beings and not as economic subjects or workhorses to slave in U.S. owned factories and fields, then our current punitive measures to protect "our" property from the people abused by it would not make sense. This point needs further elaboration.

"It is wrong to steal," according to the Judeo-Christian ethical system. Thus, it makes sense that we punish people, like the Cubans, who take "our" property. Dialogically, however, if we construct our ethics in a way that recognizes the Cuban peoples' right to have a voice, and if we look at the needs of individual women and men living in that country, and if we build an ethics based upon a sharing of experiences between their community and ours, most U.S. citizens of good will would recognize that when a country like Cuba (or Nicaragua and countless others) nationalizes its economy, it is doing so to eradicate the poverty and suffering of its own people. Such a move is intrinsically moral, even if it means that a few U.S. business people lose their "right" to extract future profits from that country, profits that contribute to Third World poverty. In explaining Protagoras' two-*logoi* fragment, Kennedy writes, "To put it another way, by agility of argument, the worse, from the point of view of common sense, is made to seem the better cause."[55] People hostile to the Sophists misunderstand Protagoras' position and criticize them for being charlatans by making the weaker position appear the greater cause. This is a superficial view that undermines the importance of Protagoras' contributions to a rhetorical epistemology, one grounded in human experience, solidarity, and community. Edward Schiappa presents a more positive interpretation of Protagoras' doctrine: "The purpose of Protagoras' theory and practice of *logos* was to challenge people for the better. The objective was understood as literally analogous to the art of medicine. The thesis that people can be made more excellent marked a departure from the traditional belief that *arete* was a function of wealth or noble birth."[56]

As Schiappa explains, Protagoras' competing logos was a form of medicine for the social body. One popular analogy in Athens was that rhetoric was for the mind as gymnastics was for the body. This sentiment is found in Gorgias, Isocrates, and Aristotle, and is derided in Plato. In each case, what is being debated is, How to improve the human being? What are the conditions of a healthy community? How best can we build a civic life?

People may disagree with the position of any of these thinkers, and they may reject the analysis in this book. But readers should leave this book with the sense that, whatever else has been discussed, I have been striving for the same thing that the people in this book were working toward: to answer the question of how best to organize society. In the humanities, at least, if not in intellectual life in general, there is no more important question to consider. It is a question that *everyone* must face: Christians, Nazis, Sophists, Communists, and Philosophers. To be perfectly honest, doctors, lawyers, professors, and every other professional must also deal with this question. A close study of their professional work reveals that they do produce their professional products with the end of such a world in mind. It may not be a world that we like, but it is one that they, to a large extent, have a responsibility in controlling.

Gorgias and Kairos

Similar to Protagoras, Gorgias was one of the most popular of the Sophists. He came from Sicily in 427 BCE as an ambassador to Athens. Gorgias was inclined toward ceremonial speaking, which he used to attract students. In these contexts, he would sometimes claim to be able to speak on any subject or topic that an audience member could suggest. In his performance, he illustrated the potential strength of his teaching. While such a claim may appear extravagant, it is really not when considering the power of *topoi*. The purpose of *topoi*, as mentioned above, is to aid in the invention of arguments. If Gorgias was the master speaker that he appears to have been, it seems reasonable to suggest that he worked out a system of topics, of set arguments or questions that he could ask of any circumstance or object, that would help him generate subjects to discuss. The purpose of bringing up the *topoi* here is not to talk about theory: Gorgias does not give us any rhetorical theory. Rather, he illustrates that people can improve their natural talent with study. He taught people to speak well, and he himself was an excellent orator. With Gorgias we start to get actual explanations for how persuasion works. We start to get texts that become subject to intellectual analysis, serving as direct preconditions for the type of rhetorical theory advanced and developed in Aristotle, like the theory of *topoi*, for example.

Also similar to Protagoras was Gorgias' position on religion and its relationship to a theory of communication. For instance, one of his important works, *On The Nonexistent*, had the following three claims: "Being does not exist; if it did exist, it would be unknowable; if it were knowable, the knowledge of it could not be communicated by one mind to another."[57] According to Gorgias, words are what are being communicated in a discourse, not meaning. Social convention alone governs language, which is little more than a doctrine of symbols. Words are imperfect for communicating since they do not reflect meaning. In other words, Gorgias taught his students to communicate effectively under the pretext that nothing is certain (which harkens us back to the principle of probability and foreshadows Aristotle's notion of the enthymeme). What becomes important in the communication process in this perspective is the timing (*kairos*) of a speech. As James L. Kinneavy notes, Gorgias "made *kairos* the cornerstone of his entire epistemology, ethics, aesthetics, and rhetoric."[58] John Poulakos explains that "Gorgias was not alone in asserting that situations exist in time and that speech as a situational response does also"[59]: "The sophists stressed that speech must show respect to the temporal dimension of the situation it addresses, that is, it must be timely. In other words, speech must take into account and be guided by the temporality of the situation in which it occurs."[60]

A speech must be opportune to time, place, and audience as well as delightful to hear. In discussing the Sophists, Jarratt elaborates on this concept: "Their effectiveness in teaching this *techne* [art] derived in part from their experiences of different cultures; they believed and taught that notions of "truth" had to be adjusted to fit the ways of a particular audience in a certain time and with a certain set of beliefs and laws. Thus they advanced concepts of *kairos* (timeliness) and *to prepon* (fitness)."[61]

Michael Carter observes that the function of *kairos* is to tap into the generative potential of opposing forces in society through timing and positioning. Carter explains how *kairos* enables the rhetor to mediate between opposing *logoi* in a non-arbitrary fashion. *Kairos,* in other words, provides "an ethical basis for [making a] decision."[62] Here we find another example of how the Sophists succeeded in providing what the Ionian philosophers could not: an alternative ethical system that was not dependent upon the foundational authority of the Gods.

The principle behind *kairos* is the notion of *kosmos,* or structure within the social community. *Kairos* is a way of recognizing the contingency of human affairs and of directing that contingency to practical ends. It is a way of building community. Community building, in such a highly political environment as was Athens during this time, is fundamentally an ethical process. This is not to say that it is morally "good," but that it involves ethical concerns. Extrapolating this to a larger discussion of rhetoric, we find that a rhetorical epistemology provides for an ethics and morality. It is one alternative that we currently have to foundationalism or essentialism in justifying a community-based ethics. Thus, in a contemporary sense, James S. Baumlin writes that *kairos* "offers a classical-based epistemology for modern rhetoric—a rhetoric that recognizes the contingent nature of reality and the way man [sic] constitutes his world through language."[63] Centuries after Gorgias, we find in Roman theories of style the concept of *ornatus.* This concept serves roughly the same function for the Romans as *kairos* did for the Greeks: it explores the contingent nature of society and the orator's influence on the community through language.

The relationship between *kairos, kosmos,* and *oranutus* is best illustrated by an analogy. This illustration comes from a fourth-century BCE Chinese Taoist parable. The story is called "Cook Ting." Mr. Ting, a cook for an Imperial court, was approached one day by a palace Lord who was impressed by Ting's butchery skills. When questioned by the Lord, Ting proceeded to explain in nontechnical terms what Gorgias was describing through his principle of *kairos*:

> A good cook changes his knife once a year—because he [sic] cuts. A mediocre cook changes his knife once a month—because he hacks. I've had this knife of mine for nineteen years and I've cut up thousands of oxen with it, and yet the blade is as good as though it had just come from the grindstone. There are spaces between the joints, and the blade of the knife has really no thickness. If you insert what has no thickness into such spaces, then there's plenty of room—more than enough for the blade to play about it. That's why after nineteen years the blade of my knife is still as good as when it first came from the grindstone.[64]

For the purpose of this analogy, equate the ox with society, and the knife with rhetoric. As Ting is able to carve the ox in precisely the way the ox is held together, the rhetorician utilizes language, informed by the principle of *kairos,* to carve reality into certain contingent and socially-useful categories at precisely their "correct" places. "Correct" here does not refer to their ontological status; it refers to its function in being able to serve the interests of the persuader.

In later Roman rhetorical theory the doctrine of *ornatus* built upon the notion that ideas derived from invention can be placed into useful configurations as a way to emphasize their social fit.[65] The Roman concept of *ornamenta verborum* corresponds to the Greek concept of *kosmos* and reveals the nature of wisdom or *phronesis* as it is manifested in that particular community. In other words, wisdom is practical and situational, as is rhetoric. The purpose of rhetoric is to derive practical knowledge, a wisdom that extends from the needs and awareness of a social community. The wise person, in this instance, is the one who can understand the structure of society. But it is not just the ability to see a particular structure in a literal sense, since one of the assumptions behind a rhetorical epistemology is that such structure does not materially exist; rather, it is rhetorically created. Wisdom involves an interpretation of the situation which, to the degree it is persuasive, enables the structure to be controlled. In other words, the structure of a society is culturally situated, and can be modified through discourse: the wise person brings order to society by creating it. Order (*kosmos*) is created out of chaos and rhetorical *kairos* (timing) is the process of matching the desires of the individual or community with the contingency of the moment in a way that redefines both. *Kairos*, then, has important philosophical as well as rhetorical dimensions. The rhetorical dimensions of *kairos* involve its sense of strategy, and its philosophical dimension involves its perception or interpretation of a society's structure. It is also an indication of how rhetoric and philosophy were joined prior to Plato. Actually, they were not even conceptualized as such prior to Plato; they had not yet been forced into distinct disciplinary frameworks. Prior to Plato, people like the Sophists would never have thought to make a distinction between rhetorical and philosophical pursuits; such pursuits were one and the same. The Sophists were interested in *language*, specifically logos, and they recognized that it is a power by which humans could transform their world. *Kairos* is a good example of this. The correct timing of a discourse is not simply its temporal appropriateness. Rather, an orator's skill in *kairos* involves a more active ability to locate the strategic spots in a particular society where a persuasive appeal can slip effortlessly between the "space" of an audience's perception and world.

Other Contributions of Gorgias

Gorgias contributed to rhetoric in several other important ways. For example, he popularized the so-called Gorgianic figures (figures of speech that Gorgias made familiar in his epideictic displays). These figures include *antithesis*, which is the comparison and contrast of opposing ideas, and *parison*, which are series of parallel structures of listed clauses. Gorgias also espoused the idea that sound itself has persuasive appeal. He exemplified what is known as the grand style of oratory. He was also known to juggle successfully many topics at once within a single piece of spontaneous discourse. Dressing and decor are also emphasized by Gorgias as being highly functional in persuasion.[66] This does not mean that Gorgias elevated style at the expense of "substance," as his and rhetoric's many detractors frequently argue. Instead, Gorgias took the position that the way that one spoke had something to do with the way that one is heard. Years later, Aristotle would reach the same conclusion: "The subject of expression . . . has some small necessary place in all teaching; for to speak in one way rather than another does make some difference in regard to clarity, though not a great difference; but all these things are forms of outward show and intended to affect the audience."[67]

Aristotle owes this influence to what he calls the "corruption of the audience."[68] Aristotle is talking about delivery and style together. The word he uses is *lexis*, which means "how something is said, style, often word choice, sometimes composition of sentences or speeches."[69]

In the "Encomium to Helen," one of the two surviving complete speeches from Gorgias, he attempts an argument from probability to exonerate Helen of Troy for her role in betraying her country and in causing the Trojan war. During this time, Helen was considered despicable, the very model of a non-virtuous woman; she was the target of ridicule and derision. Defending her publicly was not an easy task. The better for Gorgias! If he could convince his audience to absolve Helen from blame, he could illustrate his talent as a persuader and convince people to hire him as their instructor. More importantly from our point of view, he could help convince people that persuasion is a skill to be cultivated, one that affected audience perspective in fundamental ways.

In this speech Gorgias proposes four possible motivations for Helen's actions, any of which, if accepted by his audience, could transfer blame from Helen to another agent. For instance, Gorgias argued that Helen either fell in love, was persuaded by speech, seized by violence, or forced by divine necessity: "For by Fate's will and gods' wishes and Necessity's decrees she did what she did, or by force reduced, or by words seduced, or by love induced."[70] In any case, she should be acquitted of wrongdoing. The following is a more extended sample of Gorgias' argument: "If love, a god, prevails over the divine power of the gods, how could a lesser one be able to reject and refuse it? But if love is a human disease and an ignorance of the soul, it should not be blamed as a mistake but regarded as a misfortune. For she (Helen) went (with Paris) caught by the nets around her soul, not by the wishes of her mind. . . . "[71]

As this speech illustrates, Gorgias often chose unpopular or weak arguments, such as defending Helen of Troy. W.K.C. Guthrie observes that the speech was "designed to show how, with skill and effrontery, the most uncompromising case could be defended."[72]

Gorgias also provides an early pre-theoretical discussion on the power of logos itself. As he explains, "Speech is a powerful lord that with the smallest and most invisible body accomplishes most god-like works. It can banish fear and remove grief and instill pleasure and enhance pity."[73] In his elaboration of this idea, he introduces the analogy of medicine: "The power of speech has the same effect on the condition of the soul as the application of drugs to the state of bodies, for just as different drugs dispel different fluids from the body, and some bring an end to disease but others end life, so also some speeches cause pain, some pleasure, some fear; some instill courage, some drug and bewitch the soul with a kind of evil persuasion."[74]

By arguing in this fashion, Gorgias is able to elevate persuasion to a level where it is equal with love, divine necessity, and force in being able to exert influence in people's lives. Persuasion can be good or bad, but that is not the issue: highlighted for his audience is the fact that persuasion can be understood and controlled, that it is a *dynamis* that can be taught. Such is his performative argument. He is using persuasion to market a skill, not yet a *techne*, that is equal to physical force in its influence. Skill in persuasion is accentuated in Gorgias' speech. He argues rationally and linearly, a new development at the time. He provides a thesis and a set of claims that he develops and defends over the course of this discussion. He uses language and style, as well as the argument from probability, to lend persuasive credence to his unlikely proposition.

Through his view on language, Gorgias represents a fundamental development in the history of what later becomes known as "rhetoric." One such development is synthesized by Jacqueline de Romilly. She argues that Gorgias' contribution to language involves his ability to popularize a form of cultural analysis, a questioning and condemnation of the belief, prevalent in Greece at the time of the Sophists, that the Gods bestowed eloquence and that communication was inherently poetic. In other words, Gorgias represents a transitional figure in the paradigmatic shift from orality to literacy. After Gorgias, "the sound of words is no longer mysterious; it no longer implies divine intervention or even produces irrational action. It is just style, and an intellectual display of skill. The only thing it appeals to is intellectual surprise, by stirring curiosity, attention, or excitement."[75]

de Romilly's understatement notwithstanding, she does accentuate an important point: Gorgias fundamentally changed the way in which the Athenian people, and those who came after them, experienced language.

Influence of the Sophists

Before turning from the Sophists to examine, in subsequent chapters, the life and work of other prominent thinkers in Athens, it is important to note the influence the Sophists had on the domestic intellectual environment. As Bury writes, "The considerable demand for the education which such teachers could give shows how enlightenment was spreading in Greece. . . . "[76] This is an excellent point. For if we were just studying the Sophists in isolation from the larger culture, our historicization of ideas would not be complete. While the Sophists were important for who they were, they were probably more important for what they represented. They were indicative of a larger *zeitgeist*, a significant cultural condition of intellectual progress that arose spontaneously, and, it appears, independently in both the Western and Eastern worlds. The fifth and the fourth centuries BCE stand out in world history, cross culturally, as extraordinary times. Within a short time period lived Socrates, Plato, Aristotle, Buddha, Confucious, and Lao Tzu. We see the beginning of science and the flowering of culture in China as well as in Greece. To an important extent, in the Western world at least, the Sophists played instrumental roles in the development and the dissemination of this new quest for knowledge.

More fundamentally, the Sophists introduced the notion that the power of speech could be cultivated and that language itself could be used to define and articulate the human condition. From this position, the Sophists produced an early inquiry that examined what we recognize today as the epistemic nature of human communication. In contemporary terms, this is a theory of language and knowledge that maintains that human beings define and arrange social reality through their use of symbols. In this case, social reality is created through the rhetorical process of persuasion. This sentiment became immensely important, either as a sense of inspiration or reaction, in the later writings of Isocrates, Plato, and Aristotle, as well as of other important theorists of the time.

The Sophists themselves were enormously popular with the general population. Waldon writes, "One of the most remarkable circumstances connected with the appearance of the fifth century sophists was the enthusiasm with which they were everywhere received by the young men of Greece."[77] The Sophists thrived on challenging the status quo of Athenian society, challenging that society to think in different ways. Magill notes the impact of the Sophists on Greek culture: "A critical disposition of mind toward traditional values was fostered; eloquence of speech came to be admired and often to be practiced with cynical awareness that an argument need not be valid to be persuasive; and there were growing doubts of the efficacy of traditional values to govern human conduct, which was increasingly viewed as governed by nonpredictable compulsions."[78]

In cultivating doubts about the values of the status quo, the Sophists contributed to a breakdown in traditional morality by challenging the norms of the virtuous and pious. Donald Clark notes, "To the traditionalist all sophists were anathema."[79] They challenged the natural status of the aristocracies.

Because of their success, and because of their critical, anti-traditional postures, the Sophists evoked objections. Most notably, this reaction can be seen in the work of Plato, but it was felt in other sectors of society as well. The primary concern that people had with the Sophists was that they were elitists. Only the wealthy could afford the price of instruction. This could only serve as a source of frustration for the average citizen who desperately needed the skills the Sophists offered to build a more secure life for himself, or to aid his son in securing a political career. In addition, the Sophists themselves became increasingly wealthy, making it increasingly difficult for the average citizen to identify with them. Beck elaborates on this point: "It is clear then from the high cost of Protagoras' instruction that, while as a social theorist he believed education to be open to all, in practice the higher grade of training he offered . . . was available only to the elite."[80]

In addition, the Sophists were often foreigners, and Athenians tended to mistrust people who came from outside their ranks. As discussed in the first chapter, the Athenians were extremely xenophobic.

Even with the above limitations, the Sophists were tolerated and often admired for their contributions to Athenian culture. Waldon notes that the influence of the Sophists on Greek culture is "hard to overestimate."[81] Kennedy connects sophistic teaching with practices in our own culture: "The basic principle of humane law, that anyone, however clear the proof against him [sic], has a right to present his case in the best light possible is an inheritance from Greek justice imposed by the debates of the sophists."[82] Brian Vickers concurs with Kennedy on the vital importance the fifth and fourth century Sophists had in the formation of Greek and subsequent cultural and political institutions. As Vickers explains, "To the Sophists rhetoric was less an arsenal of verbal devices than a process of interaction in which the norms of justice and social order were worked out by those taking part."[83]

Clearly, a number of separate but highly related events contributed to the rise of Greek rhetoric. In particular, geographic conditions, the Homeric tradition, philosophic speculations into the nature of the material world, the influence of Egyptian culture, democratic consciousness, imperialistic tendencies, and the sophistic challenge to the status quo, created a rich environment for self-conscious oratory to develop. Rhetoric, however, was still largely in a pre-theoretical state. This condition would continue for a few decades, manifested in the writings of Isocrates, the subject of the next chapter.

Conclusion

As illustrated, the Corax/Tisias myth situates rhetoric in a political environment that privileges a democratic politics. More importantly, it establishes the principle of probability as an important perspective that can be used in understanding the relationship between people and ideas. Both of these perspectives privilege an epistemic or social constructionist role for understanding the philosophy of rhetoric. In contrast, we saw how the Ionian philosophers offered a material explanation for understanding the world. While the Ionian philosophers may be right in terms of the physics of their claims, their position does not easily point to a moral or ethical system, or toward a system of government. From the perspective of human society, the Ionian philosophers can be seen as irrelevant.

Since the Greek society of the day was starting to question its theistic beliefs, it was giving up its already established ethical and moral structures. As was discussed, religion is more than just a metaphysical comfort, and it is more than an explanation or narrative for what the world is. In actuality, religion is a system of behaviors and beliefs about how to live one's life in the day-to-day world. Without such structure, human beings easily become lost. In mediating against this confusion, all epistemologies or ideologies attempt to provide such structure, even as they offer "factual" knowledge or other sorts of ontological claims about what is and what is not true. All knowledge, as highlighted in the previous pages, involves narrative and reasoning. In giving up their traditional mythical narratives and dependence upon poetic reasoning, the Ancient Greeks sought other ways to conceptualize their world. Into this tension stepped the Sophists.

In this chapter, we have briefly explored two of the more noteworthy Sophists. There were other Sophists whose fragments survive, but they are less colorful and influential than Protagoras and Gorgias.

In the generation following Gorgias, a number of influential men were rising to meet the theoretical needs of discourse. Of these men, three were especially important. Isocrates, Plato, and Aristotle each developed a theoretical framework for the art of "rhetoric."

Notes

1. Walter Fisher, *Human Communication as Narration: Toward a Philosophy of Reason, Value, and Action* (Columbia: University of South Carolina Press, 1987).
2. *The Trial of Socrates* (New York: Doubleday, 1989), 206.
3. *Persuasion in Greek Tragedy: A Study of Peitho* (Cambridge: Cambridge University Press, 1982), 1.
4. Many of these writers are associated with South End Press and *Z magazine*.

5. See Edward Schiappa, *Protagoras and Logos: A Study in Greek Philosophy and Rhetoric* (Columbia: University of South Carolina Press, 1991).

6. "Tisias and Corax and the Invention of Rhetoric," *Classical Quarterly* 42 (1940), 61.

7. Philip Melanson, *The Martin Luther King Assassination* (New York: Shapolsky, 1991); and Mark Lane and Dick Gregory, *Murder in Memphis: The FBI and the Assassination of Martin Luther King* (New York: Thunder Mouth, 1993).

8. *1984, a Novel* (New York: Harcourt Brace, 1949).

9. For a discussion of the influence of literacy on the cultural climate of the era, see Eric Havelock, *The Literate Revolution in Greece and its Cultural Consequences* (Princeton: Princeton University Press, 1982).

10. Thomas S. Kuhn, *The Structure of Scientific Revolutions*, 2nd ed. (Chicago: University of Chicago Press, 1970).

11. Like so much of this book, the analysis in this paragraph is greatly informed by the writings of Michel Foucault. His *Order of Things: An Archaeology of the Human Sciences* (New York: Vintage Books, 1970) remains the definitive statement on this type of historical analysis.

12. See Neil Postman, "Defending Against the Indefensible," in *Conscientious Objections* (New York: Vintage Books), 20–34.

13. *God and the State* (New York: Dover Publications, 1970), 24.

14. Bromley Smith, "Corax and Probability," *The Quarterly Journal of Speech Education* 7 (1921), 24.

15. Ibid., 13.

16. J.F. Dobson, *The Greek Orators* (London: Methuen & Co., 1919), 13.

17. *Art of Persuasion in Greece* (Princeton: Princeton University Press, 1963), 90.

18. Hinks, "Tisias and Corax," 63.

19. *Contingency, Irony, and Solidarity* (New York: Cambridge University Press, 1989).

20. *Language as Symbolic Action: Essays on Life, Literature and Method* (Berkeley: University of California Press, 1966), 45.

21. *Permanence and Change: An Anatomy of Purpose* 3rd. ed. (Berkeley: University of California Press, 1984), 49.

22. "Language and Thought: Some Reflections on Venerable Themes," in *Powers and Prospects: Reflections on Human Nature and the Social Order* (Boston: South End Press, 1996), 1–30. Also, see select interviews in Noam Chomsky, *Language and Politics*, ed. C.P. Otero (Montreal: Black Rose Books, 1988).

23. *Before and After Socrates* (Cambridge: Cambridge University Press, 1932), 5.

24. Quoted in Philip Wheelwright, ed., *The Presocratics* (Indianapolis: Bobbs-Merrill Educational Publishing, 1980), 44.

25. Ibid., 187.

26. Ibid., 44.

27. Lao Tzu, *The Tao Te Ching* (New York, Penguin), 14.

28. *The Presocratics*, 71.

29. Ibid., 70.

30. Ibid., 71.

31. Ibid., 77.

32. Ibid., 187.

33. See James R. Oziniga, "Historical Materialism," in *Communism: The Story of the Idea and its Implementation* (Englewood Cliffs, NJ: Prentice-Hall, 1987), 37–52.

34. *The Sophists: Rhetoric, Democracy, and Plato's Idea of Sophistry* (Novato: Chandler & Sharp, 1987), 37.

35. *Greek Education* (New York: Barnes and Noble, 1964), 147.

36. *The Presocratics*, 324.

37. *Rereading the Sophists: Classical Rhetoric Refigured* (Carbondale: Southern Illinois University Press, 1991), 53.

38. *The Presocratics*, 326.

39. *The Sophistic Movement* (Cambridge: Cambridge University Press, 1981), 144.

40. *The Presocratics*, 237.

41. Ibid., 238.

42. *The Sophists*, 5.

43. *Great Events From History*, 286.

44. Ibid.

45. See Schiappa, *Protagoras and Logos*, for an extended development of this position.

46. *The Sophists*, 5.

47. Ibid., 73.

48. "The Age of Illumination," in *The Cambridge Ancient History* (Cambridge: Cambridge University Press, 1927), 380.

49. Ibid.

50. *The Presocratics*, 239.

51. Ibid., 240.

52. James J. Murphy, ed., *A Synoptic History of Classical Rhetoric* (Davis: Hermagoras Press, 1983), 9.

53. See Schiappa, *Protagoras and Logos*, pages 89–101 for a list of interpretations of the two-*logoi* fragment as well as a discussion of their implications.

54. The best modern articulation of this position is Paulo Freire, *Pedagogy of the Oppressed* (New York: Continuum, 1994).

55. *Art of Persuasion*, 43.

56. *Protagoras and Logos*, 199.

57. Bury, "Age of Illumination," 378.

58. "*Kairos*: A Neglected Concept in Classical Rhetoric," in *Rhetoric and Praxis: The Contribution of Classical Rhetoric to Practical Reasoning*, ed. Jean Dietz Moss (Washington, D.C.: The Catholic University of America Press, 1986), 81.

59. "Toward a Sophistic Definition of Rhetoric," *Philosophy and Rhetoric* 16 (1983), 39.

60. Ibid.

61. *Rereading the Sophists*, xv.

62. "*Stasis* and *Kairos*: Principles of Social Construction in Classical Rhetoric," *Rhetoric Review* 7 (1988), 104.

63. "*Decorum, Kairos*, and the 'New' Rhetoric," *Pre/Text* 5 (1987), 98.

64. Chuang Tzu, *The Complete Works of Chuang Tzu*, trans. Burton Watson (New York: Columbia University Press, 1968), 188.

65. Raymond Di Lorenzo, "The Critique of Socrates in Cicero's *De oratore*: *Ornatus* and the Nature of Wisdom," *Philosophy and Rhetoric* 11 (1978), 246–261.

66. Bromley Smith, "Gorgias: A Study in Oratorical Style," *Quarterly Journal of Speech Education* 7 (1921), 335–59.

67. *On Rhetoric: A Theory of Civic Discourse*, trans. George A. Kennedy (Oxford: Oxford University Press, 1991), 219.

68. Ibid.

69. George Kennedy, "Glossary" to *On Rhetoric*, 317.

70. Trans. George A. Kennedy, in *Readings From Classical Rhetoric*, eds. Patricia Matsen, Philip Rollinson, and Marion Sousa (Carbondale: Southern Illinois University Press, 1990), 34.

71. Ibid., 36.

72. *The Sophists* (Cambridge: Cambridge University Press, 1971), 42.

73. *Readings from Classical Rhetoric*, 35.

74. Ibid.

75. *Magic and Rhetoric in Ancient Greece* (Cambridge: Harvard University Press, 1975), 20.

76. "Age of Illumination," 380.

77. *The Universities of Ancient Greece* (New York: Charles Scribner's Sons, 1909), 15.

78. *Great Events From History*, 287.

79. *Rhetoric in Greco-Roman Education* (Morningside Heights: Columbia University Press, 1957), 6.

80. *Greek Education*, 161.

81. *The Universities of Ancient Greece*, 5.

82. *Art of Persuasion*, 23.

83. *In Defense of Rhetoric* (Oxford: Clarendon Press, 1988), 123.

3

Isocrates

Various historians distinguish among the strands or "schools" of rhetoric in the classical tradition. Although customary among modern scholarship, this effort is largely pedantic and reflects, more often than not, anachronistic efforts to characterize past thinkers with contemporary classifications. Such characterizations assume a larger narrative and perspective that contemporary scholars bring to past thinkers, and they position them according to their "superior" or larger explanatory viewpoint. In a sense, historians often use narratives that, in effect, create mirrors. Within the gaze of these mirrors, we see those things in the past that radiate against the backdrop of our ideological assumptions. Such scholarship is not "dirty"; rather, it is simply scholarship. The difference between the scholar and the party hack is simply the degree to which one's political identification is acknowledged. In a sense, party hacks are more honest—their integrity has been compromised from the onset, and this fact, plainly in evidence, is taken into consideration by the reader. Scholars, on the other hand, are often less honest in their dealings with their audiences. They appeal to "facts" in themselves and to the integrity of their profession, assuming, always, that their profession is beyond rebuke and outside the baseness of common politics. In their scholarly dance, one rife with ritual and mythical appeals, *all* scholars advance a politics and support an ideology. Egoistic pride and belief in outworn metaphors often prevent these scholars from acknowledging this and recognizing the rhetoricity of their professional claims. The desire to label, to characterize, to name—these are all political actions designed to reinforce belief in *some* political economy.

I cannot escape from such activity and from such critique. Similar to the scholars I criticize, I am certainly guilty of practicing the same anachronism in this text, the same positioning of the past vis-a-vis my modern subjectivities. The difference is that I do this consciously, for a reason. This *is* a book on rhetoric and I unabashedly embrace my subjectivity. I view it as a form of pedagogy. There is no education that is not at the same time a moral education. There is no knowledge besides that which we allow to touch us in deeply subjective ways. This does not mean that we merely think up the world; rather, it means that what we think about the world, and what we can hope to know about the world, are limited to those things that make "sense" to us. That is, we know what we can experience through our five senses. Since all knowledge is experiential, it is highly subjective. All of us experience the world as individuals and are thus confined to an existential subjectivity. Such subjectivity is alienating. That is why human beings gravitate toward particular ideologies, systems of vocabulary, grammar, and meaning that provide a semblance of inter-subjectivity between alien minds.

The more scholars and thinkers embrace their subjectivities, the better able they are to grow in strength as interpretative problem-solvers. Indeed, we can hardly hope to do otherwise and maintain our integrity as critical thinkers. We are guided in our task by the vision of Walter Benjamin, a theorist who reminds us that the task of the critical thinker is to "brush history against the grain."[1] We do this by questioning all the basic assumptions we make about scholarship or the past, and offer, in their place, competing interpretations and cautionary injunctions to be socially mindful. "Socially mindful" does not mean being "stupid." Rather, it means that, at least for some of us, what is more important is not getting the facts "straight" but refiguring our perspectives. "Facts," as they are, are always facts for some people that exist under conditions of certain epistemologies. For us, what becomes crucial is the force of interpretation and the new insight it gives us for the management of our contemporary lives.

Nevertheless, even under the above limitations, efforts toward the categorization of knowledge are often necessary (and useful provided we accentuate their contingent characteristics); the systematic characterization of ideas by genres or other assumed similarities is an important part of scholarship, and constitutes, to a large degree, the parameters of our academic knowledge. Such knowledge, as illustrated in this book, is highly idiosyncratic. In reflecting biases, our acts of naming (or of genre creating) reflect politics. By problematizing scholarship, we accentuate the politics of scholarship, and thus highlight the politics of our everyday interactions with knowledge. This has been, and continues to be, one important function of this book.

In distinguishing between three "schools" of rhetoric, as I will do in this and in the two following chapters, I am offering readers a more or less standard account of how historians of rhetoric have conceptualized its development. Readers, however, should not be fooled by my apparent lapse into orthodoxy. My purpose in discussing these "schools" as such is to radicalize our perceptions of scholarship by undermining our reliance in the practice of systematization. More specifically, my reliance on these characterizations is to point out their limitations. Thus, the politics of characterization is already evident—some scholars will agree on my distinctions, while others may not. For example, Kennedy discusses "technical," "sophistic," and "philosophical" rhetoric, and includes Aristotle in the category of philosophical rhetoric.[2] Furthermore, his distinction between "sophistic" and "technical rhetoric" is blurred and confusing.

No doubt Kennedy's characterizations were clear at the time he formulated them, for they made sense to the disciplinary audience that was the original consumer of his scholarship. Such audiences change as the lenses of our historicization change. The categorization of these schools, no matter under what scheme, is not important in any absolute sense. In other words, it is a way of knowing, of directing people toward a particular appreciation. The "end all" characterization of any body of knowledge should be resisted. Our knowledge keeps changing (if we let it), and this is a sign of our intellectual and cultural growth. Tolerant cultures are ones that grow and redefine themselves in relation to corresponding changes in their knowledge. Intolerant cultures cling to limited conceptions of Truth and they sacrifice their moral imaginations to the defense of the ideals they have reified.

This chapter focuses specifically on Isocrates (as the next two chapters focuses on Plato and Aristotle, respectively). Similar to the other major figures in this book, Isocrates played an important role in bringing to the fore of Western consciousness particular critical issues of language, pedagogy, and culture. In responding to the educational environment that was dominated by the Sophists, and in distinguishing himself from Plato and Aristotle, his professional rivals, Isocrates makes an indelible mark on Western thought by focusing the incipient rhetorical epistemology of the Sophists in a pragmatic way. As Edward Schiappa explains, Isocrates was "one of the first philosophers in Western history to address the concerns that we now identify with pragmatism."[3] In exploring this pragmatism, we will review the major characteristics of Isocrates' educational and linguistic philosophy, particularly its intersections with contemporary Third World pan-nationalist thought, as exemplified by Che Guevara. This chapter ends by briefly highlighting two of Isocrates' relevant writings on oratory.

Characteristics of Isocrates' Educational and Linguistic Philosophy

Isocrates was not a Sophist in the sense that Protagoras and Gorgias were Sophists. Nor was he a philosopher in the sense of Socrates, Plato, and Aristotle. Isocrates is more aptly classified as a statesman and an educator. As such, he exemplifies sort of a "middle ground" in the Greek contest between competing epistemologies. Unlike his contemporaries, Isocrates' writing and teaching sought to unify politics, education and the study of language into a single intellectual pursuit. Where the Sophists tended to treat the study of logos for its own end, and where the philosophers tried to subjugate a humanistic epistemology to the force of a monolithic principle called Reason, Isocrates' ideas were different—they were more social and practical, more politically refined. Isocrates was the champion of a conservatively liberal political economy, one in which the modern philosopher Richard Rorty would feel at home. On the one hand, Isocrates' ideas are potentially liberating (for example, in their parallels to Third World pan-nationalism); on the other hand, they reinforce certain bourgeois values (such as the sanctity of private property and the moral sanctity of the "state" apparatus).[4]

Broadly, Isocrates' ideas involved the pursuit of *philosophia*, operationalized at this time as a type of cultural wisdom derived from training in logos. In so doing, Isocrates took a broader view of logos than what was popular at the time. For him, logos involved the cultivation of culture and was a way to direct the spiritual and creative energies of people toward a perfection in political consciousness. *Philosophia*, then, involved the study of culture from the point of view of a civic *arete*.

Isocrates' position differed from that of the Sophists who at times appeared to stress success at oratory at the expense of civic *arete* and who defined politics at times as the pursuit of expediency. Isocrates' position also fundamentally separated him from the philosophers who refused to align themselves with political life or who actively sought to undermine the democratic institutions, as Socrates, Plato, and Aristotle tried to do, to some extent, through their teaching. Because similar connections between the intelligentsia and wealth exists today, and because this existence threatens democracy in no small way (in the mass media, for example),[5] this point deserves further elaboration.

Tensions Between Democracy and Wealth

As democratic political institutions in recent years have so often experienced, the Government of Athens came under direct physical attack—at least three times during its thirty years in power. Each time, national and region-wide political crises weakened the resistance of the democracy to defend itself. Democracies, in general, are highly susceptible to weakness during periods of sustained crisis; when citizens become scared, they tend to huddle in the false warmth of authoritarian figures. The appeal of such "authority" is the vision of order that it offers. The appeal of Adolf Hitler in Germany, for example, can be found in his ability to offer explanations for the problems facing people and in being able to resolve those

problems. Such "resolution" often involves taking a "hard line" (a eu-
phemism for heartless cruelty), but such excesses are legitimized by the
authorizing force and the "ends" that such policies bring (usually "order" at the expense of diversity).

Order, by itself, is not a bad thing, as all societies need a degree of
structure to be able to function effectively. But in times of crisis, "order"
often becomes operationalized as a substitute for a wider, more socially
inclusive political view (i.e. "order" for the Nazis meant the exclusion of
the Jews). Order is also established according to somebody. Society itself
has no "order." Order is the structure that a political vision imposes on a
community. In difficult times, politicians offer "law and order" in return
for our support, but we should not be confused by such an appeal. Law
and order exist at the expense of something, and act in the favor of something else. Appeals to "law and order" usually have the effect of constricting political freedom. In a real sense, they have the effect of increasing the coercive power of the state. The career of J. Edgar Hoover,
director of the FBI for nearly fifty years, and the central role he played in
the Government's policy of domestic repression, is evidence of this
point.[6] In a democracy worth the name, law only leads to order when it is
just. Unjust laws breed disorder, which necessitates police. The recently
passed crime bill, placing 100,000 more police on this nation's streets, is
the strongest argument possible for the existence of an unjust legal and
social system in the United States. For all critically minded people, "Law
and Order" should always be rejected as political goals.

Democracies, however, face other dangers than their abdication to fascism. The good will and common sense of a fair-minded citizenry, particularly those communities that have suffered from oppression in the past,
can usually resist the yokel of fascism. To the extent that they are successful, however, they invite an even more decisive threat. More often than
not, democracies are destroyed from the outside rather than from the inside. In order for this claim to make sense, I need to point out that the
"democratic political institutions" that I referred to above are not the
ones that most people immediately think of when they think of the word
"democracy." This is because most of us have been taught a limited sense
of the meaning of "democracy." For example, we tend to think of the
United States as a "democracy," when it is, in fact, a republic. Even
within the so-called "democratic" infrastructure of the U.S., we find that
its democratic characterizations are caricatures at best (although they
have been known to have marginal influence at times). As mentioned before, the United States can never be a democracy in the full sense of the
word until it establishes a world wide commitment to human rights,
which would mean democratizing and socializing its economy. Until
democracy extends to the work place, until Corporate America comes

under public scrutiny, and until we allow a wider sphere of political discussion to take place in a meaningful way, we will never live in any more gratifying society than what a selfish plutocracy allows.

In short, "democracy," in its fullest, most meaningful sense, is not what we find practiced in the United States, or even in Great Britain and France (or in any of the other industrial First World nations). Democracy, when it does exist, tends to be found in struggling Third World nations which, at great cost, exert themselves politically for a time before they are mercilessly smashed by the First World governments who seek to reestablish their economic and oligarchic control. Such democratic conditions existed in Guatemala prior to the CIA supported overthrow of the elected national government and the establishment of a fascist oligarchy in 1954. They existed in Spain during the control of the Anarchists before their defeat at the hands of Franco and the fascists. From 1970 to 1973 they existed in Chile under the Popular Unity Government of Salvador Allende. They existed in Iran for a few years before 1953 when the CIA orchestrated the coup that established the fearful and bloody reign of the bitterly hated Shah. They existed in Nicaragua for ten years under the popular, peasant-backed Sandanistas, and they exist to some extent in Cuba which has, over the years, struggled to create a humane balance between its commitment to a widespread political and social inclusion, on the one hand, and its need to defend itself from the economic and physical onslaught of the United States, on the other.[7]

Democracy, in short, is a difficult position to maintain; it runs smack into the face of capitalism and is usually defeated by the United States (sometimes with the help of Britain or France). In an important sense, all of us in the United States are accountable for the terror done by our government, at least to the extent that we could have done something to resist, and still can, but choose not to. This is difficult, I realize, since most of us are effectively marginalized from the political world that governs this country. Still, as moral beings we have a responsibility to make our lives "be a counter friction to stop the machine" to the extent that we can.[8] Caring, at least, is the most basic thing we can do.

By definition, the concept of "democracy" implies a government that is run by and for the interest of the people who occupy the country or other politically defined units. Such a position implies that all people are to be included in the political and economic decisions that need to be made with regard to running the country. Yet most people in most countries are poor. That means that "democracy," to the extent that it is real, will be concerned with equitably spreading the social wealth and power of the nation in question. Such a position is anathema to the privileged elite of the country, and to the imperialist power that is controlling the country. Thus, every democracy, at some point or another, is going to come into conflict with the powerful, the people who control the economies and the armies. Super rich people—industrialists, bankers, the large property lords—fear democracy and do whatever they can to prevent it from occurring. If it does occur, they do everything they can to curtail its effects (they call this "rolling back").

Such people are not content to achieve this goal in the international realm. They want to "roll back" domestic expressions of democracy as well (which is why we have seen an increased depravity in the U.S. under the "leadership" of Reagan, Bush, and the Republican controlled Congress). Readers should not misunderstand me: this does not mean that I support or endorse the alternative, what is popularly known as the Democratic Party. Under our current system, both major parties are equally anti-democratic; one, the Republicans, are simply more straightforward in their attempt to be fascist. The so-called "democrats" are more coy, concealing their criminal acts behind a more inclusive sounding social appeal. Both parties are fundamentally working for the same system, capitalism. Capitalism, by practice if not by "nature," prefers fascism and only tolerates individual liberty to the extent that it does not interfere with the gross saturation of profits. Thus, the industrialists of the world supported the rise of fascist power in Japan, Italy, and Germany, and that support included America's own Henry Ford and other leaders of the U.S. business community.

At least twice during what is called the "Golden Age" of democratic rule in Athens, the democracy was overthrown and unpopular tyrannies were established by the super rich. These new governments were exceedingly tyrannical, violent, and, unlike similar repressive forces today that support U.S. interests in the Third World, they were not long able to maintain their control. I.F. Stone writes, "In 411 and again in 404 disaffected elements in connivance with the Spartan enemy overthrew the democracy, set up dictatorships, and initiated a reign of terror."[9] Perhaps these governments fell because, unlike tyrannical military states of the modern era, the oligarchies that overthrew the Athenian government did not have the support of a superpower like the U.S. to suppress effectively their own miserable populations. Regardless of how well the analogy between tyranny then and now can be maintained, it is clear that the politics of both examples are very much class related. Stone elaborates, "The type of rich young men prominent in the entourage of Socrates played a leading role in all three civic convulsions."[10] In 401, there was yet another attack on the government.

These three attacks on democracy illustrate that satisfaction with the Athenian political system was not universal among elements of the population. As mentioned above, these people included the super wealthy, their thugs and cronies, and the great philosophers who argued very academically and vehemently for the virtues of oligarchy (as many intellectuals argue today in defense of the U.S. system of plutocracy).[11] Stone reminds readers that Socrates, as an instructor, frequently turned out students who were hostile to Athenian culture and who actively participated in two overthrows of the democratic government. In forecast of the practices found in the twentieth century anti-democratic forces, the tyrannies that overthrew Athens were particularly heinous. Thousands of democrats were executed, and many more were banished so that their lands could be confiscated. Once again, the lesson is clear: the present can be better understood by looking critically at the past. Only by looking at the present with the critical gaze that we can accord the past, can we learn to have some influence over our future. Ultimately it is up to us as human beings. No one will design a future worth living in if we do not do it for ourselves. This point, in particular, is akin to one that Isocrates may have made. His emphasis on the study of language reflects some of these themes and is manifested in his ideas on pedagogy and politics.

Pedagogy and Politics

Isocrates was born circa 436 and died circa 338. He began his career as a logographer, a professional speech writer, after studying under the Sophists. As previously discussed, public speaking was a tremendously important skill that people needed to have in order to participate in public and political life, as well as to protect themselves if they were accused of some criminal or civil offense (which was likely given the environment of the time). People who had more money could afford to hire a Sophist to train them to become a more effective speaker. People who could not afford this, and could not write a speech on their own, could hire, for no small fee, a logographer to write a specific speech for them. Similar to today, there was no shame in doing this. While it was considered shameful to have somebody speak for you, there was nothing preventing people from hiring ghostwriters (as most major politicians today do). Just as contemporary politicians are associated with the words that other people write for them (Presidents do not typically see their speeches until moments before they deliver them), people in ancient Greece could fulfill their political obligations by mouthing the words prepared for them by a paid professional.

Such practices, while socially respectable, undermine the principles of a "true" democracy where citizens should be the authors of their own ideas. If thoughtless people, who happen to be wealthy or in positions of political power, can "buy" ideas, then what does this say about the "value" the rest of us have for our ideas? Democracy is about amateurism (this statement is offered as a compliment, not a critique). The dynamics of our political life are changed when we introduce political "professionals," in whatever guise (professional politicians, speech writers, campaign managers, etc.). In addition, there is something wrong with our political system when the President has to have "professionals" write his speeches; this can only occur when rhetoric in politics is reduced to propaganda and the manufacturing of consent. In such cases, as the political logic of the day dictates, it makes sense that professional speech writers create the public discourse of our politicians. To do otherwise is to face the threat of "democracy" in some shape or form, which is always an economic risk.[12] Such perspective also justifies the Public Relations Industry, another major threat to the democratic state,[13] but one that the Ancient Athenians did not have to worry about.

After years of being a logographer, Isocrates accumulated enough money, prestige, and expertise to quit his profession and open his own school. In his new career, he devoted himself to a unique blend of pedagogy and politics. Isocrates valued politics above all else, and his writing and teaching tended to emphasize the political unity and beauty of Greece. In other words, Isocrates promoted pan-Hellenism, a unified Greece: "The central conviction which informed Isocrates' political teaching, and certainly the most significant for posterity, is the view of Hellenism which exalts it to the position of a religion and which gives the character of a crusade to efforts to preserve and propagate it."[14]

Greeks for Greece was not an impractical sentiment: the Macedonian threat was imminent, and ultimately successful; a politically unified Greece may have withstood this challenge. As it stood, however, the political unity of Greece was compromised by Athenian hegemony (a mixture of arrogance and greed). Because of this, Athens, and the rest of Greece, would lose its political independence and become an insignificant political and military power. Following Isocrates' generation, the only sense in which Greece (in general) and Athens (in particular) would remain significant, is in the cultural realm. Despite its subsequent political impotence, Athens would remain an important cultural center throughout the years of the Roman Republic and early empire.

What kinds of lessons can we draw from the experience of Isocrates' Pan-Hellenism? More specifically, what are the parallels between Isocrates' vision and the vision of the pan-nationalists that have risen in the second half of the twentieth century in Africa and in Latin America? Answering these questions takes us to the heart of pedagogy and politics. In exploring these questions, we learn a great deal about contemporary social movements, particularly those on the Left that struggle, as Isocrates struggled, for a more widely inclusive vision of community.

The Context of Modern Pan-Nationalism

Nationalist movements in the Third World abounded following the Second World War. These movements were largely a response to the victorious Allied Nations, in particular the United States, which moved quickly and violently to consolidate their spoils of victory. Replacing the hegemony of Japan and Germany (which were, in their turn, replacing the hegemony of Britain and France), the United States worked diligently to expand its spheres of influence throughout the Third World. To a lesser, but still significant degree, Britain and France worked to reestablish small portions of what used to be their Third World empires. Within the U.S., this rush for world domination became particularly urgent as the Soviet Union developed as a world power, competing for influence and the creation of a socialist-bloc.[15] In so doing, the Soviet Union at times offered welcomed support to countries trying to resist the dominance of the United States.

Ultimately, this jockeying for power led to the political condition known as the "cold war." The cold war was not so "cold"; it actually involved hundreds of open military conflicts and took the lives of millions of people around the world. The only thing "cold" about the cold war was the absence of nuclear war. This is yet another example of how language uses people, rather than people using language. We do not look back in horror to the cold war because it does not seem real to us. It was not a "real" war because no country suffered a nuclear attack. In a sense, conventional war has been neutered. By calling it "conventional" it is made to sound acceptable. In actuality, the cold war was an extension of the Second World War, which really never ended, and in which the U.S. replaced the Nazis as the prime antagonists. By perpetuating the propaganda of a "communist threat," the U.S., like Germany before them, used this to justify an increased terror and genocide of local populations, starting in Greece immediately after the defeat of the Axis powers.

In other words, following their official decolonization after the Second World War and the establishment of their status as independent states, the Third World nations found themselves in precarious situations: they were disunified politically, often pitted against other Third World nations, and, subsequently, subject to control by the Western powers (in what has been called a neo-colonialism). Within this context, the hope for a viable Third World independence and autonomy rested within the philosophy of pan-nationalism. Within various contexts, this was known as pan-Africanism, Pan-Asianism, and Pan-Latin Americanism. What this means is "Africa for Africans," "Asia for Asians," and "Latin America for Latin Americans." Practically, it meant solidarity: a unification of identity and resistance across national boundaries. While this philosophy recognized the uniqueness of each particular culture, it emphasized a common aspiration and goal—the resistance to imperialism and the establishment of independent economies. Politically, the method for such unity involved a form of Marxism, specifically its critique of imperialism, its alternative program for international cooperation, and its ability to serve the needs of the poor.

By the 1990s, Marxist inspired revolts in the Third World have ceased to be a politically viable option. With the exception of Cuba, the successful revolutions in countries like Nicaragua, Grenada, Guatemala and Chile were all overturned by direct U.S. military involvement or through the use of its proxies. Other revolutions, like in El Salvador and Peru, were defeated by similar forces before they could be successful. Finally, countries such as North Korea, Vietnam, and Cambodia were bombed into the dark ages, thus defeating the potential social and economic goals of their revolutions. With the exception of the Zapatistas in Chiapas, Mexico, in the early 1990s, there have not been many socialist-informed uprisings in the Third World.

There are at least two reasons for the eclipse of a Marxist-inspired pan-nationalism in the Third World. First and foremost, both the former Soviet Union and the People's Republic of China turned out to be anti-revolutionary forces. Particularly since the early 1970s when both the USSR and China sought political detente with the U.S., both nations withdrew their support for struggling independence movements in the Third World. Even earlier, as far back as the Spanish revolution, the foreign policy of the Soviets was one that was often at odds with Third World Marxism. To my mind, the lack of political unity between the major communist powers and their half-hearted support for struggling Marxist movements is one of the greatest tragedies of the twentieth century and one of the greatest set backs for the causes of justice and peace in the world.[16] Obviously, Isocrates was not a Marxist and I in no means imply that he was; we cannot take too literally the comparisons between his pan-Hellenism and the pan-nationalist movements that inspired the Third World during the decades immediately following the Second World War. Nevertheless, there are some similar political characteristics that the two philosophies share. Both philosophies stress a wider political unification incorporating more localized political entities. The ends of both movements are political strength and the creation of unity that comes from a more inclusive integration of a region's people. The effect of such political inclusion is a wider enfranchisement and better living conditions. At the very least, the effect of both political philosophies is a people free from external restraint. In addition, Isocrates argued that all Greeks had a responsibility to come together to defend the common good, the common interest. Likewise, Third World revolutionaries frequently argued that all the poor people in the Third World (most of the population) have the responsibility to come together to build a larger political movement of resistance.

Neither Isocrates nor the Third World revolutionaries (unfortunately) were successful. As suggested above, what few revolutionary govern-

ments have existed, have tended to exist precariously in a forced isolation by the imperialist powers and their colonies. They have also tended
to have limited relationships with the more successful socialist countries.
In many cases, the important new social and political gains of successful
revolutionary governments were often curtailed or even rolled back by
the military responses of the First World. In addition, in countries where
the potential for revolution has been great, fascist governments were set
up to stop an international consciousness from spreading.[17] All these factors have lead to a contemporary condition in which we are unlikely to
see the resurgence of a pan-nationalist Third World outlook in the near
future. On the other hand, the factors that motivated the spread of this
consciousness still exist and thus we can expect that, in the more distant
future, when the opportunity arises, such a philosophy may one day
come back into circulation. Its growth and progress have been greatly re-
tarded by the events of the late twentieth century, but its ideas and visions have by no means been eviscerated.

   With this in mind, we can learn from the study of history. In looking
more closely at the phenomenon of pan-nationalism we can understand
some of the revolutionary ferment that it involves. In so doing, we can
perhaps better understand the important political stance that Isocrates
was advocating, and see why it was resisted by the Athenians, the people
who had the most to lose, at least initially, by giving up their empire. By
analogy, we might learn something more about ourselves as citizens of
the First World.

   In the end, not only did Athens lose, but so did all of Greece. As all
scholarship is a narrative, and as all narratives have morals, I want to
make this moral absolutely clear: the more greedy and selfish a nation,
the more likely it is to destroy itself, and the more powerful that nation,
the more likely it is going to take down other nations with it. This is a
point we should consider as we look briefly at the career of Ernest "Che"
Guevara, this century's most notable spokesperson for a pan-nationalis-
tic unity among the diverse cultures of the Third World.

Che Guevara, Praxis, and Third World Pan-Nationalism

Che Guevara was raised in a typical Argentinian middle-class family and
earned a medical degree from the University of Buenos Aires in 1953.[18] In
his college years he traveled widely through Southern and Central America and was exposed to the squalor and depravity that characterized the
lives of most of the Latin American people during this period of U.S. economic expansion. During these travels, he witnessed first hand the CIA
invasion and destruction of the Guatemalan democracy. After gradua-
tion, Che rejected the practice of medicine to engage in political activity.

For Che, political activity was a pursuit analogous on the societal level to the physician's effort to cure disease in the human body. On this point, the parallels to Isocrates and rhetoric are clear: Ideas are to the mind as exercise is to the body. In addition, like the Isocratean model, it is the role of the trained thinker to implement his or her ideas on the social level. This takes us to the idea of praxis, which Marx took from a long tradition that starts with Aristotle, but can also be seen in the actions of Isocrates.

Praxis

Praxis is a term that is central to rhetoric. It is defined as action or practice. In the Aristotelian/Ciceronian strand of rhetorical theory, classical rhetoricians recognize rhetoric as an art that lies on the boundary between ethics and politics, and helps people to deliberate in the world of common affairs. This is very much an Isocratean ideal. While used in a pre-technical sense in Homer, praxis is given a technical meaning by Aristotle. Thereafter, praxis denotes ethical and political action that is done well and manifested through rational choice. In an Isocratean model, praxis would involve the creation of a pan-Hellenic appeal through the use of oratory.

Aristotle presents a tripartite conception of knowledge that includes *theoria* (theory), *praxis* (practice), and *techne* (art). Aristotle's treatise *On Rhetoric* establishes rhetoric as an art that takes thought (*theoria*) and applies it to a given probabilistic situation. Praxis is the part of rhetorical invention that unifies thought with expression to aid humans in realizing their potential within the contingent nature of the polis; speech builds community by stressing unity and cohesion. Praxis is an activity or action that strives towards *arete* (excellence) in political affairs. In a sense, it is good citizenship. Through praxis the speaker evokes the virtues that characterize civic life, inviting people to embody those virtues. An example of the centrality of praxis in later classical rhetorical theory can be found in Cicero's *De oratore*. Cicero, it should be noted, is very excited by Isocrates' "rhetorical" teachings. In book one of *De oratore*, Cicero, through the voice of his teacher, Crassus, argues that the orator is superior to the philosopher on the grounds that the orator has an understanding of praxis.[19] Philosophy, in this sense, is being evoked in the way that it will appear after Plato (which is fully elaborated upon in the next chapter).

While philosophers are concerned with intellectual matters, they are not able to contribute to the common good, argues Crassus. If one wants to make full light of the matter, one is obliged to turn to the orator, who has the power to explain to the populace what the philosopher can only communicate to other technical experts. The philosopher may have knowledge (*theoria*) but the philosopher does not have an understanding of praxis to translate the truth into practical wisdom (*phronesis*). In other words, ideas are worthless if they are not grounded in the experiences and needs of people. This grounding takes place through rhetoric (or socialism as the case may be). Cicero emphasizes that praxis lies in the realm of oratory and involves knowledge of the subject matter, knowledge of the human psyche, and a political awareness.

In modern times, praxis is incorporated by Hegel and Marx to designate a consciousness of historical process. Unlike Hegel who considers this process to be idealistic and grounded in *theoria*, Marx regards this consciousness as material. In such material conditions, Marx's ideology is actualized as praxis and is the dialectical counterpart of the Hegelian concept of *Geist* (spirit). Ideas achieve their true significance as action in the social realm. For Marx, praxis is a revolutionary tool for transforming material conditions and is a central concept in his philosophy. Praxis denotes the correct ideological behaviors of humans struggling to actualize justice within their materially determined conditions.[20]

Che's Rhetoric and Its Isocratean Ideal

Che's rhetorical effort to position himself as a doctor for the social body gained him the attention of Fidel Castro in Mexico. Castro persuaded Che to join in the 1956 Cuban revolution. With less than 100 followers, Castro navigated a decrepit boat from Mexico to Cuba and initiated a military campaign that succeeded in overthrowing the corrupt U.S. backed Batista regime in 1959.

As a result of this revolution, Che achieved world-wide status as a revolutionary hero. With his new status, and with his important position as a diplomat for the new Cuban government, Che had an opportunity to speak to millions around the world. Through his actions in battle, and through his discourse, Che became the representative of a collective group struggle in Third World pan-nationalist thought. Through his life and actions, Che transcended the various cultures of the Third World by illustrating how sacrifice and struggle could bring about better living conditions. In many senses, Che was an "enactment" of his argument for international cooperation, solidarity, and resistance, a living example of the internationalist perspective that a pan-Third World philosophy exemplifies. He was, after all, an Argentinian citizen who fought alongside the Cubans to liberate their country.

Karlyn Kohrs Campbell and Kathleen Jamieson discuss how speakers can aid in the acceptance of their messages if they can "incarnate" their argument and embody "the proof of what is said."[21] This, again, is very much in the Isocratean vein, and is quite rhetorical: the role of education in the classical model is to train the individual to be civically minded and to represent, though action, the breadth of one's knowledge. Translated into Marxist struggle, such an ideal becomes very much a revolutionary perspective. Arguably, Che best represents this civic sentiment in the twentieth century (although not in the aristocratic sense usually associated with classical civic thought). Even in the United States, among people who disagree with his Marxism, Che is regarded by some as a folk hero (literally, a "people's hero") for his devotion to justice. Che, in short, can be seen as a contemporary Isocrates: the two men share the view that politics and education are inextricably bound. People are not born to have a particular political sensitivity, both men would argue, and the responsibility of the educated citizen is to become a political leader by educating others to be active in the politics of the day. Such pedagogy goes beyond the injunction to "be political." Rather, it fundamentally involves the training of students in such a way to sharpen their vision so that they can "see" for themselves how best to act. Che was, above all, a teacher, as was Isocrates, who took his lessons out of the classroom and into the contested field of human culture.

With this background in mind, let's turn now to a brief discussion of how Che justifies his pan-nationalism. In this illustration, I hope to highlight the classical ideals of praxis, rhetoric, and citizenship. While Che's particular political vision may differ from that of Isocrates, the analysis illustrates the Isocratean model of education and politics.

The union between the different nations of the Third World is necessary, argues Che in a 1965 address to the Conference on African-Asian Solidarity, if a "just" Third World is to be created.[22] By first distinguishing between an unjust International Law and the potentiality of a United Third World consolidated in its opposition, Che's discourse and policies of resistance work toward the day when a more fairly representative International Law can be created, a law that reflects the interest of people living in the Third World as well as those in the First. In order to have equality among nations, however, the nations have to demand it for themselves, and that means unifying for a common end. Just as Isocrates argued that a unified Greece could withstand a foreign threat that would subjugate all the independent city states (which were already largely subjugated by Athens), Che argues that a United Third world could likewise withstand the threat from a Northern power.

As things currently stand, Che points out, International Law is simply an extension of a First World military hegemony (do not forget that the Korean War was called a "police action" by the United States). Che points out that International Law "was created as a result of the conflicts among imperialist powers and not as a result of disputes among free, just peoples."[23] His point is that the Third World is subjected to laws imposed upon them by the First World. Such "law" affects people anywhere in the

Third World. By pointing this out, Che is directing our ability to respond and to resist. More importantly, he is asking his audience to redefine its relationship to the First World. For example, International Law, Che reminds his audience, leads to the unwarranted establishment of First World foreign bases on Third World sovereign territory (such as in Guantanamo Bay). In addition, such "legal" relationships lead to the condition of a tremendous foreign debt, created by an imposed economic system that leads to mass starvation among people who live in an environment where food grows naturally in abundance. Che asks the different nations of Africa, Asia, and Latin America to reflect on this situation and to respond in the only reasonable way: to unify.

A review of Robert Ivie's research on cold war rhetoric makes Che's argument more pertinent. Ivie points out that what First World nations consider to be International Law is little more than the establishment of the privileged rights of these nations. For example, America defines war "in purpose terms, with territorial invasion and commercial injuries interpreted as attacks against America's rights."[24] Yet, as history illustrates, the United States has seldom been invaded, and never in the twentieth century, though it has been involved in hundreds of international conflicts that were resolved through the use of armed forces. This phenomenon can be explained by the U.S. practice of equating "commercial injuries" with "territorial invasion." So-called commercial injuries (i.e. indigenous people reclaiming their right to their own labor and natural resources) thus serve to justify American acts of aggression in defense of foreign owned property. This proxy, as if by magic, has been transformed into an extension of American soil. With this logic in mind, the nationalization of industry and the nationalization of foreign owned or operated property (often with reparations), which often follows the socialist ascent to state power, is defined by the United States as a situation that warrants a military response. This is the case even though there is no direct threat to the actual land or people of the U.S. United States Marine Corps Major Harries-Clincy Peterson clearly details the application of this warrant: "[T]he precedent was established that [military action] did not constitute an act of war. Functions assumed by the Marines ashore after overcoming resistance and protecting the lives and property of U.S. citizens included the disarming of natives, the training of a constabulary, and the supervision of elections."[25]

In other words, the property rights of the United States extend to foreign territory, territory that was taken by force in the first place. Notice, furthermore, that the U.S. precedent includes not only the refurbishment of North American property in the Third World, but includes also the disarming of such nations and the establishing of puppet (usually dictatorial) regimes. Had some nation, like Cuba, done this to Florida, the act would be regarded by the U.S. as an act of war. In terms of United States foreign policy, however, the use of aggression against sovereign Third World nations is justified. The rationale for such military action is cited by Peterson. He refers to a Marine handbook, the *Small Wars Manual*. It states, "The use of the forces of the United States in foreign countries to protect the lives and property of American citizens resident in those countries does not necessarily constitute an act of war...."[26] The *Small Wars Manual*, in turn, attributes justification for this form of aggression "to international law, as recognized by the leading nations of the world...."[27] In effect, the First World imperialist nations, as exemplified by the United States, have posited a circular argument. Aggression against Third World nations is justified to protect First World interests that depend upon forcing an economic and property system on the native populations.

In calling for resistance to such conditions, Che argues that political unity is essential. It is the first condition for the creation of a Third World independence. While arguing for Third World independence, Che stresses the importance of solidarity among these nations. Indeed, Che speaks in terms that are specific to the identification process. He explains, "If there were no other factors favoring unity, the common enemy would have to constitute it."[28] This is precisely Burke's principle of identification by antithesis. Burke explains, "Men [sic] who unite on nothing else can unite on the basis of a foe shared by all."[29]

As Third World nations begin to identify with Che's redescription and learn to think and act with a pan-nationalist vocabulary, they will, hopefully, reject the dominance of the threat they face from the First World. This action of self-assertion has two important consequences. First, the nations involved gain independence through their struggles. Second, as each country succeeds in gaining independence, it strengthens the positions of the others. As Che concludes, "A victory of any one country against imperialism is our victory, just as defeat for any one country is a defeat for all."[30]

This brief analysis illustrates how political unity is often dependent upon the creation of a community. This creation is always rhetorically based. As Burke explains, "Identification is affirmed with earnestness precisely because there is division. Identification is compensatory to division. If men [sic] were not apart from one another, there would be no need for the rhetorician to proclaim their unity."[31] Isocrates uses rhetoric in an unsuccessful attempt to create a wider Greek sense of community that would transcend its regional differences (and oppressions) to unify as a focused cultural and military force. Che attempted the same thing. In both cases, the community they sought to create did not exist outside of their efforts to establish it. The status quo in Greece was Athenian hegemony. Although that hegemony was certainly challenged, most notably by Sparta, it was not challenged in a constructive way, one that would lead to a stronger, more unified Greece. As it was, resistance served only to weaken Greece even further, bringing defeat not only to Athens, but to the Greek people as well.

With the above, I do not mean to deny the role that other people may have played in the creation of these visions of pan-nationalism in Greece and in the contemporary Third World; rather, I mean to accentuate the fact that such visions usually become embodied in a specific person. Isocrates stands out as an ideal. Che stands out as an ideal. Each serves as an "enactment" of his vision and gives "community" a tangible object around which to coalesce. Both Isocrates and Che Guevara best represent their visions. They both spent their lives teaching, acting, and building support for their causes.

Isocrates' Educational "System"

As noted, Isocrates was an educator, and, besides advocating pan-Hellenism, he supported a curriculum which stressed a combination of philosophy, oratory, and logic. Philosophy, it must be pointed out, was different at this point in history than it is today. In Isocrates' day, the word "philosophy" meant "literary taste and study—culture generally."[32] In a sense, Isocrates taught a form of cultural criticism—a rationality and ethic that was grounded in the language arts. Because of this, Isocrates prefigures some twentieth century philosophers, most notably Richard Rorty, whose focus on literature as a moral guide for establishing community resembles Isocrates' vision.

Philosophy was considered by Isocrates to be a literary study that stressed a refinement of educational pursuits. Russell H. Wagner elaborates on Isocrates' concept of philosophy. He writes, "Isocrates himself says that it is the art of conjecturing what should be done; that it is a theory of culture; that what gymnastics is for the body philosophy is for the mind."[33] This position differs from the characterization of philosophy that exists after Plato. Plato disciplines philosophy, making it the study of objective Truth, a characterization that went relatively unchallenged until the nineteenth century when Marx declared that "The philosophers have only *interpreted* the world, in various ways; the point is to *change* it."[34]

For Isocrates, philosophy is the way of training the mind so that the thinker can react intelligently to the world. In this pre-disciplinary sense of the word "philosophy" we start to get a feel for the way the term would be used in various strands of twentieth century postmodern philosophy and much critical theory. For Isocrates, as well as for Dewey, Foucault, Marx, Rorty, and others, philosophy is what you do when you want people to think about their world differently. In this sense, my book can be considered philosophy. This may seem strange since I have already identified this book as an expression of rhetoric. In an important sense, both characterizations are correct. When rhetoric and philosophy are approached from an extra-disciplinary perspective, it becomes clear that there is not much difference between the two lines of inquiry. It is the same for Isocrates: what existed was the word *"philosophia"* which we translate today as the word "philosophy," but we have to be cautious in doing so. What Isocrates was doing was, in a sense, a form of cultural studies. In the modern day cultural studies movement, it is difficult to find much of a distinction between "rhetoric" and "philosophy." Critical scholarship is both a philosophy and a rhetoric. Understanding this point is essential for appreciating the educational tone of Isocrates.

Another sense in which philosophy and "rhetoric" (i.e. skill in oratory) were indistinguishable is that people did not have the concept of a separate line of inquiry for the study of Truth, on the one hand, and the communication of that Truth, on the other. Indeed, they were not even interested in Truth in the sense that it becomes privileged in Plato and in the world that inherited a Platonic ontology. As Wagner states, Isocrates "may be regarded also, as he considers himself, a teacher of something more than rhetoric, of a complete philosophy of life."[35] This is an important distinction: while Isocrates is not talking about rhetoric (contrary to Wagner, Isocrates never uses the word *rhetorike* or anything similar to it); he *is* discussing the power of logos and the distinct ability that humans have to control their world through language. The method of that control is what we recognize today as being "rhetoric." This power, in the words of Burke, "is rooted in an essential function of language itself, a function that is wholly realistic, and is continually born anew; the use of language as a symbolic means of inducing cooperation in beings that by nature respond to symbols."[36]

Burke's essentializing language aside, he does clarify an important point for us. Isocrates does not have to talk about rhetoric to be talking about an important function of language. In fact, we do not have to talk about "rhetoric" at all, and most cultural theorists do not have much to say about the term. Disciplinary labels are not important. What many people are doing in the humanities is studying what Burke calls the "essential function of language"—how it is that we use language in culture and in our lives. Isocrates was one of the first people to engage in this type of humanistic inquiry. The difference is that Isocrates has a moral edge on contemporary researchers in the humanities because he recognized that this sort of study must lead to action in the social world. His vision of scholarship and education was very much grounded in the world of everyday people, in the world of events that mattered. That was one reason why he was so concerned with oratory—oratory was the way that public business got done. For Isocrates, a rhetorical philosophy was one in which the well trained mind, expressed and affected though communication, extends to the community to help re-envision that community. This, in a nut shell, is the liberal arts ideal. With it we find a moral justification for a rhetorical pedagogy, one that many scholars today would do well to emulate.

For Isocrates, philosophy is a "method of culture."[37] It is a way to analyze the relationship between self and society, and to engage strategically with the construction of both. It is a way to control one's personal habits as well as the affairs of the state: "The 'philosophy' of Isocrates meant, then, a liberal education with further qualifications that include, first, a thoroughly aroused and intense patriotism of the highest type, which would be satisfied not with voting merely, but with acting, doing, talking, planning for the best interest of the state; second, a personal philosophy of life closely akin to the Stoic idea."[38]

Still, within this larger approach that strategically engages self and society, Isocrates rejected the notion promoted by the Sophists that *arete*, or virtue, could be taught: "[H]e claimed that his course was in itself an excellent training for character. Although he did not believe in a philosophic basis for morals, he asserted that his pupils would be distinguished for their nobility of character. He said that virtue could not be taught, but that the philosopher would be virtuous."[39]

Thus, the study of philosophy is the last and highest development of a citizen's education. To speak one's mind eloquently and persuasively is the culmination of educational *arete*, and the skill of learning how to do this becomes preeminently valued. The students of Isocrates were taught that education involved the study and workings of culture. By becoming active in the affairs of the state, people accepted the responsibility to be virtuous. Isocrates did not teach people how to be virtuous, he taught them how to be eloquent; implied in the concept of eloquence was the ethical ideal. In short, Isocrates "established the ideal that each person should unite in himself the three persons of orator, statesman, and philosopher."[40] This was a standard that was to have influence for more than two thousand years.

Isocrates believed that training in philosophy and in speech involve the utilization of three qualities: Nature (Talent), Art (Education), and Practice. Natural talent is the most important trait a student in Isocrates' school could have. However, talent is not enough; education is necessary to improve upon a student's ability. Art, however cannot make up for lack of talent, and practice is necessary to refine art. Murphy explains the significance of this tripartite conceptualization: "Stressing a trilogy of Talent, Education, and Practice, Isocrates promoted a broad educational program using language study as a means of preparing for citizenship as well as for the communicative skills themselves."[41]

Finally, philosophy and education in Isocrates' school did not include the mathematical sciences.[42] This was in sharp contrast to Plato's academy, where advanced mathematical skills were used as a foundation for academic success. Above the entry to Plato's academy were the words, "Let no-one ignorant of geometry enter here."[43] Other "schools" at the time (for example, the thinkers who surrounded Pythagoras) were obviously very much concerned with the mathematical sciences.

Isocrates differed from the Sophists in that he chose his students not by their wealth or social position, but by their particular ability to succeed with his instruction. He was able to boast in his lifetime of his educational process having lasting value for his students. Furthermore, Isocrates' notions of education and culture had larger implications in Western society as he had a major influence on later theorists, in particular Cicero and Quintilian. Wagner makes this connection explicit: "The ideal of the Isocratean school—the orator-statesman—was unquestionably set up in Rome . . . "[44] Patricia Matsen, Philip Rollinson, and Marion Sousa extend this influence to modern times: "In a program centered on the highest ideals of rhetoric, Isocrates taught oratory, composition, history, citizenship, culture, and morality. These subjects, which were later adopted by Quintilian, became the foundation for the liberal arts education as we know it today."[45]

Since Isocrates' influence on the way we conceptualize the humanities is so profound, and since his focus on *philosophia* emphasizes many of the central concerns we find in our modern discussions of rhetorical theory, as well as in contemporary pragmatism, the following sections explore in more detail some of the writings of Isocrates that address these intersections.

The Writings of Isocrates

A number of Isocrates' extant works are available in English. Two, however, are particularly illustrative of Isocrates' educational and rhetorical philosophy. *Against the Sophists* and the *Antidosis* firmly position Isocrates in his role as an educator and highlight the centrality of what we recognize today as rhetoric within his sense of civic responsibility. These two texts span the breadth of Isocrates' long career. The first was written at the onset of his professional practices and the second was composed at the end of his life in defense of his teaching methods. Thus, in examining these texts, we should have an understanding of the development of his ideas on language, education, and culture.

Against the Sophists

Against the Sophists was written early in Isocrates' career, perhaps to announce and advertise the opening of his school. The work attacked the other educators of his era, especially the Sophists. Similar to the other ed-

ucators of his day, and unlike educational institutions today, various educators had to compete with each other for students. Much of Plato's and
Aristotle's writings, for instance, critique the work of other teachers; such
attacks were a way to differentiate one's own teaching from that of others.

Isocrates had seven major points to his polemic. In the first, he argues
that the art of the Sophists is not the art of the soul. He writes, "I think,
good reason to condemn such studies [sophistry] and regard them as
stuff and nonsense and not as a true discipline of the soul."[46] He contends
that the Sophists had disregard for truth and sought to deceive rather
than to enlighten. Such a critique does not differ much from Plato's, as
we will see, and it reflects the civic responsibility that Isocrates emphasized. The Sophists, it is true, were civically minded, but not necessarily
committed to the state in the way that Isocrates was. The Sophists, do not
forget, were mainly foreigners, and may have seen Athens as simply a
place to make a good living. In a sense, the Sophists may have used the
democratic environment to accentuate their rhetorically-based educational practices, but may not have been committed to the civic virtues or
even the nationalism of Isocrates' ideal. Certainly Protagoras was not,
dedicated as he was to the Periclean vision of conquest and empire.

Second, Isocrates argues that the Sophists boasted recklessly of their
power. He maintains that they talked more than they should and frequently did not back their words with action. No doubt he had Gorgias
in mind, who was not the most modest of all human beings (and who
may have been Isocrates' teacher at one time). As Isocrates writes, "If all
who are engaged in the profession of education were willing to state the
facts instead of making greater promises than they can possibly fulfill,
they would not be in such bad repute with the lay public."[47] Certainly the
Sophists open themselves to such a charge through their versatility. Furthermore, there may have been bad Sophists. Without a doubt, the *perception* of the Sophists as despicable charlatans was one that had a certain
currency in its day. This boastfulness and recklessness becomes communicated across history in the works of Plato (although Plato is clearly ex-
aggerating and he frequently forces prominent Sophists to represent positions in his dialogues that they would not have held in real life).[48]

The limitations of the Sophists notwithstanding, Isocrates' charge is
not altogether without an ulterior motive—he is trying to run a business.
More specifically, he is trying to popularize a different approach to education. Isocrates was attempting to establish a school (a novel practice at
the time), a place with a more or less codified system of instruction. The
Sophists, on the other hand, were more spontaneous, more flexible, more
accommodating in their approach to education. Thus, Isocrates' concern
might have been less that the Sophists could not deliver, but that what
they delivered was unsystematic, unaccountable, unreproducible. In a

sense, the Sophists were unaccountable for their education. Crucially, the students they turned out were like loose cannons. The whole system of the Sophists was without quality control.

If this is the case, if Isocrates was upset with the Sophists' method of education, then what we may have here is an early example of an educational *system* coming into conflict with *individual* educational practices. We see the same sort of thing today when we consider who has the right to be a professor in our modern university. To be a professor, one is expected to have a doctorate. To earn a doctorate, a person has to be part of the "system" to an extent. It is difficult to earn a Ph.D. if one is outside the system and has values that conflict with the institutional norms of the academy. By letting only bonafide doctors be professors, the system insures its continuing dominance. What is largely excluded from this picture are those people who privilege a more individual educational practice. Many smart people never go to college and many intellectuals who write a great deal and have much knowledge but no degree are not allowed to be a part of the disciplinary apparatus. Furthermore, people who have knowledge and experience that take them far from the traditional concerns of the university are also ignored. None of these people will be allowed to teach, for long at least, inside the university. And if they tried to teach outside the university, and if they got a significant amount of students, they would be assiduously attacked by recognized "scholars" for not being "professionals." Even at the primary and secondary school levels, not just anybody can walk in and teach a class; no matter how prepared they are, they are forced to go through what is often a demeaning accreditation process.

In short, the state is always interested in the economics of education, and all education, as cultural practice, is part of the larger political economy of any society. In the West, at least, we find, after the Sophists, the preoccupation with schools. Isocrates, Plato, and Aristotle all established schools, lasting for a considerable amount of time. With these schools came rigidly defined epistemologies that see knowledge in more or less foundational ways. The Sophists, on the other hand, tended to be more individualistic in their approaches to education and knowledge, thus serving as an implicit threat to these formalized schools. The result is an interesting tension that gets played out in our contemporary world when considering the relative merits between corporate and more self-styled, dialogical, and critical learning programs.[49]

Third, Isocrates claims that the Sophists charged too much money for their instruction and excluded able-minded students who simply could not afford their teaching. This critique has already been discussed. It is enough to mention here that such critique is accentuated under an Isocratean perspective because the civic responsibility of a teacher transcends an individual's material gain. This is not to say that teachers should not be paid; Isocrates himself was exceedingly rich as the result of the success of his school. The difference was that Isocrates would train people regardless of their ability to pay, provided that they had the potential to contribute to society. Plato, for his part, had a similar view. Education is something one attempts to give as an obligation. Plato's model is that the knower has the obligation to lead the unknowing into the known. With Plato this becomes a way of conditioning people. With Isocrates it is more of the liberal ideal.

Either way we look at the issue of education, its political dimensions are inescapable. From the point of view of the Sophists, or from Isocrates, or from Plato, we can see that education is always for the purpose of a political awareness. Nothing has changed in this regard in modern times; we are continually challenged not to take our notion of education for granted. One's view of politics leads one to support a particular pedagogy and a pedagogy is always a form of politics. This is the central idea behind much of James Berlin's writing. As Berlin explains, "[E]very rhetorical system is based on epistemological assumptions about the nature of reality, the nature of the knower, and the rules governing the discovery and communication of the known."[50] Berlin elaborates:

> [I]n teaching writing [or communication, generally] we are providing students with guidance in seeing and structuring their experience, with a set of tacit rules about distinguishing truth from falsity, reality from illusion. A way of seeing, after all, is a way of not seeing, and as we instruct students in attending to particular orders of evidence—sense impression, for example, in the instruction to "be concrete"—we are simultaneously discouraging them from seeing other orders of evidence—in the present example, the evidence of private vision or of social arrangements. Our decision, then, about the kind of rhetoric we are to call upon in teaching writing has important implications for the behavior of our students—behaviors that includes the personal, social, and political.[51]

Regardless of the politics education serves, and I believe it should serve the politics of a radical democratic state, one marked by economic and social freedom, it is important for readers to realize that education is itself a form of persuasion and that Isocrates, in envisioning his civic ideal, and in grounding that ideal in language, accentuates this point and underscores an important theme of this book: rhetoric is about contesting what it is that people know, feel, and believe. This is what I mean when I wrote earlier that rhetoric invites change. The way it invites transformation is to challenge the conditions of the world that we reify in our beliefs. This is precisely the theme of communication that Sonja and Karen Foss develop in what has yet to be recognized as an important public speaking text. They write that "Presentational speaking is an invitation to transformation. Speakers initiate communication with others because they are seeking opportunities for growth and change and because they believe they can offer such opportunities to others."[52]

Fourth, Isocrates claims that the Sophists distrusted their students. While the teachers presumed to teach virtue, they did not recognize the virtue within their students.[53] Along with Plato, Isocrates felt that because the Sophists' own moral position was compromised to begin with, they turned out students who may have been less than ideal: "But what is most ridiculous of all is that they distrust those from whom they are to get this money—they distrust, that is to say, the very men to whom they are about to deliver the science of just dealing. . . . "[54]

Fifth, Isocrates accuses the Sophists of not being concerned with the arts of discourse, particularly the creative or inventive process of oratory. As Goodwin F. Berquist explains, "The core of Isocrates' program was public speaking. He believed that the art of speech was the best instrument for sharpening the faculty of judgment."[55] Instead of grounding the art of speaking in the wide liberal arts ideal, Isocrates felt that the Sophists relied more on set speeches and inflexible devices for retention and delivery. In a sense, Isocrates felt that the Sophists were not teaching people how to be strong thinkers, only quick tongued persuaders. Along with Aristotle, who wrote his *On Rhetoric* not long after Isocrates wrote his tract, we get the notion that rhetoric is a power for *seeing* how to act in a given context. Isocrates is not quite as explicit as Aristotle, but his sentiment is the same. The Sophists were not teaching people how to invent ideas, or how to articulate an expanded idea developed through education. In other words, the Sophists had no larger platform to build that could be positioned upon a particular learning. Thus, the Sophists were hacks according to Isocrates (as well as to the philosophers) for seeing language as its own end and for not tying a skill in discourse to some larger rationale for culture.

Sixth, based on Isocrates' predisposition toward politics, he disagrees with the sophistic emphasis on forensic (court or legal) speaking, at the expense of deliberative (political) speaking in the Assembly (Aristotle joins Isocrates on this point). In other words, the Sophists were merely training their students to win court cases against other people, rather than to be virtuous in the arena of public self rule "since they professed to teach how to conduct law-suits, picking out the most discredited of terms, which the enemies, not the champions, of this discipline might have been expected to employ."[56] The Sophists, he felt, were concerned with winning court cases for the money they would be paid and had no concern for the justice of the trial.

Seventh, and last, Isocrates accuses the Sophists of practicing demagoguery (extreme self-serving discourse). He writes that "they pretend to wisdom and assume the right to instruct the rest of the world."[57]

Following his accusations against the Sophists, Isocrates lays out the parameters of his own educational system: mainly, that natural talent is more important than practice, and that the good teacher teaches knowledge (not wisdom). What this knowledge is, we are in no position to say. It is not clear from any of the people discussed in this book what knowledge *is*. We get theories of knowledge, particularly after Plato, but no clear indication of what specifically counts as an instance of knowledge. Knowledge, for the classical Greeks, as it is for us today, seems to be that which we believe to be true. For Isocrates, knowledge was that which stemmed from a civic, democratic, and liberal consciousness and the education that gives that consciousness a substance. For the Sophists, knowledge was that which was gleaned from the clash between two competing and mutually exclusive *logoi*. For Plato, knowledge involved the correct perception of universal forms. For Aristotle, knowledge was something demonstrable through syllogistic or inductive reasoning.

Given all these options, what does it mean to know? Well, it means many things, and we glean from this an important rhetorical lesson: words mean much more than what they appear to suggest. When we look at the word "knowledge," it usually suggests to us a singular construct. The noun form of the word implies that it is one thing, or a particular type of thing. In actuality, words are wider and more complex than the definitions we assign to them—this is why authorities like to control our use of language, in particular, our ability to define things and to explore the rich dimensions of language. Freedom to explore our language invites a playful fluidity into our social and cultural identities, and this can have revolutionary implications (in a political sense). Thus, we are largely taught that one of the thinkers in this book has to be right, and the rest have to be wrong. In effect, the philosophers who are designated "right" according to the established authority tend to be those who more closely resemble who we are today and what we value as a culture. This is because we tend to see the world through the subjectivities of our ruling elites and the intellectual class that serves them. Such perspective is limiting of what can be the human experience. We can all be much wealthier, both materially and culturally, if we have the courage to envision the human experience a bit differently.

Antidosis

The next work of Isocrates discussed here is the *Antidosis*, a printed speech which was never delivered, but circulated as a written document. The title for this document was taken from the Greek legal term "Antidosis." An antidosis was a formal challenge before the Athenian court initiated by a wealthy citizen in protest of a "liturgie," or public service. The liturgie was a sort of luxury tax on the upper class which obligated them to supply a ship, supplies, or whatever else was needed for the defense of the state. In the case of Isocrates, he was ordered by the government to supply a warship. This alone should be suggestive of how successful Isocrates' educational school was, for the state felt it necessary to tax him, and war ships cost quite a sum of money. Isocrates protested the tax in a trial and lost his case. In response, he wrote the *Antidosis* in an attempt to clear his name, as he felt misunderstood by the people of Athens. Consider for a moment Isocrates' rhetorical position: here was a man who spent his life preaching the virtues of a civic mindfulness, but who turns his back on a fundamental civic duty. In the context of his trial, Isocrates must have looked very much like the Sophists that he vehemently condemned in his youth. This had to have been an embarrassing situation for Isocrates. On the other hand, the goal of Isocrates' teaching was a civic community that transcended the provinciality of Athens. It was precisely because of this provinciality, which he had unsuccessfully warned against, that he was being asked to donate a large amount of money to the state. Had Athens listened to him, it might not have needed that warship in the first place. In this sense, Isocrates had every right to be bitter.

The *Antidosis* was composed late in Isocrates' life after the end of a long and prosperous career in education. The work is set up as a fictitious defense in court against three allegations. First, Isocrates was himself accused of practicing sophistry by engaging in the shameful deception of making the weaker appear the greater. Second, Isocrates was accused of corrupting the youth of Athens. Third, the court proposed that a man of Isocrates' wealth should give more money to the state than he did. For his defense, Isocrates points to older cases and speeches that he had written, as in *Against the Sophists*, in which he made his moral stance clear. Isocrates then points to an illustrious list of students who came from his school as evidence that he was turning out individuals who did the State no harm and who were actually quite prominent in society. Next, Isocrates challenges his accusers to find any bad student of his, a challenge, as suggested earlier, that his rivals the philosophers could never make.

Finally, Isocrates points to his wide reputation as being an indicator of his success. If I were so bad, he argues, then why do people travel long and far to become my students?: "[I]t is evident that these students cross the sea and pay out money and go to all manner of trouble because they think that they themselves will be the better for it and that the teachers here are much more intelligent than those in their own countries."[58]

About the issue of payment to the state, Isocrates makes little defense other than to downplay the extent of his wealth: "But to the others I must address myself in reply to the false charge of Lysimachus that I am possessed of enormous wealth, lest this statement if credited impose upon me greater public burdens than I could bear."[59]

Not an unfamiliar plea. Isocrates is one of the first of a long line of politicians who praise the common good but who find ways to keep from contributing to the collective coffers. It is my sincere belief that those who serve the state should serve it disinterestedly. In the modern United States, for example, politicians should receive a modest salary (that of the average public high school teacher, perhaps) and nothing more. Their earnings, and the earnings of the wealthy and of the multi-national corporations should be taxed. As it is now, many U.S. owned multi-national corporations ship jobs and industry to the Third World so that they do not have to pay American workers a livable salary. In so doing, they are free to abuse foreign labor and to avoid a U.S. federal tax burden. The foreign countries often do not tax these companies, in return for payoffs to the oligarchs who control the country and provide a "favorable" business environment by violently repressing labor. Many of these same companies, such as G.E. and Ford, are very much cultivators of American patriotism and the "American way of life" (whatever that is).

Conclusion

Clearly, Isocrates differs from the Sophists in several ways. First, Isocrates sought to establish an educational "system" that would train people to work directly for the State. While the Sophists gave people skills for public participation (speech training), Isocrates accentuated those skills with a wider philosophical and cultural understanding and education. Thus, he hoped to create not only articulate citizens, but citizens that had a sense of purpose. This purpose was civic and defined by a consciousness of culture, but it was also wider in its political vision. Isocrates stressed a pan-Hellenism which he hoped would mediate some of the tensions and abuses of his day, and prepare the Greek people for a greater era of peace and political sovereignty. In trying to establish his political goals, Isocrates strove, through his educational philosophy, to unify the moral and intellectual into a single academic pursuit. While he was only partly successful in these goals, he made a lasting influence on Western culture. As Donald Clark is able to write, "More than any other Greek rhetorician [Isocrates] left his stamp on subsequent Greek and Roman educational theory and practice."[60]

Notes

1. *Illuminations* (New York: Harcourt Brace Jovanovich, 1968), 257.
2. *Classical Rhetoric and Its Christian and Secular Tradition from Ancient to Modern Times* (Chapel Hill: The University of North Carolina Press, 1980).

3. "Isocrates' *Philosophia* and Contemporary Pragmatism," in *Rhetoric, Sophistry, Pragmatism*, ed. Steven Mailloux (New York: Cambridge University Press, 1995), 33.

4. For a similar critique of Rorty, see Frank Lentricchia, *Criticism and Social Change* (Chicago: University of Chicago Press, 1985), 15–19.

5. See Edward S. Herman and Noam Chomsky, *Manufacturing Consent: The Political Economy of the Mass Media* (New York: Pantheon Books, 1988).

6. See Omar Swartz, "The 'Faith of Freedom' vs. the Freedom of Faith: Exploring the Totalitarian Discourse of J. Edgar Hoover," *Speaker and Gavel* 33 (1996), 59–73.

7. See Howard Zinn, *A People's History of the United States* (New York: Harper-Perennial, 1980), chapter 16.

8. Henry David Thoreau, "On the Duty of Civil Disobedience," in *Walden and "On the Duty of Civil Disobedience"* (New York: New American Library, 1960), 229.

9. *The Trial of Socrates* (New York: Doubleday, 1989), 140.

10. Ibid.

11. As a current example, see, Robert W. Tucker, "The Purposes of American Power," *Foreign Affairs* (Winter, 1980), 241–274. Writing as a political scientist and co-director of The Lehrman Institute, Tucker argues that because Third World revolutionary movements "enjoy broad support. . . . Right-wing governments will have to be given steady outside support, even, if necessary, by sending in American forces" (271). The purpose of this, and of American foreign policy, more generally, is "the restoration of a more normal political world, a world in which those states possessing the elements of great power once again play the role their power entitles them to play" (273).

12. See Alex Carey, *Taking the Risk Out of Democracy* (Urbana: University of Illinois Press, 1997).

13. See John Stauber and Sheldon Rampton, *Toxic Sludge is Good for You: Lies, Damn Lies, and the Public Relations Industry* (Monroe, ME: Common Courage Press, 1995).

14. Moses Hadas, *The Greek Ideal and its Survival* (New York: Harper and Row, 1960), 90.

15. This was astonishing given the damage that Germany inflicted on them during the Second World War, and considering the isolation that Russia was subjected to for years.

16. For an analysis of the anti-revolutionary stance of the USSR in the 1930s see George Orwell, *Homage to Catalonia* (New York: Harcourt, Brace, and Company, 1980), particularly pages 56 and 57. For a study of the Chinese attempt to achieve detente with the United States and its implications for understanding Maoism as a political ideology, see Leslie Evans, *China After Mao* (New York: Monad Press, 1978).

17. See Noam Chomsky and Edward S. Herman, *The Washington Connection and Third World Fascism* (Boston: South End Press, 1979).

18. For an excellent biography of Che, see Jon Lee Anderson, *Che Guevara: A Revolutionary Life* (New York: Grove Press, 1997).

19. *Cicero on Oratory and Orators*, trans. J.S. Watson (Carbondale: Southern Illinois University Press, 1970).

20. This discussion of praxis is adapted from Omar Swartz, "Praxis," *Encyclopedia of Rhetoric and Composition*, ed. Theresa Enos (New York: Garland Press, 1996), 553.

21. "Form and Genre in Rhetorical Criticism: An Introduction," in *Form and Genre: Shaping Rhetorical Action*, eds. Karlyn Campbell and Kathleen Jamieson (Falls Church: Speech Commutation Association, 1977), 9.

22. A more detailed analysis of Che's speech appears in Omar Swartz, "Toward an Understanding of Marxist Discourse: Major Ernesto 'Che' Guevara's February 26, 1965 Address to the Conference on African-Asian Solidarity," *Speaker and Gavel* 30 (1993), 1–18.

23. ¡*Venceremos!: The Speeches and Writings of Ernesto Che Guevara*, ed. John Gerassi (New York: Macmillan Company, 1968), 386.

24. "Presidential Motives for War," *Quarterly Journal of Speech* 60 (1974), 343.

25. Introduction, *Che Guevara on Guerrilla Warfare* by Che Guevara (Washington: Fredrick Praeger), xxii.

26. Ibid.

27. Ibid., xxi.

28. ¡*Venceremos!*: 379.

29. *The Philosophy of Literary Form* (Berkeley: University of California Press, 1973), 193.

30. ¡*Venceremos!*: 379.

31. *Rhetoric of Motives* (Berkeley: University of California Press, 1969), 22.

32. Russell H. Wagner, "The Rhetorical Theory of Isocrates," *The Quarterly Journal of Speech Education* 8 (1922), 330.

33. Ibid.

34. "Theses on Feurbach," in *The German Ideology* by Karl Marx and Frederick Engels (New York: International Publishes), 123.

35. "The Rhetorical Theory of Isocrates," 326.

36. *A Rhetoric of Motives* (Berkeley: University of California Press, 1969), 43.

37. "The Rhetorical Theory of Isocrates," 330.

38. Ibid., 331.

39. Ibid., 330.

40. Ibid., 331.

41. *Quintilian On the Teaching of Speaking and Writing* (Carbondale: Southern Illinois University Press, 1987), xxix.

42. Blair, lectures.

43. Quoted in Richard Osborne, *Philosophy for Beginners* (New York: Writers and Readers Publishing, 1992), 13.

44. "The Rhetorical Theory of Isocrates," 325.

45. *Readings from Classical Rhetoric* (Carbondale: Southern Illinois University Press, 1990), 43.

46. *Against the Sophists and Antidosis*, trans. G.B. Norlin. Loeb Classical Library, vol 2 (Cambridge: Harvard University Press, 1956), 167.

47. Ibid., 163.

48. A modern representation of this boastfulness can be seen in the neo-sophistic positions of Mark Backman, *Sophistication: Rhetoric and the Rise of Self-Consciousness* (Woodbridge, CT: Ox Bow Press, 1991).

49. See Henry A. Giroux, *Schooling and the Struggle for Public Life: Critical Pedagogy in the Modern Age* (Minneapolis: University of Minnesota Press, 1988).

50. *Rhetoric and Reality: Writing Instruction in American Colleges, 1900–1985* (Carbondale: Southern Illinois University Press, 1987), 4.

51. Ibid., 7.

52. *Inviting Transformation: Presentational Speaking for a Changing World* (Prospect Heights, IL: Waveland Press, 1994), 2.

53. William Benoit, "Isocrates and Plato on Rhetoric and Rhetorical Education," *Rhetoric Society Quarterly* 21 (1991), 62.

54. *Against the Sophists and Antidosis*, 65.

55. "Isocrates of Athens: Foremost Speech Teacher of the Ancient World," *Speech Teacher* 8 (1959), 253.

56. *Against the Sophists and Antidosis*, 175.

57. Ibid., 165.

58. Ibid., 311.

59. Ibid., 273.

60. *Rhetoric in Greco-Roman Education* (Morningside Heights: Columbia University Press, 1957), 6.

4

Plato

The last chapter discussed the educational philosophy of Isocrates, high-lighting its parallels to the modern day liberal arts ideal and to twentieth century pan-nationalist thought. In Isocrates' sense of the word *philosophia*, conceptualized as a cultural method for understanding social relationships, we learn a great deal about the intersections between education and praxis. Education is training for the engaged life. The educated mind critically examines its own subjectivity as well as the subjectivity surrounding the construction of the world.

Education and Praxis: From Isocrates to Plato

Historically, the above conceptualization of education has been the liberal arts ideal. Throughout the ages there existed the notion that free "men" (the masculine standard for the adult mind remained relatively unchallenged until well into the twentieth century) could better themselves and their society through education. This said, however, it should be obvious that I am not suggesting that a revolutionary consciousness was being cultivated within the traditional liberal arts ideal; on the contrary, a classical education has most always been the prerogative of the elite, propertied classes. While education is always potentially liberating, it is more often than not used to constrain thought and to reify or justify a political order. Specifically, the "free" man of the liberal arts ideal has historically been one of independent wealth, usually slave-owning or serf-owning. In modern times, he has been the child of the industrialists, the robber-barons, and the oil tycoons. If his parents are not of this class, then they come from class of the technocrats—the doctors, the lawyers, the clergy—the professions that serve the needs of the ruling elite and that are rewarded for their services. In short, the "free" man usually derived from the aristocratic class, for whom leisure was the norm and education a way of learning the cultural customs of the ruling circle. The classical education has always been associated with money and property. It was a way to reinforce class distinctions and a conservative ideology.

Positioned in this way, what I have been calling praxis, specifically its Marxist characteristics, did not exist during the classical age. What existed was the Isocratean or Aristotelian sense of praxis—it was an education that led to an aristocratic and civic mindfulness. Education in the classical liberal arts ideal involved the civic minded oratory that Quintilian envisioned. His *Institutes of Oratory* describes the ideal education of the civic minded Republican, the patrician senator that Cicero best exemplifies.[1] Cicero lives Isocrates' vision. With Cicero at the helm, Rome exemplifies (for a short time) its own self-defining narrative of a powerful notion of civic and political *arete*.

The danger in writing this is that it glorifies Cicero and Rome, which is not my intention. For all the tribute Western culture plays to Cicero and to Republican Rome, he and it were as tyrannical and as brutal as any expansionist state in history. As noted earlier, so-called "golden ages" are times when the people we worship accumulate most of their gold. As a nation we look to this period of Rome, just as we look to John F. Kennedy's administration, with a sense of nostalgia. Here we find (or we *think* we find) innocence, strength, and glory. "The glory that was Rome" we like to say to ourselves, "the enchantment that was Camelot" we repeat like a mantra, often with misty eyes. We cheer Kennedy, as we cheer Ronald Reagan, because his rhetoric reeks of wealth and power. Americans see themselves in the rhetoric of their leaders. They imagine that this strength and power are *their* strength and power, and they refuse to see that strength and power are acquired at the cost of human blood. Americans grow intoxicated by a power that speaks for them in name only, and they suckle at its breast and feed on the blood that poses as riches. In a sense, we find gold in the rhetoric of U.S. presidents, and the presence of wealth always makes us smile, no matter how bloody are the hands that pass the coins. We smile no matter how foul the stench of the hypocrisy of our leaders who speak of "peace" and "prosperity," but who pursue policies that undermine both.

Both Kennedy and Reagan were warmongers and killers, cold-blooded and ruthless men who led a cold-blooded and ruthless international power. Both men made a mockery of the American people and helped to make America an international symbol for despair (while publicly maintaining all the time that it represents the opposite). As critical thinkers we must reject the worshipping of any state or figure and insist on measuring a society against the yardstick of compassion and political inclusion, and not on the gold that it controls. The greatness of any country must be founded on these principles. To talk of "glory" without starting here is to talk of violence, and violence can never be glorious for any sane human being.

While the politics are different between an Aristotelian and a Marxist praxis, the philosophy *behind* praxis is the same in both senses. That is what brings this book together and gives it a degree of coherence. In any sense of praxis, rhetoric is that which serves the needs of the community. Rhetoric brings people together.[2] Once people are together, they can act like savages, like many modern nations do, or they can learn to transcend the immediate self-interest of their base common interests and seek a wider sense of community and interaction with all peoples. To my mind, that is the advantage of the socialist paradigm and the reason why I assert that Marxism is rhetorical and that rhetoric itself can lead to a socialist rationality. This is praxis in its modern sense. Yet, even without this critical angle, which many people will not agree with, rhetoric is still the way to ground the human intellect squarely in the social realm. In the twentieth century, the social is socialism as the social was conceived as the aristocracy and the oligarchy during most of the age of classical thinking. To the extent that the "social" exists in the United States, it is socialistic; it is a genuine concern for the well-being of the individual as an individual and not as a consumer.

Rhetoric as praxis takes *theoria* and gives it a communal worth. "Community" used to be defined as white males with property. It has been broadened, in this country at least, to include more people, at least superficially. But it has not been broadened to include the realm of economic liberty. The freedom of the "social" is dependent upon such liberty. There is nothing social about being a slave. There is nothing social about imposing slavery on others. The social starts from a rhetorical position of established equality. But the social is always limited by rhetoric as much as it is informed and expanded by rhetoric. Within that social, however we define it, is the dynamis for history. In the rhetoric of community we privilege ideas and education.

This is as much Isocrates' classical ideal as it is our modern Marxist ideal. It is the strongest rationale for education today that I can think of. Conceptualized in this modern, critical way, education serves the interest of a more broadly construed sense of community than those practiced throughout most of all recorded history. In a sense, I am extending the range of political *arete* as practiced in Ancient Greece. Isocrates would have no fundamental disagreement with this, although Plato would, and that is the subject of this chapter. Plato would not agree with the claim that education is implicitly social and dialogical, that it exists in and for a community. Plato would not agree that education does not make sense outside of its communal properties and that its relevance increases as more people are included in its outreach. Such a view of education clashes with the traditional, Platonic, anti-humanist banking model of education that posits knowledge in a superior source to be divvied out in increments.

In the case of Isocrates, scholars can synthesize a modern approach to language, education, and resistance, as I have done in the last chapter. In this current chapter, and in the subsequent one on Aristotle, I engage in a similar analysis. In so doing, I disfigure each of these thinkers slightly, perverting standard readings, and otherwise disrupting the normality under which we commonly approach them. My license for doing so has much to do with the cultural currency that each one commands. The ideas of these thinkers hold tremendous power over our culture and our thought. While we have certainly moved beyond these thinkers in our development as a culture, much modern thought is representative of, a reaction to, or an extension of, these classical models. Similar to our experience with Isocrates, we find that Plato and Aristotle prefigure, and in many cases often directly contribute to, social controversies that exist in Western culture today.

Reification and Foundations in the Dialogues of Plato

Plato's dialogues are artfully crafted discussions that literally lay the "foundation" for the philosophical tradition in Western culture. In a rather pleasant manner, Plato reifies conceptual insights in the structure of human thought. In an important sense, Plato describes for us much of who we are. He invents us in many ways. Plato represents one "face" that is similar to that which Foucault describes when he discusses how the character of "Man" changes with the ebbing tides of history. Foucault specifically uses the metaphor of the face that is drawn in sand at the edge of the sea.[3] In Foucault's allegory, what we conceive as being "Man" today is the result of intellectual, linguistic-based inventions that took place since the European Enlightenment. As new vocabularies arise, the old ones give way. Unlike the ephemeralness of the face in the sand that Foucault describes, Plato's "face" has been carved out of stone and has more of a "temporary permanence." The stone is representative of a stronger cultural presence, yet it is still only stone. It rests on the side of the ocean with the daily ebb of the tide rushing over it, slowly grinding it down: the sand and the water slowly eat away at the stone, until nothing remains of its representation. When that occurs, we will be free from Plato. But that might take as many years as it has taken to get this far. We are not in any hurry, though, we have got nothing but the rest of Time ahead of us (barring the extinction of human beings by human or other natural calamity). Plato's philosophical edifice in Western thought is no small accomplishment; Plato should not be taken lightly. While most people today tend to treat philosophy as an irrelevant concept, philosophical ideas have had defining roles in establishing the personality and characteristics of Western culture. Ideas are the engines that drive history.

While human history and material progress is frequently demarcated by conditions of hostility and war, it is more substantially distinguished by *ideas* (ideas that perhaps contribute to conditions of war and hostility). While hostility and wars may be the negative side of ideas, they, nevertheless, distinguish, in large part, who we are as a species. Without the power of ideas, we would still be living side-by-side with the rest of the animal kingdom, a much decimated and weaker species, barely able to carry its own weight against competing species of animals who are much stronger than us in every other respect. Ideas come first, and they are proceeded by action. *Theory*, however, may be different, as theory is often a Johnny-come-lately to any type of cultural excitement.

Thus, one model of history is: idea, action, theory. For example, labor organizes because of abusive working conditions, and peasants revolt because they are oppressed; but this is not enough to enact significant social change. Organized resistance is the result of an *idea* about one's self and one's conditions, ideas about what one is as a human being. For the most part, people have to learn to resist (there are exceptions to this). A necessary condition for most resistance that goes beyond immediate self-defense (and thus potentially endangers the immediate security of the individual) is that people have to *see* themselves by their own definitions and reject the definition of "slave" or "worker" that is imposed on them by others. In the words of Neil Postman, "It is certainly true that he [sic] who holds the power to define is our master, but it is also true that he who holds in mind an alternative definition can never quite be his slave."[4] This reframing is an important function of social movements. With few exceptions, social movements are started and led by people who are educated and who have the opportunity to escape from the oppression that the larger group experiences. In rejecting this option, social movement leaders return to the communities and conditions that they successfully escaped from to *teach* their followers a new way of conceptualizing cultural conditions.[5] The Black Power movement and the consciousness raising tactics of the Feminist Movement are two examples of how resistance is a "learned" activity.[6]

With an idea or definition firmly in mind, people can envision action and thus proceed to act in novel and potentially liberating ways. Theory only comes along when people *act and fail*. Theory takes the "idea" and the "act" and studies them, offering a *strategy*. Socialism, then, is the strategy for achieving the idea of freedom and it is informed by various theories of human "nature," "knowledge," etc. Likewise, oratory has existed since human beings have first figured out how to create a rudimentary language; that is to say, since human beings first existed in a way that we would recognize as being "human." "Rhetorical" action, then, preceded theory. In this particular instance, we get the "idea" of rhetoric because of theory. With this in mind, perhaps it is better to say that there is a *reciprocal* relationship between theory and ideas. Ideas coalesce into theories and theories beget new ideas. The unit of theory, however, is still the idea, and thus we must continue to see it as a material cause (in an Aristotelian sense).

Ideas do not exist outside of our heads; they are housed within an individual's subjectivity. For example, there is, in fact, no such thing as "freedom." No living thing is ever "free." Everything that lives is constrained by what it *is* and the physiological processes that govern its existence. This is not a metaphysical assertion, but a physical one. Every "thing" is something, and not something else. Given a wider viewpoint (or a different one), what we assume to be differing structures may be redescribed in ways to accentuate their sameness. Nevertheless, there are limitations to rhetorical action, and this has to do with species-dependent constraints. This principle only becomes a metaphysical assertion if we introduce hierarchy and value into the question. Counter to Plato and, as we will discuss below, Richard Weaver, structure does not necessary denote hierarchy and value. Things can be *different* without being *better* by any absolute standard. Such statement flies in the face of traditional liberalism in this country that wants to translate difference into sameness, with a universal White/Christian/middle-class standard. In rejecting this principle, we do not reject community; rather, we simply take a more flexible approach as to what constitutes a "community."

When we talk of "freedom" we are always talking about some definition of freedom, some condition that we want to privilege over others (such as the ability to find decent work and to earn a livable wage or not to be a slave on another person's plantation). In doing so, we create an image of our idea and give that idea a cultural presence. This is an example of reification. Reification is the way we make our ideas "real" through language. Reification is how we operationalize something, like the condition of freedom. In so doing, we give it a material property. This in itself is not bad; it is the only way that we have to make sense out of our thoughts. Just as spiders make webs to live in, humans make webs out of language. Without a web, a spider's life would make no sense to it. If we were to take a spider and prevent it from making a web, and, if we were to provide it with nutrition, it would probably die because no life can exist for long in an alien environment. For a similar reason, baby monkeys that are taken from their mothers and raised in isolation go insane. They have been ripped from the web of their significance.

Similarly, people who undergo sense-deprivation often become unhealthy and, under prolonged periods, go insane and die. In a sense, they too have been ripped from their webs. We live in our webs and catch our food with them. We die without them because we lose our sense of meaning, we lose our hold on "reality." A problem only arises when we take our ideas for granted and assume they have a presence beyond their reification. Ideas invite theories, as I wrote above, but theories also invite ideas (this is part of their symbiosis). Actions are the testing ground for the idea/theory synthesis. The entire context constitutes our webs of meaning and understanding. Yet once theory has been around for a while, once ideas become like a grain of sand that is transformed into a pearl and forgets that it is only sand, we tend to forget that each has its own characterizing genesis. In other words, ideas about God and Country, Fact and Fiction, Truth and Illusion are not "givens" in nature. Rather, they are "takens," views that we hold of our world that derive from the speculations and metaphors of influential people who have lived before us.[7]

The Professionalization of Philosophy and the Linguistic Origin of Rhetoric

In Plato's dialogues we find the professionalization of philosophy, as well as the linguistic origins of rhetoric. By "professionalization," I mean that Plato gives philosophy a conceptualization by which its "essence," "structure," or "nature" could be known. In other words, Plato treats philosophy as if it were real, as if it were, say, a cow or other object that has a material presence. Aristotle, we will see next chapter, will do the same thing with rhetoric, treating it as if it were a thing, such as a cow. As if he were dissecting the carcass of an animal, Aristotle dissects rhetoric into its most intricate parts.

By professionalizing philosophy, Plato invests philosophy with an agenda—the historical task of discovering the metaphysical underpinnings of important concepts such as Truth, Justice, Ethics, and other things concerning the world as it *is* (as opposed to the world as human beings commonly understand it). With Plato, philosophy as we know it comes into being, and with Plato's characterization of philosophy we inherit certain assumptions that make us who we are as human beings in the Western world. For example, as discussed below, Plato invents the binary between Truth and Appearance. While this binary has certain socially useful characteristics, such as in helping to provide a rationale for traditional science, it also helps set the conditions for the dominance of religious thought in the West, particularly the dominance of Christianity as a repressive social and ideological force.

Furthermore, binary thinking smuggles into culture a hidden morality. In effect, Plato's intellectual strategy is itself an instance of rhetoric; it infuses a particular hierarchy and value system into Western thought. Plato privileges a *form* of knowledge over all other types and grants political privilege to those few people who are able to define what that Truth is, at the expense of everything else that becomes relegated to mere "Appearance." In so doing, Plato empowers the self-appointed champions of "Truth" to do all sorts of unspeakable things in the pursuit of their vision, since there cannot, by definition, be any compromise in the pursuit of Truth. In this duality of thought, the experience of Western culture assumes a combative tone. Right/Wrong, White/Black, West/East, and Male/Female become paired in antagonistic relationships (as opposed to being conceptualized as interactive or cooperative integrations, such as we find in the Eastern symbol of the Yin/Yang). Politically, what we find is that Male becomes positioned as being *over* Female, White dominates *over* Black, the West has the burden of *lifting* the East. Patriarchy, Racism, and Imperialism/Colonization are direct consequences of binary or dualistic thinking.

With the normalization of binary thinking in the West, the world is made to appear in a clear cut fashion, making politically viable the rhetoric of exclusion (this technically involves the tactic of "dissociation").[8] Within binary thought, what becomes important is being able to categorize well: this becomes the base of political power and it is used to mask the tensions inherent in class antagonisms and economic inequity or else to make "natural" and thus culturally secure these conditions. Within a culture that is thoroughly steeped in binary rationalities, there is always a tension between acting "correctly" and "incorrectly." Definitions for proper conduct are stipulated by those authorized to "know" and always serve the political function of supporting those in power. Professionalized philosophy, from Plato on, has had an important role to play in this cultural dynamic, for it is the art or method by which history and society can be known (as seen from the ruling class). Philosophy, in its Platonic senses, is the method for making the distinctions necessary for *accurate* characterization.

I am not suggesting that this is all that philosophy does, or that Plato has the last word on what philosophy *is*. I am only trying to illustrate that he had the *first* word; in offering his definition of philosophy, he stipulated that the "*is*" of things is important. Through his persuasive use of definitions, Plato proscribed how it is that we can think about asking questions. It has taken us a long time as a culture to learn how to think differently, and we are not even completely successful in our task (as U.S. "victory" in the cold war aptly illustrates). Nevertheless, important gains have been made by people in the nineteenth and twentieth centuries to give us hope for a new way of thinking. People like Darwin, Dewey, Einstein, Foucault, Freud, Marx, Nietzsche, and Sartre, for example, are some of the more illustrative people (in alphabetical order) who have given us new metaphors and new ways of thinking about human beings in society. Others may come up with a different list of important thinkers, but to my mind, these are some of the greatest of what we can call the "alternative" philosophers, the people who offer a different, more liberating thinking about the human presence in the world.

Notice that all the people on the above list are all white men. This phenomenon says something negative about intellectual practices in our society; we tend to honor the metaphors of white men and to remember them, and to ignore or overlook the accomplishments of women or people of color. Granted, I could have challenged myself to come up with other names, such as Emma Goldman, Mother Jones, Simon De Beauvoir, Mary Wollstonecraft, Voltairine De Cleyre, Rosa Luxemburg, or Sojourner Truth, and perhaps I should have. Nevertheless, my point still stands—it would be a *challenge* and the danger would be that it would appear as if I were stretching a bit. Even if I *did* include these names, only one of them is non-European. Sadly, the names of women and non-Europeans are not widely recognized as being paradigmatic of Western thought, and perhaps they should be. Perhaps one day we can look to bell hooks as having offered us a revolutionary way to conceptualize ourselves and other people. We would certainly be culturally richer as a nation for doing so, and probably lead lives that were more sensitive to the needs of a wider section of the population in the United States. Still, I have a difficult time imagining bell hooks being utilized in this way on a wide scale, as there is a heavily ingrained cultural resistance to ideas of her sort, as there is to the ideas of most great thinkers.

Each of the thinkers on the list is extremely controversial today. Scholars who have come after them have all struggled with expanding or refuting their ideas, and that is precisely what makes them great, their ability to generate further, and even counter arguments. This is the dialectic that leads to intellectual maturity. What is important about them is that they were introducing a rationality that rejected the binary that Plato imposed about the relationships between Reality and Appearance. They opened the terrain to popular debate, rather than setting the terms of the debate. While each of their languages have limitations, they offer a discourse that is much more inclusive of a wider range of ideas. It is the strengths, and not the limitations of these thinkers, that earn our celebration, and the same thing can be said for Plato as well.

The significance of the work of the above people, and later of continental philosophy more generally, has been to challenge Plato's characterization of knowledge and the political institutions that thrive in its image. The effect of each is to give us more conceptual room in which to imagine our lives differently. Each of the above thinkers in some way focuses history back onto the individual and his or her subjective needs. This is most clear in the work of Karl Marx, perhaps the greatest of Plato's challengers. In his words: "The question of whether objective truth can be attributed to human thinking is not a question of theory but is a *practical question*. Man [sic] must prove the truth, i.e. the reality and power, the this-sidedness of his thinking in practice. The dispute over the reality or non-reality of thinking that is isolated from practice is a purely *scholastic* question."[9]

In contrast, philosophy, in the Platonic tradition, has been conceptualized as a "tribunal of reason." This was Kant's and Descartes' vision. It is seen as the way to "polish the mirror of the mind" so as to see the world as it actually *is*.[10] When seen from a "god's eye view," all the confusions of the human world can be placed into perspective. A universal ethics and morality can be established, just laws can be written, and a governmental infrastructure can be enacted to make sure "order" reigns in the world. This was the dream of the European Enlightenment; it was an attempt to modernize Plato, utilizing the newly developed sciences, and to deduce first principles by which to solve the "riddle" of nature.

This project is largely bankrupt, although that point is hotly contested among people today. Nevertheless, the weaknesses of Plato's revised narrative should be obvious.[11] More generally, we just have to point to capitalism and to its metaphysical underpinnings to get a broader sense of the limitations we are discussing. Furthermore, as I freely admit, Marxism comes from this same tradition, and thus we can explain some, but not all, of the limitations associated with Marxist governments as they have existed in the twentieth century. Marxism, for all of its limitations, has much to say about what is potentially good about the Enlightenment project. As an ideology, Marxism accentuates both perspectives, and is thus an important and fertile ground upon which to *start* when postulating a workable social and political reality. It is not the last word, however. It is simply the beginning of what can be a powerful and transforming new set of social relationships.

One important task for philosophy (or any type of cultural analysis) is to encourage people to be effective cheerleaders for a position. If it is a position that we care about, we want to place it in its best light, and we also want to point out its limitations so that other people can get a richer idea about what it is that we want them to understand. I believe that this is one antidote for Plato. If I had to give a name to this belief, I would call it "rhetoric." Rhetoric, in a post-Platonic philosophy, becomes transformed into cultural analysis.

This brings us full circle. Philosophy, in the sense that Plato defined it, is hostile to rhetoric, a word he himself coined to differentiate his "true" form of knowledge from a base and corrupted form (rhetoric).[12] Thus, as we can see from this brief review of Platonic philosophy, Plato's hostility to rhetoric is immense. His entire project for philosophy, one that would last for more than two thousand five hundred years, is dependent upon a rejection of a rhetorical epistemology. Rhetoric cannot be the study of culture for Plato, that is philosophy's job. Both are the flip side of logos—the True and the False study of human rationality.

Who Controls Rhetoric?

Because of Plato's political commitments, it is intellectually imperative for him to keep society from engaging in a rhetorical epistemology. As we discussed earlier, all people with political aspirations, particularly those that tend to be exclusive and limiting of political rights, need to argue against rhetoric. Rhetoric always positions itself against those in power; it becomes "propaganda" when it is enlisted by the state. The state always maintains the right to utilize propaganda, but it always makes an effort to conceal this propaganda, and it does that through the demonization of rhetoric. Even in Athens, where we seem to get a sense of rhetoric's flourishing, its use was placed under severe constraints: the only people who were allowed to use rhetoric were the narrow group of people defined as citizens, and, even among those, the only people who could be trained in rhetoric were the wealthy. Thus, the revolutionary power of rhetoric was checked even in Ancient Athens, as elsewhere.

The first thing that all governments do during times of crisis (and all capitalist governments are perpetually in crisis as a result of class tensions and their imperialist policies) is to control the type of things people can say to each other. In the U.S., for example, it is technically illegal to talk against the government during times of war. Moreover, throughout the late nineteenth and twentieth-centuries, many people have been put in jail for a whole range of "subversive" activities that included talking about birth control, talking about labor rights, burning their draft cards, and condemning American imperialism. In a wider sense, as we discussed in the first chapter, the revolutionary potential of rhetoric is stifled in this country because, to be successful, rhetoric has to have an audience, and the mass audience of the modern era is controlled by a few people who own the print and electronic media.[13]

As already noted, very few societies have encouraged a rhetorical epistemology. The Greek experiment at Athens turned out to be just that, an experiment, and a limited one at that. Traditional Western society has tended to be theistic. While the Sophists were popular and while Athens was dynamic for a time, Plato, in the end, had the final word in that particular battle. But the war is far from over, as indicated above. Politically, in the United States and throughout the world, the battle is heating up. The wane of socialism as an international force has invigorated many of the old forms of limiting thought, characterized by the resurgence of ethnic and religious wars, by the deterioration of women's rights world wide, and by the declining power of labor.[14] The resurgence of each of these evils brings with it some degree of resistance and certainly disagreement and discontent, all of which create the potential for significant structural change.

Clearly, Western culture has not given up on Plato's project. Rather, philosophy since the Enlightenment takes a new turn and Truth becomes operationalized slightly differently. Truth is deflected from the spiritual to the material in a move similar to the one that the Ionians made thousands of years earlier when they stepped, for a time, into the moral void left by the decay of the Homeric gods. This materialistic, scientistic rationality is no less elitist and hegemonic as the religious episteme that it somewhat eclipsed. What it does is shift us from theocratic governance to a technocratic governance, one perfectly at home within a capitalist political economy. Replacing the priest is the "expert" and what the experts preach is that which constitutes the infrastructure of the State (its military and industrial might, its laws and its internal systems of control).[15] Thus, the same relationships exist between Truth and Power in the modern age of scientism as existed in the depraved theocracies of the Middle Ages.

All the while, rhetoric continues to be held hostage to Plato's early critique. Outside of the university, it is still the thing that good citizens are taught to avoid. Within the university, rhetoric is becoming an interdisciplinary pursuit; scholars (but not administrators) are beginning to recognize that knowledge is interdisciplinary and that the structure of knowledge is informed by a rhetorical perspective. However, even in the academy, what passes for a "rhetorical" perspective is often couched in another language. Similar to their use of "Marxism," scholars often are forced to talk about "rhetoric" using a coded vocabulary, such as "critical theory," "cultural studies," "postmodernism." Things are changing, but traditionally speaking, up until not much more than a few decades ago, where rhetoric dared to exist, it was often encumbered by elocution and grammar for the most part (or a neutered form of it was enlisted in the service of the Church).[16]

Rhetorical epistemologies, ones that help us to revision ourselves and our culture, tend to be like flowers in Spring—they blossom for a time in certain places and pollinate the air with new ideas. But many societies have shown that they cannot long survive on change and growth, and are actually allergic to the pollination of new ideas. Thus, limits are soon placed upon a rhetorical epistemology. Knowledge seldom escapes the control of its guardians, as U.S. copyright law aptly illustrates (for example). Knowledge cannot be rhetorical and communal, according to the United States, it is something *real*, it is property, it is an item that is subject to the laws of capitalism, it can be *owned*.[17] The same thing with scientific knowledge. Many Third World nations are prevented from manufacturing their own medicine and are forced to buy it from the West, paying much more money for it. As a result, many people go without medicine, who would otherwise have it if "knowledge" of that medicine was considered communal, as opposed to being considered "property."

Rhetoric, in effect, faces powerful enemies like Plato and the United States. In a sense, rhetoric is always the enemy of the ruling elites. Rhetoric *must* be such an enemy of privilege and authority, because it involves the potential that always exists to ask "Why?" Politicians have to deny rhetoric, even as they use it, for it is a permanent challenge to their own representations. Thus, rhetoric must be banished or burdened by the weight of a pedagogy unconnected with practical politics (a characterization fiercely resisted by many modern English departments who encourage a Marxist or critical orientation to the teaching of writing).[18]

Rhetorike and Theory

As the above discussion suggests, Plato's dialogues serve as important foundations for the Western intellectual and spiritual traditions. At least this has been their dominant effect. They help reify certain political, social, and philosophical orders. Yet, as previously suggested, Plato's dialogues have had another subsidiary effect, one that perhaps Plato did not intend, and one under appreciated or even ignored by the bulk of Western scholarship. Plato's championing of philosophy and derision of rhetoric served also the function of codifying rhetoric in particular ways. Otherwise put, Plato reified the very thing that he devoted his energies toward demonizing. In serving as a foil for his "true" knowledge, rhetoric itself had to be given a form and a substance. In short, rhetoric had to be made into a "thing," a specific object of inquiry. As Edward Schiappa notes, "Prior to the fourth century *logos* and *legein* were used to describe what later would be called rhetoric. Both terms are far broader in their meanings than the term *rhetorike*, hence the appearance of *rhetorike* signals a new level of specificity and conceptual clarity concerning different verbal arts."[19] Prior to Plato there existed logos and oratory but there did not exist rhetoric conceptualized as a discipline. Such conceptualization is necessary if it is going to be codified as a *techne*, which is what Aristotle does, writing from out of the shadow of Plato.

As Schiappa illustrates, the dialogues of Plato begin to develop a discussion of what we can start identifying as a rhetorical *theory* (although it is not a very useful rhetorical theory, as we will explore below). Otherwise put, rhetoric becomes a noun with Plato. As Schiappa notes:

> One rhetorical effect of entitling a new "thing" is that it creates the impression that the "thing" has been "out there" all along, waiting to be discovered and

described. Nouns, in particular, suggest things-that-already-exist. . . . Part of the rhetorical power of Plato's *Gorgias*, therefore, is that it persuades the reader that the objective referent of *rhetorike* has been around for some time. The original appearance of the noun *rhetorike*, in effect, *created* the perceived correspondence between word and thing, thereby presenting them both as already given and in place. Nouns give one the impression of something stable, even permanent and immutable, or at least beyond the immediate limits of subjectivity. Accordingly, Plato's *Gorgias* could be read (as it has been by many) as espousing timeless truths about the nature of Rhetoric.[20]

Prior to Plato, intellectual discussions on speech focused on examples of oratory or pedagogy and did not go far into the abstract realm of theory. There was no cultural or conceptual room for theory prior to Plato; the level for intellectual specification simply did not exist. With Plato, theory (both rhetorical and otherwise) comes into the world.

Theory is a natural extension of Plato's binary between Reality and Appearance. Theory, at least as it is traditionally understood, is a way of constructing an edifice of knowledge. Rhetorical theory, then, is a way of describing what rhetoric *is*. Theory helps us to separate the essential from the inconsequential. Theory, in short, is a way of describing the world, with the aim of gradually increasing one's "accuracy." Thus, within the notion of theory itself we see a tension between a rhetorical epistemology and a Platonic-informed ontology. This view of theory helps us to understand that the Sophists were not discussing "rhetoric," for a theory of "sophistic rhetoric" would be as much an oxymoron as it would be anachronistic. Any theory of rhetoric would be a limitation on the claims we can make about the strength of a rhetorical epistemology (so, in a sense, *any* "theory" of rhetoric would be an oxymoron, not just so-called sophistic rhetoric). This is another sense in which language comes to use us as much as we come to use language. The way out of this bind is to take a non-Platonic perspective on the word "theory." In our rhetorical sense, theory is a rationale for seeing, not a description of what we see.

The above helps to explain, in part, the hostility that Plato directed toward the Sophists. What they taught did not meet the test of rigor, which is an important part of the credibility of any theory in a Platonic sense, and, in effect, it was non-sense. More specifically, it was the *wrong* sense. It was emotion and not Reason that guided the oratory taught by the Sophists, and it was emotion and not Reason that guided the politics of the democratic state, which was one important forum for rhetorical discourse. The emotional foundation of non-Platonic discourse is what upsets Plato so much; at the emotional level, people are less likely to obey the rule of the Philosopher-King.

By introducing "theory" to the Western mind, Plato introduces a clear division between epistemological and ontological perspectives on the "nature" of knowledge, and he clearly associates knowledge production with politics. He does this in an interesting way, illustrating the tactic of "dissociation." He takes the word "*logos*," which had been operationalized as "reasoned speech," and declares that some reasoned speech is True and some reasoned speech is False. The True reasoned speech was "philosophy," according to Plato, and the False was "rhetoric." As a way to illustrate the problems he felt existed with rhetoric, Plato takes the most prominent Sophists of his day and proceeds to recast their personae in his light.

Plato defines rhetoric as the false art of thinking, represented by his characterizations of the Sophists. His reason for doing this is to discourage the educational epistemology of the Sophists and to undermine the moral sanction of the Athenian government that was propped up, in part, by this way of thinking. In this sense, Plato's dialogues (more specifically, his theories of knowledge) are reactionary documents. With them, Plato is trying to give an intellectual sanction for the divine monarchies that were only so recently overthrown. His foil for his defense of Monarchy is the incipient rhetorical epistemology of the Sophists, what Plato codifies linguistically as *rhetorike*, the art of the rhetor. In attacking the Sophists, Plato attacks rhetoric, thus giving a moral substance to his notion of philosophy. What we learn from this example is that theory is never neutral. Theory itself is a form of rhetorical action, a way of exerting one's political preference for the way the world ought to be.

Richard Weaver and Plato's Objections to the Sophists

As mentioned above, Plato's objections to the Sophists involved his way of attacking both a rhetorical epistemology as well as what we would consider today to be a more or less "liberal" politics. While to some degree it is not accurate to import our modern political terminology to describe the political environment of Ancient Athens, there is a very broad sense in which the categories fit. Belief in eternal Truths, forms, hierarchies of authority, and social "place" are all generally associated with conservative political philosophies. This is true in Plato, and it is true within the conservative movement today. For example, much modern conservatism in the United States acts upon the sanctity of these principles (and much of it tends to be religiously oriented). Richard Weaver, considered by many to be an important founding thinker of modern conservatism in the U.S., was overtly committed to Platonic ideals and used them to justify his political commitments. His description of society's "nature" and his antagonistic position toward "revolutionary" ideas are informative of the attitudes of our contemporary politicians. As Weaver explains: "Rational society is a mirror of the logos, and this means that it has a formal structure which enables apprehension. The preservation of society is therefore directly linked with the recovery of true knowledge. . . . If society is something which can be understood, it must have structure; if it has structure, it must have hierarchy; against this metaphysical truth the declamations of the Jacobins break in vain."[21]

Notice that Weaver engages in a rhetorical strategy that parallels Plato and much modern political discourse. For him, there are two types of society, the "rational" and the "irrational." This dissociation, a form of Plato's split between Truth and Appearance, is already communicating certain assumptions about how good a *particular* society is. Weaver would not bother to write anything at all if he was convinced that he lived in what he considers to be a "rational" society. Similarly, Plato would have never felt the need to differentiate between Truth and Appearance if he felt that people were living in Truth. For people who wholly live *within* Truth, there is no falsity. A person cannot experience "falsity," only the absence of Truth. If a person exists *within* a state of Truth, then it stands to reason that that Truth is all he/she knows, it is the sum total of his/her awareness. Seen from another perspective, Truth can only make sense in relationship to error. As a concept, Truth only makes sense to people who can perceive error (in effect, non-Truth). To talk about Truth, therefore, a person has to be outside of it, looking in. This is why Plato's description of Truth is dependent upon his idea of Truth's formal characteristics. Truth exists in relationship to its form. Such forms are perfect representations. By definition, even for Plato, we can never achieve them. By definition, from a wider Christian perspective, we exist outside of Eden; we live in a condition that exists after the Fall (in whatever metaphorical sense we take that to mean). Still, common experience illustrates we all have our place inside the hierarchy, and that means that some of us are better able to perceive Truth. Hence the need to struggle. Hence the need for politics. Hence the need for *theory*. Hence the need for Plato's idea of monarchy.

For Weaver, there is a standard of Truth, and that is the logos. But logos can be True or False, according to Plato. The logos that Weaver discusses is the philosophical logos, not the rhetorical logos (although Weaver was himself a rhetorician). While Weaver was a rhetorician, he did believe that some arguments were metaphysically better than others.[22] He uses the metaphor of the mirror in the above passage. Truth becomes mirrored in rationality; political truth is deduced by reason from hierarchical principles. Society, in other words, has a correct structure, one that can be logically deduced from first principles. Weaver discusses a "formal structure" which constitutes a "natural" arrangement. Our "apprehension" is determined by that structure and by how well we can study it and learn it. Thus, humans do not invent society, imply Weaver and Plato, they perceive their proper place within it. Our institutions, then, our government, our police, our schools must be designed to reflect its essences.

Weaver goes on to link the future of society with our understanding of these first principles and with our ability to adapt ourselves to their structures. Society that breaks from this True knowledge is doomed to destruction (as the allegory of Sodom and Gamora is utilized in Christian pedagogy). But what is this True knowledge? Knowledge is of structure, but, as Weaver makes clear, structure is dependent upon hierarchy. Hierarchy, for Weaver, is the ultimate standard of the Good. However, hierarchy can be viewed in a radically different way. Hierarchy is another form of inequity. Systemic inequity is hierarchy. Hierarchy is authority divorced from reasonability. It is authority for its own sake. Now, hierarchy may have practical functions, but that is not to say that it has metaphysical significance. Weaver, however, holds hierarchy as evidence against the French revolutionaries, and against revolutionaries in general. Hierarchy is the standard by which we can know and live peacefully in the world. Revolution, that terrible thing, is, after all, the attempt to do away with hierarchy. Certain forms of socialism, anarchism for example, recognize this anti-hierarchical position as the decisive principle behind all revolutionary theory.[23]

Weaver's Platonic position can be contrasted to that of the Sophists, generally, and to a rhetorical epistemology, particularly. Basically, Weaver, like Plato, would have many objections to the Sophists (and thus to modern day liberals or people farther to the Left). They would feel that the Sophists had disregard for Truth and were completely ignorant of the basic structure of reality. Likewise, any counter-conservative position today would be based upon a subjective understanding of Truth, one that saw contemporary hierarchies as fundamentally unjust. Such a position rejects the doctrine of forms, and thus rejects the notion that some people can have a better perception of how nature structures society. Rather, people on the Left tend to argue that society should best be structured so that it meets the needs of as many humans as possible, and not so that fits a system that denies the contingency of human community. Conservatives like to imagine that human needs do not change, while contrary positions argue that human "nature" is ever changing, and that society must be suited to keep definitions as flexible as possible. Flexible definitions of human nature, however, are not encouraged by our government; they do not lead to stable investment opportunities, particularly in the Third World, and they tend to give people democratic control over their lives. But since Truth is hierarchical, according to the conservatives, that necessarily means that some people are better at perceiving Truth than others, and democracy simply lets the "worst" perception win out over the "better" (in effect, their specific critique of rhetoric).

Rhetoric, for Plato, and for conservatives generally, is not concerned with the True and the Just, but with the appearance of each. This is the main crux of Plato's polemic against the Sophists. Rhetoric, we will see, is positioned by Plato as a false wisdom, a flattery: it is the knack for making the lesser appear the greater. In more graphic terms, a rhetorical epistemology, one that empowers people to be the masters of their own fate, is the equivalent of rape. It quite literally involves the rape of nature (although not in terms of the Leftist critique of capitalism). Rhetoric, like sexual deviancy, is a perversion of human "nature." Similar to homosexuality and masturbation, it corrupts God's commandment to procreate by "mistaking" one body part for another.[24] For Plato and for many conservatives like Weaver, human action that is not molded on the "nature" of the world leads to dis-ease. Many Christians like to argue that people are dis-eased (not at ease) when they do not walk in the spirit of God. Actual medical disease does stem from similar conditions. Disease occurs in the human body when something is out of order, when it is not working correctly. Poor diet, lack of exercise, smoking, and alcohol all lead to disease because they interfere with an individual's ability to maximize his or her health—specifically, the person is not molding his/her actions to match the "truth" of the human body. The person is living "incorrectly" in terms of the physiological needs of the body.

Similarly, the rhetor flatters his/her victims, and later debases them. Rhetoric is like sugar or cigarette advertisements: it invites disease in the social and human bodies by getting people to act out of accordance with "nature." In a sense, rhetoric is a violation of the public trust (not a bad argument against the phenomenon of advertising). For Plato, anything that leads people astray of the True path creates disharmony in the hierarchy of order that he establishes when he creates the binary between True and False knowledge. The goal of philosophy is to teach wisdom. The wise person is able to perceive the hierarchy of nature and to order the political world in such a way as to bring people into accordance with God's (or Nature's) master plan. All other teaching is wrong and dishonest. For Plato, the Sophists represented such teaching. In modern times, the political Left is similarly positioned by conservatives. As Donald L. Clark notes, "To Plato the sophists were dishonest in their pretensions to wisdom and their claim that they could teach wisdom."[25] Wisdom for contemporary conservatives is wrapped up in the ideology of capitalism and the "free" market. All claims to the contrary are considered "emotional," "misguided," or even "wrong," as the capitalist hierarchy is equated with God and other eternal forms.

Because the Sophists taught a relative truth with human consciousness being the center of judgment, rhetoric's purpose was to articulate the reality that served human and, from Plato's point of view, corruptible purposes. Truth, under a rhetorical epistemology, is socially defined and subject to the needs of historical contingencies. This position clashed fundamentally with the Platonic position which held that Truth was only available to those philosophers who engaged in dialectic, an intellectual process designed to help the soul remember the Truth already ascertained during the process of death and reincarnation. Plato's belief in ahistorical Truth forces him to believe in reincarnation. It is not unreasonable for Plato to conclude that if the Trueness of a thing corresponds to its permanence, then value of the human is measured by its relationship to that permanence.

Furthermore, if Plato's world view is such that he recognizes a difference between the world people perceive (illusion) and the world as it actually exists (Truth), what else can we expect from him? Metaphysics, by definition, is the study of things that are beyond the normal senses. Plato's idea is no different than the idea central to all religions, and to a conservative ideology. Some things are right because we *know* them to be right, and we know them to be right because people we respect, people better than ourselves, are able to enlighten us with their experience. This is an important role that the Priest and the Politician play in our society. Authority, then, is an important hallmark of a conservative, anti-rhetorical ideology. The more something is an authority, the more it can perceive something that the rest of us cannot, and the more we must listen to it. The Sophists, if they were nothing else, were anti-authority. The very fact that they argued for a plurality of positions is, in itself, an affront to authority (even if it does not mean that they were all democrats in any meaningful sense).

Plato's Philosophical Views

Now that we have seen the relationship between philosophy and rhetoric according to Plato, and have gained a larger sense of the political economy of Plato's theorizing, I want, in this section, to fill in some of the details regarding Plato's philosophical views. After I do so, I can specifically discuss Plato's theory of rhetoric.

I mentioned above that Plato believed in reincarnation and I pointed out that such a belief was consistent with Plato's commitment to ahistorical Truth and to his hierarchy of values. If people are to be *unequal* in this life time, there has to be a reason for it, some structural justification that will lead people to believe that they are, in fact, unequal. The Hindus have such a philosophy that they use to justify their rigid class structure (the mass of "untouchables" in India are lorded over by an elite Brahman class). This class structure is so ingrained in Indian society that even Mahatma Gandhi was unable (or unwilling) to alter it. The Hindus believe that social inequity corresponds to spiritual justice. Certain Christian sects share a similar philosophy (Calvinism and Protestantism, for example). They believe that material prosperity corresponds to the level of one's standing in God's grace.

Finally, the United States promotes a certain version of this myth in its propaganda. We are God's most blessed nation for we have the wealth and the power that the almighty has conferred upon us (or something to that effect). *We are the chosen people,* our politicians have been telling us since the foundations of our Republic. The "New World" was to be the "new" Jerusalem, in the foundation myths of this nation. The fact that the rich are rich and the poor are poor is God's design, not the intentional outcomes of a human designed political and economic system. There will be winners and losers, that is the "nature" of things, we are told, and thus the poor cannot be helped, *they will always be with us.* To help them is at best foolhardy, for it wastes meager resources and "impoverishes" the wealthy. At worst, it is a crime against "nature" to help those whom God has cast His displeasure upon. Nature has to be protected from human moral transgression (but not from our physical transgression), and that is why Plato was careful to plan for a large police force in his *Republic,* to make sure that the masses of people did what the authorities thought was best for them. The health of any social community depends upon the proper maintenance of the hierarchy. This brings us to another of Plato's arguments against democracy. All people are *not* born equal, according to Plato. To treat people as if they were equal would be to violate nature's "order." People are born with a certain amount of status or worth, corresponding to the amount of "knowledge" they have. For Plato, this knowledge is dependent upon previous lives and one's ability to learn from the experience of the birth/death process. The more one learns, the more one will be able to act morally (have the "right" political ideas, according to the people who hold power). In other words, we are all responsible for our life conditions—we simply need to pay more attention to the way things "are" and to adjust our lives accordingly. Society has no responsibility for how we turn out, besides providing for the "correct" education. Our failure as individuals only proves that we were unworthy of help in the first place. Under Plato's system, we are measured by an internal standard that pre-determines our social existence. The government, once it sets up its "True" and "Just" system (as the U.S. government purports to have done), does not have to be responsible for people; "nature" takes care of the details. This is the "trickle down" theory of responsibility: if the government takes care of the privileged, and if the privileged act according to "nature," then they will occupy a moral position. This will have a reverberation throughout the social community so that ultimately everyone benefits from the "ideal" order. People who for some corruptible reasons fail to appreciate their place in the hierarchy are labeled "criminals" and are simply removed from society. Seen in this way, any theory of reincarnation is very much a political position, accentuating one important intersection between religion, capitalism, and government.

Basic to Plato's theory of reincarnation is a concept known as the transmigration of souls. Plato believed that reality was broken up into two worlds, one of the here-and-now, which, since Kant, has been known as the "phenomenal" world, and a world beyond the physical realm, which is known as the "noumenal" world. Truth was considered by Plato to be the absolute knowledge of an object's essence as it existed in the noumenal world. Truth, as found in the noumenal world, served as the archetype for the illusions of the phenomenal world. These are the forms, the structure behind everything that exists in the world. Objects in the noumenal world existed in their ideal state of perfection. As noted above, his doctrine of forms is the metaphysical underpinning of Plato's philosophical system and substantiates his distinction between Truth and Appearance.

What humans find in the phenomenal world are mere approximations of these perfect entities. In effect, what humans have to work with are imperfect copies of the noumenal archetypes. This automatically puts all of us at a disadvantage, makes us like sheep in need of a leader. Anyone who can point out to the rest of us the True "nature" of the world, naturally is in the position to be our leader. Fortunately for that person, no matter who it is (Plato, Hitler, Kennedy, etc.), there are ways of getting an edge up on other people, of creating the appearance of being wiser than the rest of us. The first is to be born rich. Kennedy had that advantage, and perhaps Plato did as well, as he was a wealthy individual. Hitler, however, did not have that advantage, and thus had to use the second way. The second way, as mentioned earlier, is to be aware of one's own inner light, one's self-evident appreciation of Reality. This was Hitler's claim. He "saw" something that the rest of us did not see, a Truth more real than the "illusions" that were bringing disorder to Germany. In the "brightness" of that greater glory, Hitler built for himself a nation.

One explanation for the strength of Nazi Germany, at least from the point of view of the Nazis, was that Hitler had "awakened" the German people to act morally. While the rest of the world may reasonably condemn Nazi "morality," we must keep in mind that in the reality that Hitler was constructing, a different sort of moral relations existed, just as a different set of moral relations exist between the United States of 1998 and the United States of 1798, when it was considered "just" to return the property of one man's runaway slave (and "just" to exterminate the Native Americans). In both cases, a moral universe was constructed, and to the extent that both German and U.S. societies were perceived as being "strong" at these times, there was a tendency for people to think that they were getting things "right." The West, after all, was "won," and Germany *did* manage to lift itself by its bootstraps and assert itself politically and militarily in the world.

As these instances show, it is up to individual people to tell us what is just. Hitler tried to do that, but so did Dr. Martin Luther King, Jr. Unlike Hitler's, King's vision was and continues to be extremely reasonable. Still, to believe that King had the last word on "justice," no matter how appealing his conceptualization, would be to limit our moral growth for the future. It would keep us squarely in Plato's moral universe. For instance, the United States tends to cherish the image of King that we find standing at the foot of the Lincoln Memorial in Washington D.C. in 1963 (although we were not so excited about him then). We hold that instance and that image as the model of "justice." But justice, ethics and morality are not stagnant like Plato suggests, and that is why we have to reject his vocabulary. King, himself, soon developed beyond his "limited" morality that he expressed in Washington. By the time he was assassinated in 1968, he envisioned the struggle for African-American civil rights within the larger context of the global Third World struggle against imperialism and poverty. In a series of talks he gave over Canadian radio in November and December of 1967, only five months before his death, King made overt this linkage:

> I have said that the problem, the crisis we face, is international in scope. In fact, it is inseparable from an international emergency which involves the poor, the dispossessed, and the exploited of the whole world. . . . It is clear to me that the next stage of the movement is to become international. . . . We in the West must bear in mind that the poor countries are poor primarily because we have exploited them through political or economic colonialism. Americans in particular must help their nation repent of her modern economic imperialism.[26]

Having killed the messenger, we conveniently ignore his message, focusing our understanding in limited, although still vastly progressive ways (compared to how things were before).

Michael Eric Dyson extends this critical theme of King and society in his work. He explains that "King's legacy is viewed as most useful when promoting an unalloyed optimism about the possibilities of American social transformation, which peaked during his 'I Have a Dream' speech."[27] Dyson goes on to explain, as I did above, that such view is superficial and ignores the mature vision of King that proves to be a more substantial critique of American society. "Corporation-sponsored commercials that celebrate King's memory—most notably, television spots by McDonald's and Coca-Cola aimed at connecting their products to King's legacy—reveal a truncated understanding of King's meaning and value to American democracy."[28] This is my point exactly with regard to the hoopla and panegyrics of the Olympics, and the evocation of King's image in that context. The cooptation of radical thought serves the function of neutralizing its more threatening characteristics. This is one reason why imagery (its structure of narrativity) is infused with a political economy.[29]

Before rejecting Plato's "inner light of Reason," we need to look more specifically at how it worked for Plato. As mentioned, souls transmigrate. This transmigration gives us direct access to the world of forms (the noumenal plane). Once in the noumenal world, the soul is able to see Truth and understand the sum total of all there is to comprehend. Having partaken of this knowledge, the soul then can proceed to travel back to the phenomenal world. The problem, however, is that on returning to the phenomenal world the soul must first drink from what Plato called the river of forgetfulness. Thus, the soul is born to the phenomenal world in a state of ignorance and is susceptible to the allure of illusions. Depending upon the strength of the particular soul, this amnesia will be experienced in different degrees. The point of Platonic education is to find people with the potential for working through their amnesia and to help them. Those weaker souls, helplessly lost in forgetfulness, simply need to be tended so that they do not hurt themselves or the social body (the "management" principle of governance).

Dialectic comes in as the method that Plato utilizes for remembering the soul's experience in the noumenal world. It is Plato's tonic against moral and political amnesia. The purpose of dialectic is to aid in recovering the Truth that the soul was once exposed to but has forgotten. Dialectic is not used to discover Truth, but to remember what one has known, to become aware again of knowledge. Plato's point is that Truth is something independent of human beings. We can never discover it, as that assigns too much agency to the human mind. We simply have to acknowledge it, appreciate it, and let it guide our lives. Later, philosophy and science develop into having a more central goal of "discovery." Nevertheless, in both cases, the assumption is that the pursuit of knowledge is the pursuit of something non-human that can serve as a warrant or an authority by which we can ground belief. Ideas come first, then comes the appreciation of the wise. Indeed, "authority" is dependent upon such appreciation or "apprehension" (to use Weaver's term). Because of these traits, Plato affectionately refers to dialectic as "the midwife art" because it assists in the rebirth of ideas.

Plato's strategy of dialectic involves the collection of material to account for every possible instance that a topic occurs, the definition of the topic being discussed, and the division of a topic into its infinite points and sub-points. This is otherwise known as the "Socratic Method." Murphy notes that Plato uses this questioning to determine the following ends:

1. definition of key terms
2. the statement of propositions or definitive declarative statements about the subject
3. the identification of possible contradictions
4. the application of ideas[30]

The motivation behind this process is the duty that the knowing have to help the unknowing come into the known. As much as I have been harping on Plato, I should point out that he did have an intense civic consciousness (as did Hitler). Similar to Christianity, Plato's and Hitler's ideologies demanded attention from other people. Each demands total acceptance by as many people as possible. Christians, Platonists, and Nazis all have at least one thing in common: they all maintain that their beliefs have an *a priori* presence in the world and that everyone else must accept that fact, through persuasion or force. Just as Christians have the obligation to share the "good news" whether anyone else wants to hear it or not, and just as the Nazis felt obligated to "share" their political reality with the greater part of Europe and Northern Africa, Plato felt that it was the moral duty for the wise person to help those he could to grow morally. Dialectic, and not rhetoric, was the superior method for this task because it ensured moral growth—by definition, at least one participant in the conversation has been exposed to Knowledge. His/her task is to raise the other out of ignorance. Rhetoric fails in this task since the rhetorician is, by Plato's definition, ignorant of Knowledge and is simply espousing to a mob what it wants to hear. Dialectic leads to understanding, and rhetoric leads to confusion.

The biases behind Plato's conception of dialectic and rhetoric illuminate his political views. If rhetoric is false knowledge produced for the vanity of an audience, then what hope is there for the democratic process? In Plato's view, none at all. He felt that human beings, when left to their own devices, would inherently act unwisely. Consequently, in sharp contrast to a democratic system, Plato supported a utopian aristocracy led by philosopher kings. His idea was that one who is fit to rule should rule and that a philosopher was the only one who had the wisdom to know whether or not he was fit to rule.

Plato's Gorgias

Now that we have a sense of Plato's ideas in terms of their larger political and social implications, we can turn to a specific discussion of Plato's views on rhetoric. Plato discusses his theory of rhetoric primarily in two dialogues, the *Gorgias* and the *Phaedrus*. In both dialogues, as throughout his writing generally, Plato speaks through the voice of Socrates. Thus, in the analysis to follow, the two names will be used interchangeably to designate Plato's ideas. Also, keep in mind that Plato is lampooning his political and educational rivals, and that their actual positions are not being fairly represented.

In the *Gorgias*, written early in his career, Plato has Socrates ask Gorgias to define his occupation. The reply is that Gorgias is a teacher of rhetoric. In the process of answering Socrates, Gorgias' student Polus interferes with the dialogue and shows himself to be foolish as he attempts to answer questions for his master, thus slighting Gorgias' ability to instruct and thereby casting doubt on his character and his claim to teach virtue through rhetoric. With the limitations of Gorgias' teaching fully accentuated in his student, Gorgias is finally permitted to step in and boldly proclaim that rhetoric is the art of persuasion and that the subject matter is "the greatest of human concerns . . . and the best."[31] Gorgias comes to this grandiose conclusion via the following line of argument: power is the supreme good, and rhetoric is the supreme tool in achieving power; therefore, rhetoric is the supreme art. With this reasoning, Gorgias concludes: "Since it is perfectly true that by virtue of this power you will have at your beck and call the physician and the trainer, that business man of yours will turn out to be making money for somebody else! Not for himself will he make it, but for you who have the power to speak and persuade the vast majority."[32]

Such argument is pure nonsense, yet its obvious transparency was overlooked for centuries by scholars eager to jump on the anti-rhetoric bandwagon. As illustrated in the discussion of Gorgias in chapter two, such argument does not flow from his composition principles as we know them. Nevertheless, this is the view of the Sophists that Plato wants to convey to posterity. It is also convenient for Plato because it sets up his next argument.

Plato has Socrates take issue with Gorgias' line of reasoning and replies that persuasion is little more than the ability to induce belief (*doxa*) at the expense of knowledge (*episteme*). Here we find a clear articulation of Plato's important binary between the Real and the Apparent. "Logos" as a concept has now been replaced by at least two more specific concepts: *episteme* and *doxa*. The first is the end of philosophy and the second is the end of rhetoric. Notice also how the moral injunction has been smuggled in—if knowledge exists, why on Earth would anyone want to have anything to do with belief? Why waste time with rhetoric when one can have a more substantial knowledge? Plato makes it clear that knowledge and belief are not anywhere close to being the same thing, and that they often conflict with each other. Belief is nothing more than opinion, and human opinion is unreliable at best, thought Plato. F.M. Cornford elaborates on Plato's sentiment: "The states of mind differ in that knowledge is *infallible*, whereas opinion may be true or false. It is inferred that the objects of knowledge must be completely *real* and unchanging, while the objects of opinion are not wholly real and are mutable."[33]

Socrates claims that rhetoric, in producing persuasion, is only creating belief in an audience and procures only the appearance of knowledge. Rhetoric cannot be an art because apparent knowledge is not True knowledge. A rhetorician cannot be a better doctor than a doctor, as Gorgias absurdly is made to claim. Rhetoric, therefore, can only be a knack for creating belief; it may sweeten or embitter, but it is not the meal itself. Consequently, Socrates likens rhetoric to cooking or cookery. Both rhetoric and cooking, concludes Socrates, merely flatter the physical body without offering substantive knowledge. Socrates extends the analogy between rhetoric and the arts of the body. Cooking is a false art while medicine is a real art. Cosmetics is a false art while gymnastics is a real art. Likewise, sophistic and rhetoric are false arts of the soul while philosophy and dialectic are real arts of the soul. Socrates says, "as make-up is to gymnastics, so is sophistic to legislation; as is cookery to medicine, so is rhetoric to justice."[34] Notice how Plato's analogy challenges his rival, Isocrates, who claimed that training in speech is to the mind as exercise is to the body.

Sophistic and rhetoric only imitate Truth rather than discuss the Truth. Rhetoric only pretends to be philosophy. Rhetoric instills belief at the expense of Truth for the benefit of the mob. Socrates concludes, "Now you have heard what I say rhetoric is: the counterpart of cookery in the soul, as cookery is its counterpart in the body."[35] Furthermore, the real crux of Plato's condemnation of democracy in general and the Sophists in particular, is that rhetoric is more extreme than cosmetics and cookery in terms of consequence. A bad cook only makes his master ill, and bad cosmetics can only hurt the one who fools him or herself by appearance. Plato thought that rhetoric, in the hands of a democracy, is dangerous and leads to poor government, war, and dis-ease (it leads to a social order that is out of balance).

Plato's Phaedrus

As seen in the *Gorgias*, Plato, early in his career, had no tolerance for rhetoric. Over time, however, it may appear that Plato changed slightly in his opinion of rhetoric. For instance, one problem that Plato may have encountered in his later years is that without some kind of communicative art it was difficult for the philosopher ruler he envisioned to communicate Truth to large numbers of people. Whatever the reason, in the *Phaedrus*, Plato's later dialogue, the reader is exposed to a different attitude toward rhetoric. This view is more tolerant of rhetoric, but suggests that rhetoric is an unattainable art, one that resembles modern practices of state propaganda.

The *Phaedrus* itself contains three speeches. All three speeches concern the topic of love. The thesis of the first is that it is better to make love to a non-lover than to a real lover. Socrates disagrees with the substance of that speech and offers a speech of his own in which he defines love. Socrates is then ashamed for having given a better speech than the first on a shameful subject-matter and feels that he has to redeem himself by giving yet another speech. The third speech, the main substance of the dialogue, explores the nature of love in relation to the soul. Oscar Brownstein explains that love and the lover "serve as analogues for another object of desire—knowledge of truth—and for the means of attaining and transmitting it."[36] Consequently, Socrates builds the case for dialectic and philosophy, and then proceeds to discuss the character of rhetoric, the definition of rhetoric, and the requirements of a noumenally correct rhetoric. In contrast, Brownstein notes, the corrupt rhetoric is "characterized by a false love, truly a nonlove, which is selfish whether it is passionless or lustful."[37] It is, in the sense discussed earlier, a form of rape, a violation and defilement of the social body.

In the dialogue Plato defines rhetoric as an art, reversing his earlier decision that rhetoric is not an art, and suggests that rhetoric has the power to lead the soul in both trivial and important matters. Plato offers the following definition of rhetoric: "Is it not true, then, that rhetoric, taken as a whole, is an art of influencing the soul through words, not merely in the law courts and all other public meeting places, but in private gatherings also? Is it not the same when concerned with small as with great matters and, to put the matter in the right light, is it to be esteemed no more when involved with important affairs than it is when occupied with the trivial?"[38]

This is the first formal definition of rhetoric that we have. It is "an art of influencing the soul through words." For someone who hates rhetoric, this is not a bad definition, although it is not very useful. For example, could the above definition not be applicable to dialectic? Indeed, as Plato acknowledges, rhetoric is only *one* of the arts of influencing the soul, and perhaps it is the weakest and most corrupt of them all.

Plato expands this definition when he has Socrates outline his requirements for a True rhetoric. The first requirement for a rhetoric that fits in the Platonic world view is that the rhetor must know Truth. A speaker, in order to be Truthful must first engage in dialectic to gain a perspective on Truth before he or she can begin to formulate a line of argument. In a sense, rhetoric is subservient to dialectic. Rhetoric is not a way of know-ing, but a way of transmitting knowledge that is uncovered or known by other means. Next, the speaker is obligated to have a working knowledge of the nature and types of men's souls. What Plato means by this is not much different than what modern theorists mean by "audience analysis" and "audience adaptation." Plato, however, offers a sinister twist to this knowledge. For him, the reason to understand the "nature" and "types" of peoples' souls is so that the speaker can control them more easily. The next thing Socrates says is that the speaker must know the various types of speeches and the relationship between the types of speeches and the nature of men's souls. Finally, the speaker must know the relationship of a situation to the type of a speech:

> A man must first know the truth about every single subject on which he speaks or writes. He must be able to define each in terms of a universal class that stands by itself. When he has successively defined his subjects according to their specific classes, he must know how to continue the division until he reaches the point of indivisibility. He must make the same sort of distinction with reference to the nature of the soul. He must then discover the kind of speech that matches each type of nature. When that is accomplished, he must arrange and adorn each speech in such a way as to present complicated and unstable souls with complex speeches, speeches exactly attuned to every changing mood of the complicated soul—while the simple soul must be pre-sented with simple speech. Not until a man acquires this capacity will it be possible to produce speech in a scientific way, in so far as its nature permits such treatment, either for purposes of instruction or of persuasion.[39]

Plato's definition raises important questions about rhetoric. For exam-ple, is rhetoric an art that can meet the expectations of Plato? Are Plato's conditions for rhetoric just a roundabout way of saying that rhetoric, to be good, must be philosophy? On the other hand, now Plato's potential philosopher-king has the tool of rhetoric available to him to help run the affairs of the State. We have to ask, however, is this an advantage? If rhetoric is stripped of its epistemic and reality-questioning characteris-tics, what good is it? Do we need such an eloquent description of propa-ganda? Do we need to justify propaganda by calling it rhetoric?

In terms of the history of ideas, can we draw the conclusion that Plato grew more tolerant in age with regard to his view of rhetoric? I think not. A rhetorical epistemology, as mentioned above, is the most formidable challenge to a Platonic position, and Plato responded to its implicit threat with a full fledged attack. Intuitively or consciously, Plato feared rhetoric, as politicians and tyrants after him did, even though he had to use rhetoric, as do tyrants, in order to curtail its influence. Some scholars, however, disagree with this interpretation of Plato's view of rhetoric. Ed-

win Black, for example, concludes his influential study of Plato by arguing that "Plato did not despise rhetoric, but only the excesses of the
Sophists."[40] In justifying his position, Black implicitly endorses Plato's
politics and argues that for some of rhetoric's propagandistic and "educational" functions, "no apologies need be offered."[41]

Indeed, Black rejects the "clamorous spirit of fanaticism at large in the
world, sustained by rhetorical discourse."[42] In doing this, Black is rejecting the epistemic function of rhetoric that Plato rejects. Writing as he did
in 1958, Black can only be referring to Communism, although he never
mentions the word. Thus Black seems to imply that rhetoric is okay if it is
being used in the service of the State, but it is not good when it is being
used to question those reifications. He even leaves us with this final comment, "[W]e may begin to suspect that, after all, Plato was even wiser
than we had thought."[43] Maybe one day some enterprising young
scholar, as Black was in 1958, will say the same thing about Hitler. After
all, Hitler was "right" about communism, and thus he could not have
been all that bad (only perhaps a little excessive to the Jews who might
not have been "all" communists).

If Plato is not reversing himself on the question of rhetoric, why does
he take the trouble to discuss it in the way he does in the *Phaedrus*?
Brownstein provides one possible answer to this question: "Perhaps
Plato's doctrine of Forms and his integrity have in a sense trapped him
into conceiving of a Form of Rhetoric, an ideal rhetoric of which the
rhetoric of the Sophists is a mere shadow; in any case its function here is
to demonstrate the practical impossibility of such an art."[44]

As Brownstein notes, the dialogue of the *Phaedrus* does little to alter
fundamentally the previously established relationship between philosophy and rhetoric. While rhetoric may abstractly be an art, it is in effect a
worthless method for communication in the everyday world. Plato is still
placing philosophy in a position primary to rhetoric, and he believes that
rhetoric is purely dependent upon philosophy. Rhetoric still is incapable
of finding Truth and only serves the purpose of communicating Truth
once it has already been established. What is historically important about
the *Phaedrus* is that Plato acknowledges the study of communication in
his conceptualization of philosophy, unlike that presented in the *Gorgias*
where rhetoric is completely severed from philosophy. Because of this, he
gives Aristotle the conceptual room he needed to compose his famous
work on rhetoric (discussed in chapter five).

Platonic Versus Rhetorical Analysis

To illustrate further the limitations of a Platonic/systemic perspective of
communication, let us turn to a contemporary example of oratory and

apply to it a Platonic analysis.[45] In his 1986 Libya speech, which was delivered immediately following the bombing of key targets in Libya, Ronald Reagan called the action "self-defense." As Reagan argued:

> [F]or us to ignore, by inaction, the slaughter of American civilians and American soldiers, whether in nightclubs or airline terminals, is simply not in the American tradition. When our citizens are abused or attacked anywhere in the world, on the direct orders of a hostile regime, we will respond, so long as I'm in this oval office. Self-defense is not only our right, it is our duty. It is the purpose behind the mission undertaken tonight—a mission fully consistent with Article 51 of the United Nations Charter.[46]

To a careless listener, this would appear to be significant justification in light of the named terrorist activities directed at Americans. In addition to self-defense, Reagan appeals to "tradition" and to "International Law." He also responds as if he were a philosopher-king, and not just the President of the United States. A president, after all, is no different than anyone else, and that is what distinguishes a representative democracy from a monarchy or an empire. Kings and Emperors lay claim to a divine sovereignty, which we assume implies some sort of a divine knowledge, or access to such knowledge. Presidents, however, are supposed to act on behalf of the people. That means that the voice should come from the people to the president, and not from the president down to the people. It is not the president who should order the attack, but the people of the United States, in the event that they feel threatened. Yet since the people felt no threat, it becomes the President's job to create the illusion of threat. America, after all, was not attacked at any time by "terrorists" (another name for the enemy's armed forces). People targeted for attack were American soldiers *in uniform* stationed overseas. The presence of these soldiers threatened military occupation, if it did not already constitute an act of military occupation.

In acting as Plato's philosopher-king, Reagan gives the U.S. people his definition of the event and encourages us to believe in this definition through the force of his authority. Being "in the know," Reagan comes across as being much smarter than we are; after all, Reagan can magically perceive all sorts of threats to the U.S. that the rest of us cannot. For example, Reagan can see the downfall of America in the tiny Island of Grenada and in weak, but proud, Nicaragua. He can also see that the rest of the world loves us, with the exception of a few criminals and communists (the same thing, according to this world view). Because such resistance to U.S. prerogatives is criminal and communist, and because criminals and communists hate America, anything we do to them is in "our" "defense." Reagan can see this, and this is perhaps why he is our leader, as he has access to a higher form of knowledge than the rest of us, people who cannot see the world as according to Reagan.

Because of his "superior" vision, Reagan justifies the bombing as self-defense. Reagan, however, is not being a very good Platonist, and even the most sympathetic of critics can find ground to challenge his characterization. To be a good Platonist, that is, to give some sort of intellectual credence to his weak and criminal position, Reagan would have to approach his speech from a clearer sense of definition. Reagan, for instance, does not give us a definition for "self-defense," he simply asserts that this action can be characterized this way. What we would expect from a more mature Reagan would be what constitutes a state of self-defense. For example, Reagan could have turned to the dictionary and defined self-defense as "the act of defending one's person when physically attacked, as by countering blows or overcoming an assailant."[47] For most people in this country and throughout the world, this would have been at least a reasonable starting place. According to Reagan, however, who did not define his terms, military action against the civilian population of another country constitutes self-defense in this instance. He argues, "We believe that this preemptive action against his terrorist installations will not only diminish Colonel Qaddafi's capacity to export terror—it will provide him with incentives and reasons to alter his criminal behavior."[48]

Based on a strictly Platonic position, Reagan's position constitutes an ontological fallacy. It is difficult to imagine Plato condoning this act. From a practical perspective, however, justification for the action depends upon the interpretation of the act—thus it is probably more worthwhile to talk about this act from the point of view of a rhetorical epistemology. Because Reagan defined what he intended to do as self-defense, then the action had its rationalization (even if it was a weak one). In fact, Reagan might have actually persuaded many people that what he did was "just." Reagan was certainly a popular president, even though he resided over an administration that had the most legal and ethical charges raised against it in U.S. history, and even though Reagan was personally responsible for the devastation of millions of lives among people living in Nicaragua, Grenada, and El Salvador. Rationalized or not, that hardly means that the American bombing of Libya was "just" in any philosophical or moral conception of the word.

A Platonic critic would not agree that Reagan's actions were done for the justification of self-defense, nor can we do so from a rhetorical position. Such a critic, in exploring the implications of the argument, would move beyond questioning "self-defense" and explore, by definition, "self," "defense," and "threat." For example, in what sense can Reagan translate a resistance to U.S. military might in foreign or occupied territories as an attack against the American people? In what sense can the

American people be identified with the interest of their corporate rulers? In what sense does the American notion of "self" extend beyond its borders? Similar questions can be raised regarding the bombing of the U.S. Marine base in Beirut in 1984 and the bombing of a similar base in Saudi Arabia in 1996. In what sense can these attacks be considered "terrorism?" Those, like Plato, who claim to "know" and associate that knowledge with American business interest, make precisely the claim that these acts constitute terrorism and thus justify "self-defense." The rest of us, however, should be more cautious. How many foreign countries maintain military bases on U.S. soil? Such a proposition is unthinkable. That being so, why is it "reasonable" to many that we have our troops stationed around the world? What function do these troops serve? Why has the U.S. not fought a war on its own soil since we last fought the British, and exterminated the Native Americans, and stole half of Mexico? What does that say about the "nature" of wars involving the United States? What does this say about our values and ideology? More importantly, why can't most people "see" this?

Reagan, for his part, might dismiss this analysis as philosophical or rhetorical meandering and could respond to this criticism by saying that the evocation of "self defense" in his speech was metaphorical rather than literal. Yes, a Reagan supporter could say, bombing Libya sent a message to Libya and perhaps other nations that the United States could be provoked, and perhaps the chances of future hostilities were less after the bombing. Such would be a rhetorical response, and one not altogether unreasonable if we could suspend or bracket our political values. But that is exactly the point—rhetorical arguments self-consciously demand that people participate from within their political values. This is exactly why Plato rejects rhetoric. The Platonic critic would base his or her evaluation of the U.S. bombing of Libya on the logical element of the argument and not on the metaphoric sense of Reagan's claims. This illustrates a weakness in Plato's theory in that, with strict definition, there is no room for a rhetorical perspective, no allowances for differing interpretations of the same event. The doctrine of forms denies dual perspectives and is functionally a philosophy of absolutes. Thus, we have to condemn Reagan both rhetorically *and* philosophically in this speech. Rhetorically, his speech does have some savvy, and Reagan's savvyness may explain, in part, his tremendous success. Unfortunately, one thing that rhetoric can do is to turn monsters into heroes. But that is an acceptable risk, since, by the same token, rhetoric has the power to turn heroes into monsters, an important critical edge. Plato, however, did not recognize the benefits of such critical perspective. He liked his monsters to be monsters and his heroes to be heroes, and never the two shall meet (except for on the battlefield, as in Homeric epics). In the every day world of human affairs, it has become increasingly difficult to tell monsters from heroes and that is why the critic's task has become particularly important.

Conclusion

Plato's discussion of rhetoric and the Sophists is largely composed of a polemic against the concept of *doxa*, or popular opinion. Central to the position of the Sophists is the premise that popular opinion constitutes the essence of democratic life and popular ways of knowing. This was certainly the stance held by many of the citizens of Athens. In this sense *doxa* is "a collective view which absorbs the opposed arguments and transcends them in a judgment accepted by all parties."[49] Such an intellectual position is a central part of a rhetorical epistemology.

With the precept of *doxa*, Plato worried that philosophy becomes impotent under the dominance of rhetoric and mismanaged by a mob sentimentality. Plato felt that philosophy, snubbed by popular opinion, led to the ineptitude of the Athenian government. Isocrates' concerns about the need for a larger political identity were not unfelt by other people, although Plato had a very different response to the exigency, as did Aristotle, who was forced to flee Athens after its defeat by Macedonia. (Aristotle had been purged from the city for his pro-Macedonian attitudes, having grown up as a physician's son in Phillip's court, and having tutored the young Alexander). Furthermore, Plato was convinced that the compromise of philosophy led to a corruption of society. In order to remedy societal ills, Plato proposed an "ideal" society devoid of popular opinion and under strict ideological control. His dialogue, the *Republic*, describes in great detail a society based on the assertion of a philosophical aristocracy.

It is debatable as to whether or not Plato's ideal world ever materialized; yet it is clear that Plato's rift between "philosophy" and "rhetoric" remains. His dialogue the *Gorgias* succeeds in separating philosophy from rhetoric and in positioning the two concepts against each other. While the *Phaedrus* presents a less hostile relationship between philosophy and rhetoric, it allows only Plato's concept of philosophy to have access to the Truth. Either way, rhetoric is severely crippled, and the epistemic nature of human communication is denied.

In short, a reading of Plato's two dialogues on rhetoric reveals an extreme view, but a view well worth noting. Plato's arguments against the rhetoricians expose the audacity of the Sophists and the fallibility of humanist reasoning. Furthermore, the susceptibility of human beings to be confused by false pretext is highlighted. Plato's *Gorgias* and *Phaedrus* warn of the limitations of the art of rhetoric. Plato's criticisms of rhetoric have a degree of time-worn relevance (perhaps what Professor Black was trying to communicate in the above quote). For example, the extremes of rhetoric and popular opinion created the Nazi state and countless other tyrannies. The existence of the United States alone stands as an indictment of rhetoric, as well as rhetoric's greatest challenge. For the U.S. exists through its reliance on propaganda, and that is the disgrace of rhetoric. By the same token, however, it means that the U.S. is extremely vulnerable. If we can defeat its propaganda with our rhetoric and show people how to see the monstrosity of their country, there is a real chance to change things. Whatever we choose to call it, language is important. It helps us to understand our world and to become active agents in its creation.

If Plato's view on rhetoric went uncontested, the rhetorical tradition would have suffered a premature demise from the uncompromising conditions of Plato's attacks. This was not to be the case. Plato's student, Aristotle, expanded the *Phaedrus* and made it applicable to the phenomenal world. W. Rhys Roberts substantiates this claim by remarking, "The points of contact between the *Rhetoric* and the *Phaedrus* are obvious and admitted. . . . "[50] Aristotle defends rhetoric against Plato's severe condemnation and legitimizes the art by detailing the parameters of its use.

Notes

1. Tran. H.E. Butler in 12 volumes, (Cambridge Harvard University Press: The Loeb Classical Library, 1976).

2. Or, as Burke points out, rhetoric can be used to take communities apart: "[O]ne need not scrutinize the concept of 'identification' very sharply to see, implied in it at every turn, its ironic counterpart: division," *A Rhetoric of Motives* (Berkeley: University of California Press, 1969), 23.

3. *The Order of Things* (New York: Vintage Books, 1970), 387.

4. *Conscientious Objections* (New York: Vintage Books, 1988), 25.

5. Social movement leadership in the twentieth century included the following college educated and/or professional people: Fidel Castro, Mahatma Gandhi, Che Guevara, Abimael Guzman, Martin Luther King, Jr., Huey P. Newton, Abbie Hoffman, Vladimir Ilyich Lenin, Subcommandante Marcos, Ho Che Minh, and Mao Tse Tung.

6. See James W. Chesebro, John F. Cragen, and Patricia McCullough, "The Small Group Technique of the Radical Revolutionary: A Synthetic Study of Consciousness Raising," *Speech Monographs* 40 (1973), 136–146.

7. See John Dewey, *The Quest For Certainty* (New York: G.P. Putnam's Sons, 1929), 129.

8. My discussion of "dissociation" has been scattered throughout this book. For a more specific discussion, see Edward Schiappa, "Dissociation in the Arguments of Rhetorical Theory," *Journal of the American Forensic Association* 22 (1985), 72–82.

9. "Thesis on Feurbach," in *The German Ideology* by Karl Marx and Frederick Engels (New York: International Publishers, 1970), 121.

10. Richard Rorty, *Philosophy and the Mirror of Nature* (Princeton: Princeton University Press, 1979).

11. For an expansion of this idea, see Douglas Kellner, *Critical Theory, Marxism, and Modernity* (Baltimore: The Johns Hopkins University Press, 1989).

12. Edward Schiappa, "Did Plato Coin Rhetorike?" *American Journal of Philology* 111 (1990), 460–73.

13. See Howard Zinn, "The Control of Information," in his *Declarations of Independence: Cross-Examining American Ideology* (New York: HarperPerennial, 1990), 210–220.

14. For a particularly good example of this, see Michael Parenti, "Sexism, Capitalism, Socialism," in his *Land of Idols: Political Mythology in America* (New York: St. Martin's Press, 1994), 148–153.

15. See Charles Derber, William A. Schwartz, and Yale Magrass, *Power in the Highest Degree: Professionals and the Rise of a New Mandarin Order* (New York: Oxford University Press, 1990).

16. This was the result of Saint Augustine's actions at the end of the Roman Empire. He was able to divest rhetoric of its epistemology and make it serve the Platonic function of communicating Truth. Augustine's argument for a Christian rhetoric appears in his *On Christian Doctrine* (New York: Macmillan Publishing Company, 1958).

17. For a discussion of so-called "intellectual property" and how it effects the developing Third World peoples, see Fidel Castro, "Communism Will be Abundance Without Egoism: On Intellectual Property," in *Communication and Class Struggle* v. 2. eds. Armand Mattelart and Seth Siegelaub (New York: International General, 1983), 288–295.

18. James Berlin, "Poststructuralism, Cultural Studies, and the Composition Classroom: Postmodern Theory in Practice," *Rhetoric Review* 11 (1992), 16–33.

19. *Protagoras and Logos: A Study in Greek Philosophy and Rhetoric* (Columbia: South Carolina University Press, 1991), 41.

20. "*Rhetorike*: What's In a Name? Toward a Revised History of Early Greek Rhetorical Theory," *Quarterly Journal of Speech* 78 (1992), 9.

21. *Ideas Have Consequences* (Chicago: University of Chicago Press, 1984), 35.

22. *The Ethics of Rhetoric* (Davis: Hermagoras Press, 1985).

23. Daniel Guerin, *Anarchism* (New York: Monthly Review Press, 1970).

24. It must be pointed out that this is more of a contemporary analysis, as the Ancient Greeks felt nothing wrong with homosexuality and probably did not have the taboo against masturbation that exists within the Christian paradigm.

25. *Rhetoric in Greco-Roman Education* (Morningside Heights: Columbia University Press, 1957), 6.

26. *The Trumpet of Conscience* (New York: Harper and Row, 1989), 62.

27. *Making Malcolm: The Myth and Meaning of Malcolm X* (New York: Oxford University Press, 1995), 27.

28. Ibid.

29. The rest of Dyson's analysis deserves mention in this note. He explains that much public commemoration of civil rights does not describe its opposition in detailed terms (perhaps because its ugliness is too close to home). "On such occasions, the uneven path to racial justice is often described in a manner that makes

progress appear an inevitable fact of our national life," (28). In other words, there is little mention of the efforts by everyday Americans and politicians to prevent social progress in the United States. Thus, such representations "deny King's radical challenge to narrow conceptions of American democracy," (28). In short, "not enough attention is given to the vicious cultural contexts that called forth such heroic action" (28). Dyson's critique continues on pages 99–106, where he clearly situates the politics of "representation" and of "civil rights" in their class orientations/limitations.

30. *A Synoptic Historic of Classical Rhetoric* (Davis: Hermagoras Press, 1983), 17.

31. *Gorgias.* Trans. W.C. Hembold and W.G. Rabinowitz (New York: Library of Liberal Arts, 1956), 9.

32. Ibid., 10.

33. *Plato's Theory of Knowledge* (London: Routledge & Kegal Paul, 1935), 29.

34. *Gorgias*, 26.

35. Ibid.

36. "Plato's *Phaedrus*: Dialectic as the Genuine Art of Speaking," *Quarterly Journal of Speech* 51 (1965), 392.

37. Ibid., 393.

38. *Phaedrus* trans. W.C. Hembold and W.G. Rabinowtiz (New York: Library of Liberal Arts, 1956), 48.

39. Ibid., 72.

40. "Plato's View of Rhetoric," *Quarterly Journal of Speech* 44 (1958), 374.

41. Ibid.

42. Ibid.

43. Ibid.

44. "Plato's *Phaedrus*," 397.

45. This analysis was suggested to me by Carole Blair, Lectures on the Origins of Rhetoric. Davis: Summer 1990.

46. "The Fight Against Terrorism," *Vital Speeches of the Day* (May 1, 1989), 419.

47. *Websters Encyclopedic Unabridged Dictionary of the English Language.* 1989 ed.

48. "Fight Against Terrorism," 419.

49. Brian Vickers, *In Defense of Rhetoric* (Oxford: Clarendon Press, 1988), 123.

50. *Greek Rhetoric and Literary Criticism* (New York: Longmans, Green, and Co., 1928), 20.

5

Aristotle

The previous chapter explored how rhetoric as an area of intellectual inquiry becomes conceptualized in the dialogues of Plato. Emphasized was the importance of naming as a political/rhetorical strategy in accentuating an area of "knowledge." With this discussion, this text explored the fundamental tensions that exist between what contemporary scholars recognize as a rhetorical epistemology, and what Plato was developing as a philosophical ontology. The tensions between ontological and epistemological perspectives of knowledge, and their relationship to communication and politics become, after Plato, generative of much cultural conflict and development. As a way to develop this point, the following two sections discuss some of these issues. The first section, "Foucault, Knowledge, and Language," offers a contemporary view of these problems that Plato posed, and the second further emphasizes the political salience of these issues. This leads back to the question of incommensurability, and segues into our discussion of Aristotle.

Foucault, Knowledge, and Language

In the twentieth century, Foucault's archeologies and genealogies trace the interconnections between knowledge and power, and highlight their intersections with communication. By tracing the origins of knowledge in specific cases—i.e. medicine, biology, history, sexuality, criminology, and education—Foucault illustrates how they are grounded in "statements." These statements are conceptualizations that have a bio-political significance. In Burkean terms, "statements" roughly correspond to "terministic screens" that direct sight. Yet, we do not just "see" with our eyes, we see with our total being. The bio-political significance of language involves the effect that thought (in terms of power) has on molding the human body in particular ways. For Foucault, as well as for Burke, "reality" is what things do to us. In the human world, what we take to be our "bodies" and our lives involve our subjectivities, and these are always molded by language. The "things" that are done to us, our experience of "reality," involve education, medicine, punishment, and disciplinary training.

A similar principle applies to the food we eat. Some scholars argue that we "mask" our violence done to animals with our language, just as we mask our violence toward people. For example, Carole J. Adams writes, "We do not see our meat eating as contact with animals because it has been renamed as contact with food."[1] Moreover, "By speaking of meat rather than slaughtered, butchered bleeding pigs, lambs, cows, and calves, we participate in a language that masks reality."[2] But Foucault would never write that language was a "mask"; rather, more crucially, *language invents a specific rationality* that creates our knowledge of "food" as well as our desire for particular forms of it. Knowledge, in short, is derived from relationships that authorize behaviors. What Foucault offers is a more rigorously applied historicism and theoretical apparatus that, in effect, substantiates Burke's more opaque philosophy of language. What we take to be our lives, both Burke and Foucault argue, is the world that our particular language structure enables us to perceive. The configurations of these relationships result from power and that power and desire get enabled or enacted through discourse. As Carole Blair explains: "Foucault described power not just as a capacity or a potential of discourse to effect change, but as an essential or definitive function of discourse. From this vantage point, power is a function of discourse, and discourse is at the same time a function of power. To study any discourse without considering its political function is to derive an incomplete view, for the act of discourse *is* an act of power."[3]

Foucault's work is a clear affirmation of a rhetorical epistemology and an excellent counter-argument to the Platonic tenor of the current political atmosphere. Indeed, we should expect to find Foucault discussed more thoroughly in the history of rhetoric in the years to come, since his work represents an extension of the conflict that Plato created between "Reality" and "Appearance."

Taken with Marx and Nietzsche, two of Foucault's intellectual peers, the rhetorical tradition has met with its most powerful allies. Arguably, they are even more important than Aristotle and Burke. Aristotle and Burke describe rhetoric *per se* and give scholars a vocabulary to talk about it. While this is crucial to our understanding of rhetoric as a disciplinized study, it is itself limiting. As argued in the Introduction to this book, "rhetoric" cannot be confined to one culture or to one set of disciplinary practices. While Nietzsche, Marx, and Foucault seldom talk about rhetoric in the sense that it is talked about in the tradition of Greco-Roman rhetorical theory (of which Burke is a twentieth-century extension), they are functionally countering Plato and thus are enabling of a rhetorical epistemology.

Their work is far from complete, however. While Western history can be seen as a dialectic between epistemological and ontological tensions, leading to understandings of "nature" and knowledge, it is the Platonic, philosophical, and totalitarian side that typically becomes accentuated and incorporated into the political and cultural infrastructures of our society. In the West, the governing rationality has been authoritarian. With few exceptions in its twenty-five hundred year history, the West has practiced a barbarism that is frequently hidden by its loud rhetoric proclaiming "civilization." We in Western culture are heirs to Plato much more than we are heirs to the Sophists, and that says something rather unpleasant about the political economies that exist in the West today. In facing this fact, we may be motivated to imagine different ways of doing things in the future. This, at its base, is the root of all political revolution.

Platonic Tendencies in Western Society

It is not entirely surprising that Western society has embraced more of an ontological view, at the expense of a rhetorical epistemology. The belief in a realist ontology that drives science, for instance, carries with it a strong degree of cultural ethos. While the limitations of scientism are becoming increasingly apparent at the close of the twentieth century, its popular appeals remain strong. While science may be responsible, in part, for the genocidal destructiveness of our weapons and the pollution of our environment, people still believe that the solutions to the above problems can be found strictly in the scientific and technological, rather than in the moral or political realms. For example, the U.S. government's response to nuclear threat is to build *more* bombs and to invest *more* money in the technology of war rather than to pursue policies that reduce world tensions while increasing human respect and dignity across the globe. In addition, the response of the American Medical Association to pollution in the environment (air, water, and food) is individualistic. If *you* are sick, we have medicine that might be able to help *you*. Yet this association makes no political effort to point out that much sickness in the world is the result of structural abuses that benefit the owners of industry (the major polluters of the environment). This illustrates a blindness or a willful neglect of what it is that science is capable of. Its benefits are extolled, while its costs are silently spread to the people who suffer from the exhaust fumes of "progress."

Aside from the positivistic aura that continues to surround science, there are other aspects in which Plato's world continues to be, in some sense, our own. The superstition of religion still rears its ugly head throughout the world. This appearance is not just apparent in the rise of militant Christianity, Islam, and Judaism—and in the increased barbarity of fundamentalist states that claim to represent each faith. Rather, the superstition of religion has a more subtle impact. Its influence is evidenced by its appearance in taken-for-granted places—on our currency, for example, and in the pervasiveness of Churches and of other religious centers. These religious centers litter the landscape of the United States, taking resources that can be used for homeless shelters or food kitchens. To be fair, some Churches, Mosques, and Synagogues are committed to the poor and to the needy, but they are far from the norm. These institutions are to be praised and should be considered worthy of our highest respect. Religion does not have to be alienating, as the Liberation Theology movement in Latin America and the Church Solidarity Movements in the U.S. aptly illustrate.[4]

With few notable exceptions, much current politics in the United States, including those that are racist, sexist, and classist, are couched in a religious vein. Furthermore, *all* U.S. presidents evoke a Christian deity as a way of establishing community. For example, after the June 1993 U.S. bombing of Iraq, President Clinton was quoted as feeling "good" about the attack, while he was "on the way to Church," the newswriter clearly noted. The fact that Clinton made his official pronouncement (of the attack) to the American people in the context of a religious setting betrays one way in which we authorize our leaders to commit murder.[5] As mentioned in chapter four, Robert Ivie illustrates how U.S. war appeals are often couched in religious terms.[6] In recent years, Ronald Reagan became very successful as president by exploiting this imagery. We Americans have God's blessing, Reagan frequently told us, and it is our duty to fight the "evil empire"— meaning Russia and just about everyone in the Third World.

Granted, most Presidential appeals to God are rhetorical flourishes in the popular, pejorative sense of the term. It is difficult to take seriously the thought that Reagan, Bush, Clinton, and all the other monsters from the American political past were pious Christians, even though they bloodied the world for Christiandom and for the American "way of life." All thoughtful Americans should be embarrassed for their country whenever they hear God evoked in defense of the "National Interest." Certainly, pious Christians should be angered by such sacrilege and hypocrisy (although, historically, "sacrilege" and "hypocrisy" have seldom bothered the institution of the Church). The apparent naturalness and the relative hospitality and enthusiasm with which religious appeals in politics are received by the American public indicate that more is at stake than a passive tolerance on behalf of American atheists. In this vein, the people of the U.S. still have not given up on religion and other forms of dogmatic, essentializing thought in the public realms.[7]

Incommensurability and the Invitation for Aristotle

Bringing a sense of closure to the issues discussed above and in the last chapter, we are once again faced with the question of incommensurability. This question was raised in the second chapter when we discussed the condition that exists when mutually exclusive paradigms come into conflict. When there are two or more different ways of interacting in the world, which one do we choose? How do we choose it? What are our criteria? How do we justify our choice? Aristotle helps us to answer some of these questions. With Aristotle we learn that human happiness is a primary virtue and the end of a just political state. With Aristotle we get our first meaningful sense of rhetorical theory. As part of this theory, Aristotle offers us logic and other systems of rationality that privilege a civic consciousness. We may not care for the limitations that Aristotle places on his notion of a civic body. Nevertheless, we are always challenged to expand those boundaries. Aristotle's theory of rhetoric is instructive in helping us to make decisions when decisions need to be made. Aristotle leads us away from the condition of incommensurability and enables us to ask practical questions about our political and social worlds.

At some point we as agents need to commit to a reality and invest our resources in some world that can be trusted. Aristotle helps us by mediating the tensions that Plato creates for rhetoric. Aristotle does this by giving rhetoric a social purpose, defining it as a "practical art." Rhetoric is useful for politics and thus for human happiness, which is the result of politics, for Aristotle. With Aristotle, rhetoric becomes a *techne*, an art. With it we are introduced to a practical way of thinking (*phronesis*). In constituting rhetoric as civic art, Aristotle saves it from the propagandistic function that it is limited to in Plato's monarchy, making it serviceable to a wider political body.

Introduction to Aristotle

In ways similar to Plato, Aristotle is a paradigmatic figure in Western culture. His ideas of knowledge, politics, language, and society inform the conceptualization of communication and community that dominate contemporary political life.

Aristotle was born in 384 BCE and was intellectually proficient in many diverse areas, as his surviving treatises suggest. Of the hundred treatises he is said to have written, only thirty are extant. Within this diverse corpus there exists Aristotle's lecture notes on rhetoric. In his book, Aristotle offers the first "complete" view on rhetoric that exists. Prior to this time there existed only theoretical speculations on the nature of logos, as well as Plato's general description of rhetoric as an unattainable concept. With Aristotle we find a qualitative difference in the conceptualization of rhetoric: "Aristotle embarked upon a scientific and descriptive investigation of the entire domain of persuasive communication, viewing rhetoric, not so much as the technique of persuasion, but rather as the discovery of all those elements which, in a concrete situation, would contribute to the process of convincing and being convinced."[8]

Arguably, Aristotle's book is "the most philosophical (or scientific) work ever composed on the subject."[9] Aristotle's nearest "competitor" in offering a "total" theory of rhetoric is Kenneth Burke, a scholar writing in the twentieth century. Yet Burke, self-consciously extending from Aristotle, needed eight major books to accomplish his task. Even so, Burke does not accomplish what Aristotle did in one short treatise (which may not have even been intended for publication).

Aristotle was a student of Plato for twenty years. Failing to inherit Plato's Academy when Plato died in 348, Aristotle opened his own school, the Lyceum, and turned to the study of what we would recognize today as the biological arts. Aristotle sent students out to collect and document specimens from all over Greece and Asia. From his experience as a "biologist," which depended upon categorization, Aristotle began to develop a systematic study of knowledge. This process corresponds to Plato's sense of dialectic—i.e. the process of defining the subject being studied, then dividing the subject into its parts, then exploring the interrelation of those parts with the goal of understanding the relationship between the parts and the whole. When divorced from metaphysics, this is a useful model for studying material things. The format of Aristotle's treatise on rhetoric usually follows this sequence.

Aristotle's view of rhetoric differs from that of the Sophists and from that of Plato. The Sophists said that rhetoric was an "art," but not necessarily a practical art, and Plato said that rhetoric was no art (or if it was an art it served no function other than that of state propaganda). Aristotle, in contrast, promoted the view that rhetoric is a "practical" art like ethics and politics. Aristotle discusses three kinds of arts which he called theoretical, productive, and practical. Theoretical arts are law-like and universal as in the art of physics or those which work toward an understanding of the physical sciences. Productive arts are those which lead to the making of something. These are non-absolute, like poetry and cooking. The practical arts are those which lead to statesmanship, right action, and happiness. Poetry is considered a productive art (it leads to the construction of a poem), while rhetoric is a practical art (it leads to the condition of political *arete*).

In arguing that rhetoric has practical implications, Aristotle gives to rhetoric the moral justification that was lacking in Plato's conceptualization of knowledge. Here we learn from Aristotle that rhetoric is that which we use to do something—such as start a revolution. Obviously, Aristotle is not arguing for this, nor does he mention it. Nevertheless, this is one model that describes how revolutions work. Revolutions work only when they are rhetorically inspired. Revolutionaries have first to imagine the potential for change and articulate the conditions upon which that change can emerge. Finally, revolutionaries have to invite people to participate in that vision and to provide a method for bringing into being the conditions that lead to a restructuring of society. These conditions are not "objective" as scientistic Marxists have tended to argue in the past, but are *artistic*. Revolution is an art not unlike rhetoric. When it is mechanistic and formulaic, a revolution is seldom persuasive; it appears forced and contrived. But, similar to rhetoric, when it is creatively approached, when it attempts to meet the needs of people, when it focuses our attention in new ways, then it has the potential to create human happiness, which is its purpose. Revolution, in its basic structure, is fundamentally "good," as rhetoric is fundamentally "good" (although both rhetoric and revolution can be misused, as the example of Hitler's social movement illustrates).[10]

Rhetoric, Aristotle felt, is judged by action—the degree to which it can actualize the common good. A revolution would have to be judged by the same standards. Revolutions, like rhetoric, do not have themselves as an end. Rhetoric, when it does this, becomes panegyric. Revolution, when it does this, becomes tyranny. The perfect system of rhetoric for Aristotle is one that helps people to gain a large enough scope of knowledge so that they can persuade anyone. Similarly, the perfect revolution would be one that met the needs of the people it served. Happiness is the result of both rhetoric and revolution. In a sense, the two concepts go hand-in-hand: they both strive to build community by re-envisioning people's relationships from within a social system. While the relative "completeness" of a particular revolution is impossible to ascertain, the relative "completeness" of Aristotle's rhetoric is accentuated by his meta-rhetoric.

Aristotle's Meta-Rhetoric

In Aristotle's view, many diverse topics, now classified as individual fields, are interrelated. Just as my book on rhetoric engages with both the political and the moral, Aristotle recognizes that rhetoric cannot be understood apart from its wider social influence. Unlike contemporary scholars, Aristotle attempts to look for the larger unity of all things; his view on rhetoric accentuates this perspective. Aristotle privileges synthesis above most other things in his writing. His notion of harmony can be found, for example, in the "Golden Mean." Contemporary critical thought owes a great deal to Aristotle on this point: it tends to reject the rhetoric of the extreme and seeks, instead, as its political and cultural goals, integration, synthesis, and intersubjectivity.

By extending from this vantage point, we can see that many of Aristotle's treatises are central to the ideas found in his writing on rhetoric. In a significant sense, they can be considered Aristotle's meta-rhetoric.[11] As Richard Enos and Ann Blakeslee warn, "Reading the *Rhetoric* in isolation from Aristotle's other treatises is a disservice to his objective of harmonizing knowledge...."[12]

James Murphy elaborates on the concept of a meta-rhetoric: "Metarhetoric investigates what a rhetorician needs to know in order to be a rhetorician. It examines the first principles, either stated or left implicit, upon which a rhetorician bases his [sic] whole activity."[13] Many of Aristotle's important works, while contributing fundamentally to the creation of their own disciplines (i.e. political science and psychology), emphasize the centrality of rhetoric to Aristotle's system of philosophy. For example, the following treatises of Aristotle concern the rhetorical process, yet they also are peripheral to rhetoric—they appear in separate contexts: Aristotle's *Politics* supplies the context for rhetoric. His *Ethics* provides a system of correct action in speech. The *Posterior Analytics*, *Prior Analytics*, and *On Sophistical Refutations* introduce a system of logic and argumentation to public communication. The *Topics* provides instruction in the gathering and inventing of material. Finally, Aristotle's *Poetics* offers advice on the thematic nature of language and its relationship to human psychology. Thus, it is reasonable for Murphy to argue that "Students of Aristotle's *Rhetoric* should understand the basic concepts appearing in his *Ethics, Politics,* and Psychology (*On the Soul*), as well as the *Poetics.*"[14]

While I agree with Murphy's sentiment, I do not believe for a moment that Murphy takes this view seriously. Certainly, Murphy is academically committed to this synthesis, and he teaches his graduate seminar on this principle. But what does it mean to take ethics and politics seriously when considering rhetoric? In Aristotle's sense, it means little more than what we do today. His *Ethics* and his *Politics* are models of aristocratic or bourgeois virtue. Thus, public discourse today very much engages in, or implicitly recognizes, Aristotle's meta-rhetoric. The implication of this view is that we have the "right" to hear but not the "right" to speak. The great politicians clash on the television while the rest of us silently watch at home. This is called "democracy" in our society. Certainly, in this context, rhetoric is connected with ethics and politics, but not in a way that is grounded, first and foremost, in community. Rather, it is grounded in the appearance of community, or community as corporately defined. Such a world is frequently protected by Aristotle's view of rhetoric and by the view of scholars who work from out of an Aristotelian paradigm.

With the above limitations in mind, how does Murphy's comment change when it is reimposed on an extra-disciplinary rhetorical context (such as this book)? Repositioned, it challenges us to take ethics and politics seriously. This means going beyond the Aristotelian sense of the above and engaging seriously with the Marxist and critical interpretations of politics and social change. In this view, politics is always *contested* politics. Ethics is always *contested* ethics. Both take seriously the complete psychology of the individual, not just its most self-serving and egotistical dimensions. Furthermore, such meta-rhetorical view engages in the psychology of *all* people, not just the privileged people of the narrowly defined political polis. Such a view of meta-rhetoric leads us, ultimately, to books such as this—books on rhetoric that take seriously the intersections between power and communication and trace their effects to the suffering peoples of the world.

The *Rhetoric* of Aristotle

Aristotle's *Rhetoric* was written between 334 and 324 BCE.[15] The treatise was known throughout the Roman Empire. After the fall of the Empire, the *Rhetoric* became largely unattainable, although some of its ideas circulated in various forms. By the Renaissance, parts of the *Rhetoric* regained circulation and interest. The treatise was fully recovered by the twentieth century and became widely influential in the disciplines of Communication and English Composition, as well as in critical theory, generally.[16] In what follows, some of the main ideas contained in Aristotle's *Rhetoric* are explicated. In discussing Aristotle's concept of rhetoric, we can see rhetoric emerging as a *useful* activity. What we do not find in Aristotle, however, is rhetoric as a *critical* activity, and one of the purposes of this chapter is to accentuate this conceptualization and to infuse it with Aristotle's discussion of rhetoric.

Relationship Between Rhetoric and Dialectic

Aristotle's concerns with invention characterize Books I and II of the *Rhetoric*. In an important sense, Aristotle's treatise is about thinking in terms of opportunity. For Aristotle, "opportunity" literally means persuasion, and Aristotle is extremely focused on this task. For us, however, "opportunity" means something different. It first and foremost means a thinking beyond, a reimagining of our most sacred beliefs. Rhetoric is a way for inviting this opportunity, but it must be a critical intervention of self into society for the transformation of both. Thus, my view of rhetoric and Aristotle's view of rhetoric are both situated in the primacy of invention. The ends of a critical rhetoric are different, however, as it does not limit itself to "persuasion" or "effect."

Aristotle's preoccupation with a limited form of invention is clearly seen in the first pages of the treatise, in which Aristotle challenges Plato's condemnation of rhetoric. Aristotle asserts that rhetoric is the "counterpart" of dialectic. In writing this, Aristotle is claiming that rhetoric has an important role to play in the phenomenal world. While it may not lead to

"Truth" in Plato's sense, it can lead to happiness. Along with dialectic, rhetoric is the method by which people gather and work out their political lives. Such meeting is useful for Aristotle, but does not involve the critical consciousness evoked in my book. As should be recalled, women, slaves, and non-citizens are excluded from his political/rhetorical body. Similarly, today, the voices of minorities and other people who do not fit completely into the world view propagated by the two dominant political parties of the U.S. find themselves outside of the rhetorical situation as envisioned by Aristotle (and by Bitzer, who uncritically perpetuates an Aristotelian politics in his useful theory of contemporary rhetoric).[17] Those who fall outside of the rhetorical situation also fall outside of the moral or ethical parameters that guide interaction within a rhetorical transaction. Napalm, enforced starvation, wage slavery, and laws constricting abortion await those non-people who are unlucky enough to be excluded from the civic community of the powerful and the elite.

The Greek term Aristotle uses for counterpart is *antistrope*. A *strope* is a set of lines delivered by an actor in a Greek play. For example, a performer may muse out loud before the audience, "Should I marry her?" This would be an example of a *strope*; it is discourse that recognizes that a larger audience exists for the play and evokes that audience without ruining the integrity of the spectacle. Since audience members are not normally able to participate physically in the drama, the chorus of the play was responsible for uttering the *anti-strope*. The chorus would speak for the audience. In speaking for the audience, it would represent its interests (its desire to know and its desire to extend itself empathetically into the moral drama of the play). In a sense, the Chorus would also *control* the audience in particular ways. All representations can be co-opted by an audience. As Greek plays usually evoked political themes, it was important that the audience "got it right" in terms of its political education. Then, as today, culture was corporate. Communicated art is largely sponsored by the media (or in Ancient Greece, by the government) and it largely takes the form of propaganda.

These corporate-defined identities and representations have to be presented so that they resist subversion by critical mis-readings. A good example of this in modern times is the Walt Disney Corporation. Disney serves an important function in promoting and reifying American ideology (both at home and abroad), and it is constantly on guard to prevent critics from reinterpreting its icons and messages. Woe to the university professor or other critic who in class or in print takes a Disney image and attempts to subvert its "preferred" innocuous meaning. Beneath the facade of the smiling mouse is a vicious rat (and a team of high powered lawyers) who will stop at nothing to protect its illusion of childhood innocence against adult forms of critical interrogations.[18] Beneath the celebration that Disney offers are disturbing thoughts about who we are as Americans. Disney's desire to hide these thoughts is an example of a system of thought control that emanates from the corporate community.

In the particular instance of the above Greek example, the chorus would retort to the actor playing Oedipus Rex, "No, don't marry her, she is really your mother." The *anti-strope* clashes with the strope to aid the audience in comprehension. This theatrical device helps the audience to follow the plot, especially when the characters themselves are oblivious to their situation, as King Oedipus is in Sophocles' famous tragedy.

The *strope/anti-strope* dialectic in Greek drama illustrates two important dimensions of Greek and subsequent rhetorical perspectives. First, it emphasizes the importance that antithetical reasoning played in the development of Greek thought.[19] Any notion of the "true" within the conditions of a rhetorical epistemology must be the result of some sort of antithetical reasoning. By pairing statements against each other, the wider implications of a particular position can be explored. Modern contrarian thought has its origins in such a view. As society becomes more and more committed to particular ways of experiencing the world, contrary positions must be introduced to unsettle the foundations that have been established and reified as Truth. This is one important way of keeping society from taking any of its beliefs so seriously that it is unable to recognize the limitations of any one particular way of seeing (in Burke's sense).

Second, and perhaps more importantly, the *strope/anti-strope* dialectic anticipates much of what Aristotle would later identify as enthymematic reasoning. The enthymeme, as discussed below, is considered by Aristotle to be the most important part of rhetorical persuasion. Generally, the enthymeme involves the audience in the construction of the argument so that it can "see" for itself the value of the conclusion. The conclusion is believable to audience members precisely because they helped construct it in their own image. By "inviting" the audience to participate in the drama, the "argument" of the play becomes more personalized for the viewer. Playwrights, after all, have to create a condition in which audiences come to believe in the universes they have created, and that means getting the audience to commit, psychologically, to a form of persuasion.

As no play can perfectly recreate the conditions of life, certain incongruities have to be hidden from the audience, and others have to be positioned in such a way that audiences voluntarily overlook them. By getting the audience involved in the development of the plot, playwrights encourage viewers to commit themselves emotionally or intellectually to a particular narrative logic, and thus to a particular conclusion. If this is done well, then the audience and the playwright reach a similar conclusion. In this way, the structure, the flow, and the effect of the play are synchronized and the dramatic experience is culminated. Drama, like all art, is always a negotiation of belief that is constructed between an artist and his/her audience. By being conscious of their own narrativity, and by exploring its dimensions through drama, "the early Greeks quite literally invented invention, and with it the link between narrative and what is not. . . . Without this concept we cannot observe the intricate connectedness of narrativity to reflectivity."[20] This sentiment provides an important insight into the development of a rhetorical consciousness in ancient Athens.

Both the *strope* and the *anti-strope* are of equal importance in Greek theatre and contribute to the unfolding of the drama. Thus, Aristotle makes it clear at the beginning of his treatise that rhetoric is *equal* to dialectic. While rhetoric serves a different function than does dialectic, it is nevertheless important. In Kennedy's words: "The functions of rhetoric and dialectic, Aristotle means, are parallel movements, virtually identical in content; both deal with matters which are common subjects of knowledge among men [sic]; neither falls within any distinct science."[21]

Through the rest of Book I, chapter one, Aristotle proceeds to explain the similarities and differences between the two arts.

In terms of similarities, both rhetoric and dialectic lead only to probable conclusions. Both deal with human opinions and with contingent knowledge. Both arts are methods of doing something; they are practical in Aristotle's view; neither art is particularly substantive in and of itself. In other words, both rhetoric and dialectic are universal in that they are not reserved for specific subjects or for individual people. Any educated person, not just the True philosopher, can, with training, engage in either practice. With these comparisons, Aristotle raises the status of "opinion" and rhetoric, and lowers the status of Plato's dialectic.

The differences between rhetoric and dialectic, according to Aristotle, has to do with the character of the audience. Rhetoric has a popular audience, that is, an audience made up of different types of people from a wide range of occupations. Furthermore, each of these people brings to the communication context a variety of internal conditions. To engage in rhetoric, the speaker must be able to sense his/her audience's reactions, and to adjust his/her message accordingly. Dialectic, on the other hand, focuses its address on an explicit and specific audience of a few chosen people. In many cases, these people have a similar educational or cultural background; thus, it is much easier to stipulate definitions and to reach consensus on particular propositions. In neither case are the audiences for the two arts constituted of widely dissimilar people. What Aristotle seems to be saying is that persuasive communication can take place among Senators on Capital Hill (dialectic) as well as when the President of the United States speaks on television to rally support for the illusions of the State (rhetoric). While Plato would dismiss the function of rhetoric in the second instance and endorse the communication among the Senators, Aristotle encourages us to think more broadly about the relationship between communication and politics. In this sense, my book does stand on the "shoulders of giants" when it argues for *even broader* thinking of the relationship between communication and politics.

The goals of rhetoric and dialectic are different. According to Aristotle, the end of rhetoric is persuasion, while the end of dialectic is criticism and the refinement of ideas. The above paragraphs have challenged this standard characterization of Aristotle. In Kennedy's view, "Dialectic usually deals with philosophical or at least general questions, rhetoric with concrete or practical ones."[22] Such a view still perpetuates certain Platonic formal assumptions. Seen more critically, dialectic itself is a type of rhetoric. This helps us to see education, traditionally conceived as a form of dialectic, as rhetorical and political.

Uses and Definition of Rhetoric

According to Aristotle, rhetoric has four uses. First, rhetoric helps truth and justice prevail when they are being threatened by ignorance or malice. Second, rhetoric instructs people of the facts in a case (for example, members of a jury in a criminal trial). In other words, rhetoric is the method of engaging with a popular audience. This point is the foundational assumption that largely guides the construction of Aristotle's treatise. Third, rhetoric helps a speaker to see both sides of a question and hence to be able to make the best decision. Fourth, rhetoric is used for self-defense against attack in the civil and criminal law courts. Having justified the use of rhetoric, Aristotle proceeds to define it and to explicate its properties.

Aristotle defines rhetoric as "an ability, in each [particular] case, to see the available means of persuasion."[23] The sense in which Aristotle evokes rhetoric in this definition is as a *dynamis*. In a broad sense, *dynamis* means "power" or "potentiality." It is the ability to distinguish what is important from what is superficial, ideologically, within a communicative interaction. In a sense, Aristotle's definition of rhetoric invites the type of perspectivism that guides Kenneth Burke's theory of rhetoric. In Burke's words: "Any performance is discussible either from the standpoint of what it *attains* or what it *misses*. Comprehensiveness can be discussed as superficiality, intensiveness as structure, tolerance as uncertainty—and the poor *pedestrian* abilities of a fish are clearly explainable in terms of his [sic] excellence as a *swimmer*."[24]

Rhetoric, under Aristotle, becomes an art of choice, one of emphasis. The persuader must learn to accentuate certain things at the expense of other things, to see, in Burke's words, "the thisness of a that, or the thatness of a this."[25] Burke is specifically referring to the function of metaphor, which he equates with "perspective." As one of the four master tropes, metaphor aids in the construction of rhetorical meaning and persuasion by inviting the audience to imagine novel relationships among formally dissimilar things. Rhetoric, at its base, invites meaning, and meaning can be understood in terms of relationships. While Aristotle does not use this modern language, he *is* talking about the ability to see things differently when he defines rhetoric in the way that he does. The rhetorician understands this point and emphasizes the particular arguments or perspectives that lead to specific visions of the world. To do this well, without thinking, is Aristotle's goal for students.

In short, rhetoric is the strategic use of language for a predetermined end. With such definition, rhetoric gains its most important characteristics, as well as some of its more severe constraints. As discussed in earlier chapters, Aristotle's notion of rhetoric is measured by its success, and it is infused with a combative ethos. With Burke, this limitation is modified somewhat. For him, rhetoric is always the potential to see differently, to invite different perspectives. This view differs from Aristotle who writes that an orator must choose carefully from the causes or means of persuasion. In the process, the speaker can make "wrong" decisions ("wrong" from the point of view of "success"). As "success" and "community" may be different things altogether, and as rhetoric has been defined in my book as fundamentally concerned with community, Aristotle's particular objectification of rhetoric imposes limitations on sight, from a socialist point of view.

Rhetorical Proof

What does Aristotle mean by *pistis*, or the "means of persuasion"? Aristotle's concern is how to influence people to change their behavior or attitudes. With this in mind, can the offering of a bribe be considered persuasion? Does the use of force constitute a persuasive act? Aristotle makes clear that there are dimensions of persuasion that do not fall into the realm or scope of rhetoric. Such influences are called inartistic (*atechnoi*) proof; they are nontechnical and extrinsic to rhetorical invention. The word "proof" refers to the means of persuasion. Inartistic proofs, then, are those persuasions that do not involve the art of rhetoric; they fall outside the art. For Aristotle, appeals to existing laws, witnesses, contracts, oaths, and torture fall outside the realm of artistic rhetorical proof. As inartistic proof, they are beyond the orator's ability to produce through rhetoric. In order for a proof to be considered artistic, a rhetor would have to be responsible for developing its effect.

Notice that "torture" is specifically mentioned by Aristotle as being a form of persuasion that does not involve the art of rhetoric. From our point of view today, it seems odd that Aristotle would casually mention "torture," particularly in a list of legal terms. Aristotle did so because torture was institutionalized in Ancient Greece. Testimony from slaves was not considered reliable unless that testimony was gathered through the use of torture. This is another point that is often deemphasized when politicians and other cultural agents appropriate the ancient world to justify contemporary cultural representations. The "wonderful" legal apparatus that follows so easily from democratic rationales was built upon the blood of the people whose labor constructed the Ancient World, just as the modern United States was built from the labor of Africans who never (even now) fully benefited from the fruits of their labor. It is also built from the labor of poor people in the Third World who slave for Multi-National corporations. Just as Aristotle takes for granted the acceptability of torture in extracting testimony from witnesses, we take for granted the blood that has spilled daily from the beginning of our country until the present time. The "red" in our national flag represents more than the blood of patriots; it more directly represents the blood of our victims.

In contrast to inartistic proof, Aristotle discusses what he considers to be the three types of artistic (*entechnoi*) proof. The first artistic proof is called *ethos*. Ethos is the perceived character of the speaker as it is revealed to an audience through the speech. In other words, ethos is the sense of credibility that is communicated through a discourse and is negotiated with an audience. For example, ethos is the phenomenon associated with the presidency that authorizes and privileges presidential discourse at the expense of a critical interrogation of that discourse. Because presidents are seen as being credible by virtue of their office, their individual sinisterness is often overlooked. While much partisan criticism is directed at our presidents, these criticisms seldom interrogate the legality or morality of much presidential action. In short, the ethos of the office shields the criminality of the actions that take place within that office.[26]

The second artistic proof is called *pathos*. Pathos is the state of mind of the audience that becomes modified through emotional appeals. Appeals to patriotism are often couched in a pathetic allure. Much of this discourse takes on the form of "ideographs," single term representations of an ideological structure.[27] For example, when a politician in this country appeals to "God" and "Country," and to "Freedom" and "Democracy," he/she is emotionally linking dissimilar terms, or unfamiliar terms with common sentiments. None of the above concepts are bad, but none of them have any clear referent. They are all concepts that have positive value in our society, even though no one clearly knows what they mean. Furthermore, they are often evoked to mean the opposite of what they are. Appeals to "God" are exclusionary, a particular God is being evoked and not the universal fraternity that the concept of God generically implies. Appeals to "freedom" usually mean the freedom of capital to do what it wants, diminishing the freedom of the rest of us to experience an agency in our lives. Appeals to "democracy" usually mean that we should support the repressive oligarchy of this nation and that we should not consider alternative, more democratic politic expressions. Because of the emotional cloak that covers these words, gut responses are encouraged at the expense of critical introspections.

The last artistic proof, *logos*, involves the words used in a discourse through a logical argument (specifically, the enthymeme and the example). This proof will be discussed in the next section.

Aristotle primarily concerns himself with the available means of persuasion in Book II of the *Rhetoric*. For example, when Aristotle discuss the state of mind, or pathos, he does so by discussing each state in light of its four causes: formal, final, material, and efficient. Each state of mind can be understood in terms of these elements. For example, Aristotle defines the formal cause of anger as "desire, accompanied by [mental and physical] distress, for conspicuous retaliation because of a conspicuous slight that was directed, without justification, against oneself or those near to one."[28] Aristotle defines the final cause of anger as "a kind of pleasure [that] follows all experience of anger from the hope of getting retaliation."[29] The material cause of anger, Aristotle says, includes "contempt, spite, and insult."[30] The efficient cause of anger is the person who thinks him/herself greatly superior "by ill-treating others."[31] For Aristotle, an orator can rationally appeal to these various states in his audience in order to persuade. According to Larry Arnhart:

> The success of the rhetorician in handling the passions suggests that the passions must somehow be rational. For in trying to persuade an audience to adhere to some passions and give up others, the speaker must assume that speech alone is sufficient to alter men's [sic] passions. And such an assumption is verified not only by rhetorical practice but also by more common experiences: men are continually talked into or out of their passions, either by themselves or by others. Passions do respond to arguments. . . . The rhetorician changes the passions of his listeners by changing their minds.[32]

Chapters twelve through eighteen deal with *ethos*. The following is a possible list in an Aristotelian style which may describe the contemporary persuasive person: education, status, age, past history, experience, wealth, attractiveness, good will, and immediacy. Aristotle, however, only discusses three elements of ethos: goodwill, good sense or intelligence, and good character. Notice how these traits are culture specific. While Aristotle's list appears to be more applicable across cultures, the contemporary list of "credibility" reeks of a capitalist bias. To be credible in our society, one must have wealth. Wealth breeds education, gives people the potential for useful experience, enables people to pursue positions of status, and enables them to be more attractive. From this list, which positions itself as being natural, where would we find the working person, the average laborer of this country? Or the average person in the world, for that matter. In what sense can they be considered "credible"? They are denied education, wealth, status, and the wide-ranging experiences that more privileged people benefit from. Furthermore, their attractiveness is compromised by premature aging through malnutrition, disease, and poor working conditions. Are these people to be deemed "non-credible" because they do not meet the expectations and demands that society cruelly puts on all of us?

Logos was, for Aristotle, a more important construct than ethos, though ethos could easily be the deciding factor in a persuasive situation. In Book III, Aristotle, while discussing style, makes clear his bias. He argues, "To contend by means of the facts themselves is just, with the result that everything except demonstration is incidental."[33] By this Aristotle means that logos is the privileged proof. Nevertheless, auditors are subject to "corruption" and thus the arts of style and the effect of the speaker's character are of no small concern. While Aristotle devotes a book to a discussion of style, it appears to be an appendix or an afterthought to his more central ideas concerning logos and the construction of rhetorical arguments.

Two Types of Rhetorical Argument

As suggested above, Aristotle discusses two types of rhetorical arguments. The first, the enthymeme, is a rhetorical deduction. Aristotle considers the enthymeme to be the counterpart of the dialectical syllogism and to comprise the "body" of rhetorical persuasion.[34] The second, Aristotle called the rhetorical example, which is a rhetorical induction. In order to understand how the enthymeme and example work, a more thorough discussion of Aristotle's formal logic is necessary.

Aristotle was the inventor of formal logic. Formal logic relies on the "form" of an argument and attempts to ascertain the validity of an argument rather than its "truth." Within the discipline of formal logic there are two types of argument: deductive and inductive. An instance of the deductive argument is the syllogism. Syllogisms work categorically and formally as in the classic example of Socrates' mortality. To conclude that Socrates is mortal after establishing the premises that people die and that Socrates is a person is to make a formally correct observation. The conclusion, in this case, happens to be true, but does not have to be in other instances of syllogistic reasoning. An argument can be formally correct, yet be false if one of its premises is false. Deductive arguments start with a major premise, one large generalization, which is followed by a minor and more specific premise. The conclusion is based on the two premises. The enthymeme is a rhetorical deduction in the formal sense discussed above, but differs from a formal syllogism because it takes as its starting point premises or positions that are acceptable to the audience (or even offered wholly by them). Lloyd Bitzer offers the following explanation of Aristotle's enthymeme: "The enthymeme is a syllogism based on probabilities, signs, and examples, whose function is rhetorical persuasion. Its successful construction is accomplished through the joint efforts of speaker and audience, and this is its essential character."[35]

This is an important strategy of rhetoric. People who feel involved in part of an argument are more apt to be affected by a message than if they feel alien to its construction. In short, audiences find messages more appealing when they deduce a conclusion for themselves rather than being told what to think. Audiences can foresee the conclusion because they have helped supply the premises through their opinions as part of a syllogistic argument. In addition, the formal syllogism, which depends on orthodox structure, can be insulting to an audience if its points are made too obvious, which is why the enthymeme can be more effective.

Induction, on the other hand, argues from specific cases to a general conclusion. Unlike deductive arguments, inductive arguments can never be formally valid. To observe that A, B, and C are instances of a class of things and to conclude that all things of that class have the traits of A, B, and C is a position of truth that can never be verified. It would only take one example of something that is of that class but differs from the attribution to destroy the argument. Since it is impossible to examine every "thing" in a class that has, does, or will exist, inductive claims can never be known to be absolutely correct. Nevertheless, induction is an important way for human beings to gather information and ascertain knowledge. In the best of cases, a proper sampling is needed to make sure that a large enough data base is accumulated before reaching a conclusion.

The rhetorical example is an inductive form of argument that moves from a specific case to a specific case. In Aristotle's words:

> It is reasoning neither from part to whole nor from whole to part but from part to part, like to like, when two things fall under the same genus but one is better known than the other. For example, [when someone claims] that Dionysius is plotting tyranny because he is seeking a bodyguard; for Peisistratus also, when plotting earlier, sought a guard and after receiving it made himself tyrant, and Theagegnes [did the same] in Megara, and others, whom the audience knows of, all become examples of Dionysius, of whom they do not yet know whether he makes his demand for this reason. All these actions fall under the same [genus]; that one plotting tyranny needs a guard.[36]

Consider a modern instance of rhetorical example. A popular bumper sticker in the United States during 1980s read, "No Vietnam in Nicaragua." The concern of this slogan is that there should be no United States hegemony in Nicaragua, or by implication, anywhere else in Central America. From a rhetorical point of view, what becomes important is that a similarity is implied between Vietnam and Nicaragua that the audience is supposed to accept. If that semblance is recognized, then a significant political, historical, and moral linkage has been established by the persuader.[37]

The conditions of the war forced upon Vietnam by the United States are well known, although often ignored or excused. The conditions of the war forced upon Nicaragua are less known. In this case, the known condition (past) represents the unknown condition (present). If an audience member denies this inference and sees no relationship between the two countries in terms of U.S. foreign policy and criminal aggression, then that audience member is not likely to give much credit to the bumper sticker, and an important attempt to build support for political resistance in the U.S. against the policies of the Federal Government will fail. In order for such resistance to be imaginable, the implied similarity between the two cases of a rhetorical example must be recognized. In this way, moral condemnation can be transferred from one case to another. Such linkage is important as it emphasizes the continuity of U.S. criminality, giving more people reason to resist, and to resist with a greater intensity in the future.

The rhetorical example and the enthymeme often work in conjunction. Examples are frequently used to build enthymemes. In the following illustration, both forms of arguments are used to generate a complex argument: "No Vietnam in Nicaragua, boycott Folgers coffee." When made explicit, the full line of reasoning can be understood as follows: U.S. business interests significantly contributed to the U.S. invasion of Vietnam and its subsequent destruction. This situation was not desirable for either the Vietnamese or for the citizens of the United States. A similar relationship exists between U.S. business and U.S. involvement in Central America. In particular, one company, Folgers, is responsible for encouraging U.S. violence and aggression in Nicaragua (and in El Salvador) and for the ultimate overthrow of the popular government there. Boycotting the product of this cruel company is an act of social responsibility that will send a message to Folgers that its behavior will not be tolerated by conscientious U.S. citizens.

The above is implicit in the phrase, "No Vietnam in Nicaragua, boycott Folgers coffee." Yet since both parts of the argument appear as separate bumper stickers, its representation needs to be concise. All that is stated in the actual argument is the initial example and a conclusion. The audience must figure out the relationship between the two premises. That is where the enthymeme comes in; it is a way for the audience to make the conceptual leap required to decipher a complex argument. Those that make the connection will be more strongly affected by the argument, and may even be moved to action by the new insight. Those who fail to see the relationship have to be told explicitly the nature of the situation, and they will less likely be affected by the comparison, as there will be more opportunity for them to disagree with any of the implied premises.

The Topics

As part of his discussion of the enthymeme, Aristotle introduces the concept of *topoi* ("seats of arguments") or topics. The topics constitute the materials from which an orator develops artistic proof: they are the place where arguments are located. Robert J. Brake explains that *topoi* "are pigeonholes from which dialectical and rhetorical syllogisms draw their premises and forms."[38] In other words, topical systems are used for the invention of arguments. Ijsseling explains how the topics are "a kind of table of empty forms that can be of assistance in looking for arguments."[39] Another metaphor used to describe the topics is the "storehouse." Eugene Garver elaborates on the relationship between the topics and thought. He explains, "A topic is sometimes expressed as a term, and sometimes as a direction or relation between terms, and sometimes as a question; whatever its verbal form, its function is to provide a direction for thought without predetermining the thought."[40]

Take, for example, the legal question of "motive." Motive is an important *topoi* in the courtroom. In asking what advantages a suspect may have in his or her relationship to a crime, the prosecuting attorney has opened up a field of inquiry that results in further questioning. Likewise, a defendant can build his or her case on the same question. In this instance, motive, as a *topoi*, directs arguments in both the prosecution and defense of the defendant.

Two significant *topoi* lists are found in the *Rhetoric*. The first list, in Book I, is genre specific. The *topoi* deal with peace-war, means (place, location, locus), and ways (good or bad). Material *topoi* (*koina*) are found in Book II, chapter twenty. These genres are unrelated and deal with more-less, possible-impossible, and past fact. The special *topoi* (*eide*) that Aristotle mentions include time, definition, opposites, logical division, consequence, and effect to name a few.

A *topoi* list is good for locating the lines of an argument, the material premises, and the location of possible things to say. A modern example of a classical *topoi* list can be found in journalism: who (*qui*), what (*quid*), where (*ubi*), by what means (*quibus auxiliis*), why (*cur*), when (*quando*), and how (*quem ad modum*). If each of these questions is properly addressed, no question should be left about a certain news event. The same is true for a rhetorical situation.

The *topoi* are a thinking tool, an inventional device used to locate the argumentative aspects of a speech. In the classical allegory, the rhetor is positioned as a hunter, the argument is seen as his/her quarry, and the topic a locale in which the argument may be found.[41]

Aristotle's topical system and the two types of argument, the enthymeme and example, combine to form logos, as logos is used to denote the logical end of rhetorical discourse.

Three Genres of Rhetoric

There were, in Ancient Greece, three primary areas that called for the artistic use of persuasion: the courts, the assembly, and the public ceremony. Within the courts, the question of justice was determined through the use of forensic/judicial speaking. In the assembly, oratory involved the deliberation of policy and the pursuit of expediency. This type of oratory was known as deliberative speaking. The ceremonial speaking that took place in public civic events was known as the epideictic address.

Each type of speaking had a different goal and a different approach to the issue of time. The forensic speech was given in the courtroom. The goal of forensic speaking is to determine justice and injustice. This genre of speaking concerns the past, focusing on accusation and defense. The questions raised in forensic oratory explore whether or not a past action occurred or if it occurred in the manner suggested by the prosecutor. Deliberative speaking took place in the Assembly of Athens or in similar assemblies in the ancient world. Deliberative speaking is concerned with what should or should not be done. This genre of speaking is concerned with future events and with exhortation or dishortation. The question raised in deliberative speaking involves the expedient or inexpedient.

In the last genre, epideictic speaking, there is no immediate practical end, but there is an important goal. Speeches of this nature were given in public arenas, particularly during religious and athletic celebrations. The goal of an epideictic speech is to determine honor or dishonor, praise or blame of a person, place, or thing. Epideictic speaking deals with the present and the values that support the politics of the day. A clear illustration of this can be seen in the example of the funeral oration. Funerals exist to give comfort to the living as well as to acknowledge the end of a person's life. They are used to reinforce a culture's values as exemplified in the present. People reinforce their own values when attending a ceremonial situation, and these values exist in the present. These values, however, are never neutral, and the disruption of a community caused by a death is always potentially subversive. Human death always forces the living to reconsider the things that they believe in, and these beliefs are tied to some sort of communal infrastructure. Death makes the living insecure, and insecurity is always an affront to political stability.

A closer examination of Pericles' "Funeral Oration," as it appears in Thucydides' re-creation, serves to illustrate the above points. The speech appears at the culmination of a civic ceremony to honor the recently slain in the war that Athens was having with Sparta, resulting in the eclipse and decay of Athens' imperialism and power. In the ceremony, Pericles commemorates the valor of the fallen soldiers and the importance of their service to Athens.

Pericles is facing a community torn with grief, as any community would be in a similar situation. The enormous weight of their loss and suffering can cause the Athenians to question the worth of their sacrifice. To the dismay of politicians and other warmongers, then and now, distant objectives and national "honor" often appear insignificant to citizens when confronted with the harsh reality of bereavement. At this politically volatile time it is necessary for the state to gather the community and persuade it to reaffirm its basic values (which are often exploited in nationalistic war rhetoric).

Pericles, the literal embodiment of Athenian "democracy" and imperialism, reminds his audience that its position in the conflict with Sparta is "just" and "worthy" of its sacrifice in blood. This is a *present* concern, a concern for the immediacy of the moment that must be accentuated if the war is to continue to have a minimal level of popular support. In this vein, Pericles shamelessly reaffirms the "democratic" values of the Athenian polis, and contrasts those values with those he reifies in the Spartan enemy. For example, Pericles explains, "We are free and tolerant in our private lives; but in public affairs we keep to the law. This is because it demands our deep respect."[42]

Similar to today, appeals to "Law" and "Order" had deep propagandistic effect in Ancient Athens. Respect for the law was the obligation of each citizen, and through that law Athens experienced its "liberty," as well as its license to steal. However, with liberty comes civic duty. According to Pericles, "[W]e do not say that a man who takes no interest in politics is a man who minds his own business; we say that he has no business here at all."[43] Pericles here symbolically constructs the "heart" of the community, making explicit the rationale behind all its institutions, perpetuating the illusion of justice. The war is just, Pericles seems to be saying, because the Athenians are a "just" people. Their "freedom" is held up to them as a sign of their moral superiority. Such demagogic appeal is popular in all nations that pretend that "democracy," in name, is itself its own path to the ethical high ground. Furthermore, Pericles realizes, or acts as if he realizes, that the institutions that he holds up to his people for allegiance need themselves to be reinforced and even defended during the difficult times of a protracted, and, ultimately, un-winnable war. While the dead are buried, the living need to be instructed to return to their struggles and to accept the "wisdom" of the state that justifies the sacrifice in blood.

Aristotle: A Summary

As illustrated in this survey of Aristotle's more important contributions to rhetorical theory, his disagreement with Plato's opinion of rhetoric led to the creation of a methodological approach to the study of human communication. By expanding upon Plato's *Phaedrus*, Aristotle created a practical system of communication to engage with the everyday interactions of the phenomenal world. Furthermore, when Aristotle equalized dialectic and rhetoric, and when he recognized the power of the enthymeme in bridging the distance between the speaker and audience, he took an important step in legitimizing the study of rhetoric in the Western world.

Such legitimization, however, is not without its limitations. Aristotle did not write the final word on rhetoric. What he did was to give rhetoric disciplinary space in which its study and practice could flourish for particular people and within specific contexts. With Aristotle, rhetoric becomes a way of thinking, but a constrained one. Rhetoric becomes relegated to rigidly defined state-sponsored functions. Whether in the courtroom, Assembly, or the context of the public ceremonial address, rhetoric was that which served the function of containing subversive thoughts. Rhetoric sought a civic arete and a political community that narrowly pursued its own material interests. Because Aristotle is both practical and limiting, his work is a good place to begin when we start to reconceptualize the role of communication in our contemporary society.

With the above discussion of Aristotle, this book concludes its historical study of the rise of rhetoric. With Aristotle, rhetoric has "risen" and becomes an intellectual force of its own. Development in rhetorical theory occurring after Aristotle is found in Rome, where Greek rhetorical ideas become amplified and refined. In the Roman world, treatises on rhetorical theory proliferate and rhetoric expands in importance with the rise of the Roman Republic. By the time of the empire, rhetoric becomes infused in the Roman schools, and from there becomes transmitted to the modern world.

Notes

1. *The Sexual Politics of Meat* (New York: Continuum, 1990), 66.
2. Ibid., 67.
3. "The Statement: Foundation of Foucault's Historical Criticism," *Western Journal of Speech Communication* 51 (1987), 377.
4. See Phillip Berryman, *Liberation Theology* (New York: Pantheon Books, 1987).

5. *Purdue Exponent* (109, no. 93, June 28, front page).

6. "Images of Savagery in American Justifications for War," *Communication Monographs* 47 (1980), 279–291.

7. When I tried to argue this position for the *Partisan Review* I was rejected. In that paper, I argued that religious thinking is inappropriate for the public life of a liberal democracy. My paper, "God, Redescription, and Cruelty," or some variation of it, may appear in print one day.

8. Samuel Ijsseling, *Rhetoric and Philosophy in Conflict: An Historical Survey* (The Hague: Martinus Nijhoff, 1976), 29.

9. W. Rhys. Roberts, *Greek Rhetoric and Literary Criticism* (New York: Longmans, Green, and Co., 1928), 35.

10. See Omar Swartz, "The Nazi Social Movement: A Consideration of Co-Active, Legitimization, and Nonsummative Rhetorical Strategies," *The Pennsylvania Speech Communication Annual* 49: (1993), 3–21.

11. James J. Murphy, Graduate Seminar in Classical Rhetoric, University of California, Davis, Fall Quarter 1990.

12. "The Classical Period," *The Present State of scholarship in Historical and Contemporary Rhetoric*, revised edition., ed. Winifred Byran Horner (Columbia: University of Missouri Press, 1990), 11.

13. "The Metarhetorics of Plato, Augustine, and McLuhan: A Pointing Essay," *Philosophy and Rhetoric* 4 (1971), 202.

14. Unpublished notes on the instruction of graduate and undergraduate courses in classical rhetoric. These were given to me by Professor Murphy in 1991.

15. See Paul Brandes, *A History of Aristotle's Rhetoric* (Metchen: The Scarecrow Press, 1989).

16. George Kennedy, "Supplementary Essays," in *Aristotle: On Rhetoric*, trans. and with notes by George A. Kennedy (Oxford: Oxford University Press, 1991), 309.

17. "The Rhetorical Situation," *Philosophy and Rhetoric* 1 (1968), 1–14.

18. For an example of Disney's control of its representations, see John Shelton Lawrence, "Donald Duck vs. Chilean Socialism: A Fair Use Exchange." This essay appears as the appendix to Ariel Dorfman and Armand Mattelart, *How to Read Donald Duck: Imperialist Ideology in the Disney Comic*, trans. by David Kunzle (New York: International General, 1971), 113–119.

19. *A Synoptic History of Classical Rhetoric* (Davis: Hermagoras Press, 1983), 5.

20. C. Feldman, "Oral Metalanguage," in D. Olson & N. Torrance, eds., *Literacy and Orality* (Cambridge: Cambridge University Press, 1991), 124.

21. *Classical Rhetoric and its Christian and Secular Tradition from Ancient to Modern Times* (Chapel Hill: The University of North Carolina Press, 1980), 65.

22. Ibid., 66.

23. *On Rhetoric: A Theory of Civic Discourse*, trans. George A. Kennedy (Oxford: Oxford University Press, 1991), 36.

24. *Permanence and Change* 3rd ed. (Berkeley: University of California Press, 1984), 49.

25. *A Grammar of Motives* (Berkeley: University of California Press, 1969), 503.

26. By "criminality" I do not mean the crimes associated with Nixon and Watergate, or the allegations that Clinton sexually assaulted a woman when he was

governor of Arkansas. Rather, I am talking about more substantial presidential
crimes, such as Reagan's funding of the Contras, Nixon's attack on Laos and
Cambodia, and Bush's invasion of Panama, to name only the most obvious few.

27. Michael McGee, "The 'Ideograph': A link Between Rhetoric and Ideology,"
Quarterly Journal of Speech 66 (1980), 1–16.

28. *On Rhetoric*, 124.

29. Ibid., 125.

30. Ibid.

31. Ibid., 126.

32. *Aristotle on Political Reasoning: A Commentary on the "Rhetoric"* (DeKalb:
Northern Illinois University Press, 1981), 115.

33. *On Rhetoric*, 218.

34. *On Rhetoric*, 30.

35. "Aristotle's Enthymeme Revisited," *The Quarterly Journal of Speech* 45:
(1959), 408.

36. *On Rhetoric*, 44.

37. This and the following example were suggested to me by Carole Blair of the
University of California, Davis.

38. "A Reconsideration of Aristotle's Concept of Topics," *Central States Speech
Journal* 16 (1965), 112.

39. *Rhetoric and Philosophy in Conflict*, 30.

40. "Demystifying Classical Rhetoric," *Rhetoric Society Quarterly* 10 (1980), 76.

41. Michael Leff, "The Topics of Argumentative Invention in Latin Rhetorical
Theory from Cicero to Boethius," *Rhetorica* 1 (1983), 24.

42. Quoted in Thucydides, *The Peloponnesian War*, trans. Rex Warner (London:
The Penguin Classics, 1954), 117.

43. Ibid., 119.

Conclusion

Throughout this book, I have explored various intersections between knowledge and politics. I have used as my backdrop important historical figures and ideas from the rhetorical and socialist traditions to emphasize my points. In so doing, I offered interpretations of a variety of cultural phenomena. Some of these phenomena faired well in my analysis, and some faired less well. This is all a part of historical memory and of earning one's world.

To those readers who may disagree with my positioning of key historical figures, I offer the following challenge: examine carefully the role these people have played in history. Examine their actions and their policies from different angles and from different perspectives. Consider the effects of their actions and the history of their ideology. Be suspicious of my characterizations and go study history independent of the biases of this book. My assumption is that, to the extent that people are open minded, and to the extent that they are motivated by questions of justice, fair-minded people will learn and grow from the experience. This growth is the basis for any progressive political action.

In accentuating the intersections between knowledge and politics, this book is unabashedly offered as an example of a politicized scholarship. Knowledge, I have argued, never exists for its own sake; it is always contextualized as knowledge by the communities that affirm it. This book, for example, can be positioned as "knowledge," or it can be positioned as "rhetoric" (in Plato's sense). For me, this book is rhetoric in an epistemic sense. I am trying to create a *practical* knowledge of our past as well as a workable, more livable future for Americans and for people living throughout the world.

Scholarship and Radical Democracy

As clearly stated throughout this book, my purpose is to further the ends of what is known in current political language as a "radical democracy." This concept means different things to different people. For me, the ideal form of such political term is a socialist state—not one designed on the formally articulated Stalinist models, but one that stems from a more domestic model, envisioned in the struggles for democracy that have a long and dynamic tradition in this country.[1]

The term "radical democracy" becomes operationalized in various ways, but one of its clearest expressions is by Michael Eric Dyson. Dyson's discussion of "radical democracy" appears as he is considering the "meaning" of Malcolm X. By reviewing Dyson's observations on Malcolm X, we get a better sense of what he means by a radical democracy.

Malcolm X was a man who was both revered and demonized in his day. He was culturally misunderstood by many, and he suffered an assassination and then, thirty years later, experienced a spiritual rebirth at the hands of the media. Malcolm X was a man who refused to be pigeonholed, yet, ironically, he serves as an icon to many—representing a diverse range of feelings, emotions, ideologies, and resistances. To different people Malcolm X represents anger, pride, misogyny, racism, socialism, and merchandising. Since many of these positions contradict each other, Dyson's inquiry is valid: what does Malcolm X *mean*? More importantly, given that Malcolm's current representations have much to do with the agenda of his racist and classist opponents (the people who positioned Malcolm X in the film *Malcolm X*), how do those of us who need to learn from Malcolm X "hear" his message?[2]

As Dyson concludes, Malcolm X has multiple meanings, and no one can lay claim to the superiority of any one of them. He is all the above things, and perhaps more. The same can be said of the phenomenon known as "Ancient Rhetoric" or of U.S. "democracy." As concepts, Malcolm, classical rhetoric, and U.S. democracy all have multiple meanings. This book has emphasized some of the cultural currencies of these concepts, accentuating how the meanings of the above must be understood in their historical context. In discussing these contexts, particularly as they involve questions of knowledge and knowing, we look at where the concepts impose limitations on thought and understanding and where they direct us toward avenues in which we have the opportunity to experience moral growth. For the same reasons we remember Malcolm X, Dyson reminds us, we engage in this intellectual and, ultimately, cultural activity, because we have a commitment, on some important level, to build a more inclusive community and society.

This building of a more inclusive community and society is the "essence" of a radical democracy and of the politics constructed in its image. As Dyson explains, "[T]he term seeks to accent the emancipatory elements of political practice, signifying a broad emphasis on popular participation in the affairs of the citizenry."[3] He goes on to explain how "radical democrats view issues of race, gender, sexuality, the environment, the workplace, and the like to be crucial spheres where negotiation over identity, equality, and emancipation takes place."[4]

As accentuated throughout this book, the perspective of a radical democracy, and the critical apparatus that leads to it, is not much different than that perspective that goes under the formal name of "Marxism," especially when Marxist struggle is divested from the dogmatism and essentialism that people often attach to it.[5] By itself, Marxism is revolutionary and historical. It is rhetorical, it is emancipatory (sorry, Foucault), and it has as its goal social democracy. What has happened in history is that its champions have sometimes cloaked its strengths with rigid ideological straight jackets, turning it into an anti-revolutionary force. To make things worse, its class enemies have also reified Marxism in unsavory ways so that its current representations come to us somewhat tarnished. In neither case has Marxism (or anarchism or socialism) itself been attacked. What has been condemned is Stalinism, and rightly so. This is another valuable lesson in representation. Fundamentally, politics is about representation, and Marxism is about politics and democracy. This is to say, as I have said, politics is about language and rhetoric and the human being's place in society as an agent in the construction of history. This broadly has been the message of this book.

My purpose, once again, has not been to vilify the U.S.—its actions, its history, its economics have done that more forcefully and thoroughly than my modest effort to represent it. I have no interest in casting needless aspersions on the nation in which I was born and raised, and for now at least, continue to live. My work is not for deconstruction, but it is not for abdication to authority either. Rather, my work stands to challenge such authority—authority in scholarship, authority in history, authority in representation. I believe in the time-honored adage that authority unquestioned is not authority at all; rather, it is tyranny.

Representation, its politics and its economy, is why I wrote a book on the rise of rhetoric and its intersections with contemporary critical thought. My focus has been to illustrate two points. First, to show that scholarship itself is rife with issues of representation. My critical reading of the past is nothing more than one of many competing representations. As a critical reading, it offers certain advantages over traditional readings, but it also suffers from certain limitations, as well. No representation can be a Xerox copy of Truth. There are, I have said many times, *better* and *worse* readings. What I have attempted to give is a "better" reading of history and theory, one accentuating the point of view of its victims.

I recognize that my critical reading is decidedly at odds with the larger political environment, and that immediately makes my claims suspect. However, as the political environment changes, and I hope it does change for the better, then some of the controversy that surrounds my representations will be abated, and perhaps my ideas may even be embraced. The claims themselves do not change, but the environment in which they are received does.

Second, I have shown how conflict *within* the history of rhetoric, and the cultural permutations of these conflicts within Western society, involves representation. In one form or another, all the people discussed in this book—from the Rhapsodes to the Sophists, from Isocrates to Aristotle, and from Che Guevara to Martin Luther King, Jr.—were all struggling over the fundamental question of what it means to "know" and who has the "right" to define the parameters of knowledge.

We find even in the struggle over what constitutes U.S. "history" that we cannot escape the question of representation and politics. Why, for example, is the understanding offered in this book better than more traditional (or "normalizing") accounts of history? As readers have probably noticed, the history of the U.S. offered here is significantly different than the history of the U.S. to which most people in this country are committed. The difference has to do with the amount of struggle we are willing to undergo in order to understand the past. To digest the histories of the U.S. by our politicians is certainly an easy thing to do; it does not constitute any effort, no struggle for representation or understanding. Indeed, it does not involve any concern at all. For people who accept standard accounts of history, history is unimportant, it has no relevance to the present. There is no need for memory. For these people, memory has been assassinated—people are robbed of their consciousness of being historical beings, they are made to be one-dimensional (in Marcuse's sense).[6] What is being maliciously hidden from these people is the fact that the struggle for memory is the most important political task in which any of us can engage. The struggle for memory is the first principle behind all critical analysis, thus all humanizing activity.[7]

There is not one Truth, but many "truths," and the study of history gives credence to this position. This plurality of positions, all constituting what we can consider to be small "truths" is what the guardians of Truth today do not want us to see. If we as a nation do not like the dominant version of Truth that is being lorded over us by Capitalism, then we have to acknowledge our responsibility as human beings to struggle to change this Truth. Truth is never self-evident, it is often imposed from the top. The purpose of a radical democracy is to recognize and to defend the fundamental ability of *all* people in the world to accept responsibility for the construction of their lives. This is a "truth" that was only partially acknowledged in Ancient Athens, and one that has had only a limited currency, at best, in the hectic and violent years of the twentieth century. Democracy—in its Marxist, Athenian, Christian, or Capitalist forms—has largely remained unactualized. We must challenge this state of affairs with all our might, all of our intellect, and with all our will. As we face the twenty-first century, and as we have failed as a species to resolve the problems of the twentieth century—problems that have pushed us well beyond the brink of a localized genocide and invite us to imagine more gruesome terms—we are faced with one immediate question that refuses to go away: what do we do now?

Notes

1. For a vivid sense of this struggle and how it manifested itself in the desires and lives of the working classes in the late nineteenth and early twentieth centuries, see Emma Goldman's two volume autobiography, *Living My Life* (New York: Dover Publications, 1970).

2. While the film's director Spike Lee is an American of African descent, he nevertheless is constrained by the backers of the film, by Hollywood authority, and by his own biases. Since Lee is able to "make it" in the White world, Dyson correctly assumes that, to a certain extent, Lee is playing by the rules of the White world. A fundamental tension exists in the film because Lee represents the more bourgeois elements of the African-American community while Malcolm's fundamental message was situated in the experience of the international African proletariat.

3. *Making Malcolm: The Myth and Meaning of Malcolm X* (New York: Oxford University Press, 1995), 197.

4. Ibid.

5. See Cornel West, *The Ethical Dimensions of Marxist Thought* (New York: Monthly Review Press, 1991).

6. Herbert Marcuse, *One-Dimensional Man* (Boston: Beacon Press, 1964).

7. See Howard Zinn, *The Politics of History* 2nd ed. (Urbana: University of Illinois Press, 1990).

Index